William Burgess

Land, Labor and Liquor

A Chapter in the Political Economy of the Present Day

William Burgess

Land, Labor and Liquor
A Chapter in the Political Economy of the Present Day

ISBN/EAN: 9783744645553

Printed in Europe, USA, Canada, Australia, Japan

Cover: Foto ©Suzi / pixelio.de

More available books at **www.hansebooks.com**

LAND, LABOR AND LIQUOR

A CHAPTER IN THE POLITICAL ECONOMY OF THE PRESENT DAY.

BY REV. WM. BURGESS

Pastor of the Congregational Church, Listowel, Ont.

WITH INTRODUCTION BY

W. H. HOWLAND, ESQ., MAYOR OF TORONTO.

"All men must think for themselves; and so all men must be taught how to think. It is therefore, worth while for public educated discussion to put forward in the foreground axioms, self-evident truths."—JOSEPH COOK.

S. R. BRIGGS,
TORONTO WILLARD TRACT DEPOSITORY, TORONTO.
1887.

Entered according to the Act of the Parliament of Canada, in the year one thousand eight hundred and eighty-seven by SAMUEL ROBERT BRIGGS, in the office of the Minister of Agriculture at Ottawa.

PARKDALE TIMES PRINTERS.

INTRODUCTION.

IN the pages of this volume a long-felt want has been supplied. The opponents of Temperance Reform have often questioned the figures and statistics of the evil trade in Canada, given by temperance men as being of doubtful accuracy, owing to the differences in the estimates made by different speakers. We have now, in this volume, carefully prepared and most complete statements and arrays of facts and figures which can be utilised as a basis for the future. In many ways in addition to this, the volume commends itself to the public in this age of quickened interest in Temperance work. The thoughtful and massive presentation of facts showing the wasteful character of the Liquor Manufacture, its small employment of labor and its immense injury to both the tradesman and the laborer, from an economical point of view, will help to convince many a fair mind as to the blessings that would result to this country were the whole liquor traffic banished from our soil—may God grant it soon,—but more for the sake of the dear flesh and blood wasted than for any money that would be saved.

As the writer points out, the working man has awakened to the fact that the great weapon in the hands of oppressors and monopolists—the great weight on the back of the wage-worker, hindering his rise (which would otherwise be natural and rapid in this freest of all countries) is the liquor trade, and thank God, that realization once expressed as a square issue at the polls will settle, once and for all, the fate of this worthless and evil trade in this fair Canada of ours. "Soon shall we see the glorious dawn."

BLYTH COTTAGE,   W. H. HOWLAND.
  Toronto, March, 1887.

AUTHOR'S PREFACE.

IN preparing this work for publication, I have been inspired by its objects and purposes, rather than by the mere pleasure of adding one more to the countless number of books.

My first object was to answer the call for reliable facts and Canadian statistics. For several years past I have felt the need of such a handy volume as would fill the place of a text book for temperance reformers, especially on the subjects relating to labor, capital, trade, &c., &c. I entered upon the task fully conscious that it was one of great magnitude and importance, demanding the treatment of a more skilful and experienced hand than mine. In fact, I have frequently urged the importance of the work upon those whom I thought competent to deal with it.

The statistical work has been even greater than I supposed. The figures have been collected mostly from Government Blue Books, and were not found in such a form as to be easily placed into tables.

My second object has been to present what I believe to be the most important fact in the treatment of the labor problem. It appears to me that social reformers and political economists who recognize the terrible burdens and afflictions under which the masses groan and suffer, and yet ignore the intimate relation of the liquor traffic to every form of social depression and woe, are simply baling out water from a leaky ship while its timbers are being rotted and scuttled.

Last and not least, my hope is that this little work may hasten the final overthrow of the most gigantic of all evils. I see no possible redemption of Society from the numerous social wrongs which degrade, impoverish and demoralise our people, without the complete overthrow of the liquor traffic as an organized force and a legalized institution. The political power and dominating influence of this huge system must be broken before the masses of civilized lands can be emancipated from degradation and grinding poverty.

I am indebted to officials of the Dominion and Ontario Governments for kindly supplying the requisite documents for reference, and to many whose works I have quoted, without permission, I tender my thanks for the aid they have afforded me. I am especially indebted to the Chief of the "Bureau of Statistics of Labor" of Massachusetts for a copy of their last report, and also to several public officials and others for kindly supplying important information.

W. B.

CONTENTS.

	PAGE

CHAPTER I. OUR NATURAL RESOURCES. Our country—its territory—its capabilities—land—lakes—rivers—springs—minerals 17

CHAPTER II. OUR NATIONAL WEALTH. Natural resources and national wealth not identical—Wealth defined—Sir Isaac Newton quoted—Prof. Fawcett's definition — Adam Smith — Henry George—Value of the national wealth of Canada 20

CHAPTER III. LABOR. Productive labor defined —John Stuart Mill's definition — Education and labor—Washington Gladden — Dr. Channing—Elevation of labor 26

CHAPTER IV. PRODUCTIVE AND NON-PRODUCTIVE LABOR. Production the glory of labor—Unproductive work is drudgery—Court-martials—The Treadmill — Unproductive labor defined — Billiard rooms—Professional sport and gambling —A plea for recreation 31

CHAPTER V. DESTRUCTIVE LABOR. Definitions and illustrations—Dynamite as a servant and a destroyer—Hell-gate and anarchy — War and labor — The war debt of Europe — Cost of modern wars—Standing armies and War-ships — Labor and Liquor — Labor expended in liquor not productive—Henry George's "desire" theory examined — Market prices not always proof of value—Liquor factories and lotteries—Alcohol the ashes of food................. 36

CHAPTER VI. LABOR EXPENDED IN LIQUOR MAKING DESTRUCTIVE. Brewing not cooking—War sometimes justified—Alcohol sometimes of value.................................. 49

CHAPTER VII. WHAT CAPITAL IS. Definition by various authors—Capital and labor not antagonistic but co-operative—Capital and labor one in slavery, but competitive in freedom—Labor may be trusted — The capitalist and the laborer equals 52

CHAPTER VIII. CAPITAL MISDIRECTED. Burglar's tools his capital—Gain of a few not always increase of wealth—Capital at war with capital —Amount of capital in breweries, distilleries and liquor stores in Canada—Boots and shoes *versus* liquor—Capital responsible for its effects. 58

CHAPTER IX. DESTRUCTION OF FOOD. Grain consumed in liquor making—Official Canadian statistics.. 66

CHAPTER X. OVER-PRODUCTION. What it means! —A fallacy—Lord Derby's stocking illustration —Millions without stockings—Why?.......... 72

CHAPTER XI. OVER-CROWDING THE LABOR MARKET. The-too-many-workmen theory — Immigration—Statistics of over-population.... 79

CHAPTER XII. CO-OPERATION. Its value to the labor problem—Its use and progress—Co-operative production—Profit sharing—Co-operative coopers—M. Leclaire's great enterprise and faith—What weakens co-operation—What Canadian workmen lose—How 25,750 workmen in Canada might be capitalists...... 83

CONTENTS.

CHAPTER XIII. KNIGHTS OF LABOR. Secret origin—Its rapid growth after secrecy was abolished — Its policy and constitution — Mr. Powderly and moral sentiments—Opposition to strikes and boycotts — Workmen and International peace 97

CHAPTER XIV. LABOR UNIONS AND THE LIQUOR TRAFFIC. The action of various bodies against the traffic—Mr. Powderly and Mr. Trevillick speaks—Mene, Mene, Tekel, Upharsin 106

CHAPTER XV. THE ROOT OF THE EVIL. Monoplies and Millionaires — A coal combination swindle—National blood-poisoning — Cardinal Manning's Catalogue of Evils 111

CHAPTER XVI. MORE WAGES AND LESS LABOR. Cost of living in Canada and Massachusetts—Productive power of machinery—Carlyle, Mill and Gladstone quoted—Why wages are low—Why labor is in competition with labor—Liquor bill of Toronto — How to spend $1,500,000 118

CHAPTER XVII. WAGES AND WHISKEY. Labor employed in making liquor—Trades that live by destruction—Mr. Canada, farmer and his barley—Caledonian Distillery contrasted with Sheffield Iron Works—Gooderham and Worts' distillery contrasted with Toronto Manufacturers—Annual income and number of employees compared—Important statistical table—Wages of Canadian industries compared........... 128

CHAPTER XVIII. OUR NATIONAL DRINK BILL. Statistical Statement—Total direct cost for 18 years—Indirect cost—Waste of food—Its cost—Coals consumed—Labor Wasted—Hands employed—Capital wasted—Cost of Crime—Millions borrowed—Our National debt—How to pay it? 140

CHAPTER XIX. COMPARATIVE VIEW OF OUR NATIONAL LIQUOR. United Kingdom and United States drink bills—Three National drink columns—Canada favorably compared—Christian Church and Education Expenditure—Table of comparisons........................... 158

CHAPTER XX. FURTHER STATISTICS AND ILLUSTRATIONS. Waste of food illustrated—Yonge Street paved with bread-loaves—A procession of baker's teams—Spirits, Beer and Wines consumed—Where it all goes—The number of people who don't and who do drink—Quantity of drink per head of population 166

CHAPTER XXI. IS THE MONEY WASTED. Money is not wealth—Productive Expenditure—Three parties to a fair bargain.................. 173

CHAPTER XXII. WHAT'S TO BE DONE WITH THE BARLEY? An alarmist's cry—Richard Cobden's Illustration—High wages and little corn—Drink and farm produce—Historical facts of London and Ireland famines—Canada's barley market—How to improve our markets—Barley as a feeder—Scientific evidence of same—Boys worth more than grain—Printing Press 178

CONTENTS. xiii

CHAPTER XXIII. FARMERS AND THE FOREIGN MARKET. England asks for Canadian produce—What the British public buy and where from—The Canadian cheese export—Its growth—Butter exports—Why it stands still—Eggs—What one man exports from Canada—Farmers not dependent upon brewers for a market..... 191

CHAPTER XXIV. LIQUOR AND CRIME. British, U. S. and Canadian statistics all agree—Strong words of Canadian Legislative Assembly—Montreal, Toronto, and Ottawa Police Statistics—Cost of Crime—Ontario prisons—Actual number of criminals and drunkards—500 inmates of Penitentiary—27,000 criminals...... 196

CHAPTER XXV. INSANITY AND ALCOHOL. Insanity in Canada—Cost of same—Insanity and drink—Statistics of Ontario Asylum—Alcohol abolished in some of them—Testimony from English authorities—Earl Shaftesbury's opinions and statements—Dr. F. R. Lees quoted....... 215

CHAPTER XXVI. DRINK AND PAUPERISM. Workhouse system in Britain—Its radical defect—Jews Board of Guardians—Number of paupers in England and Wales and cost of same—The Cause of pauperism—Report of Convocation of Canterbury and other testimonies—Pauperism in Canada—Vagrants in Ontario—Dr. Howard Crosby on drink and poverty—The Canadian Legislative Assembly's report—The Senate's report—Ears but hear not 227

CHAPTER XXVII. THE ECONOMIC VALUE OF MAN. Man greater than institutions—The Bible for man—Life's value—Alcohol kills—Medical testimony—Insurance and Mortatlity Statistics—Richard Cobden on life without liquor—The higher life and drink........... 240

CHAPTER XXVIII. THE CHRISTIAN JUGGERNAUT. Mr. Gladstone on the evils of drink greater than those of war, pestilence and famine — Annual human sacrifice — 500,000 souls per year—More than Canada's population in ten years—Drink a god of Christian nations.—The devil's chain—Look on this and on this. 259

CHAPTER XXIX. THE LICENSE SYSTEM IMMORAL AND DEGRADING. Buxton the Brewer and the war between heaven and hell—Mr. John Dougall and license—Licensed vice—Prof. Sheldon Amos on the subject—Hon. Ed. Blake and Prohibition—Law as an educator—Mr. Gladstone on the duty of the State—John Bright's picture of war—An angel of death—Hope in prohibition.................................. 268

APPENDIX A. STATISTICAL TABLES of Land, Mineral, Railway, Industrial and other values in Canada 282

APPENDIX B. TESTIMONY OF EMMINENT AUTHORITIES on the relation of drink and crime—British and American Judges—Lord Brougham—Earl Shaftesbury—John Bright—Cardinal McCabe—etc., etc 288

APPENDIX C. HOW DRINKS ARE DOCTORED.... 297

APPENDIX D. KNIGHTS OF LABOR—Preamble to Constitution 308

APPENDIX E. FIRE INSURANCE AND DRINK 311

APPENDIX F. COMPENSATION 312

STATISTICAL TABLES AND DIAGRAMS.

Showing War Debt, per capita of Europe	39
Showing loss of Life by War	39
Showing number of Standing Armies in Europe	40
On the Waste of Grain in Canada	69
Seven years immigration to Canada	80
How to spend one and a half millions	125
Comparison of fifteen industries with liquor factories	137
Value of all Canadian industries compared	138
Showing Cost of Drink in Canada in 1885	142
" " " " " " " 18 years	143
" Grain consumed in 18 years	145
" Value of Grain consumed	146
" Number of Persons engaged in Liquor Traffic	146
" Annual Cost of intoxicating drinks in Canada	151
" Cost of Drink in 10 years in United Kingdom	160
" " " " " 4 years in U. S.	160
" Drink Expenditure compared with other items	164-5
Giving 18 years consumption of Liquor in Canada	168
Showing average consumption per head of population	172
Years of Famine in Ireland compared with ordinary years	182
Colonial imports to United Kingdom	193
Prisoners arrested in Montreal in different years	198-9
" " " Toronto and Ottawa	200-1
Cost of maintenance of Penitentiaries	204
" " Crime in Canada	208
Alcoholic stimulants used in Asylums	219
Insanity in United Kingdom	220
Causes of insanity in United Kingdom's Asylums	222
Paupers in England and their cost	230
Showing Sick and Death Rate of Abstainers compared with Moderate Drinkers	246
Death Rate of two sections of United Kingdom Temperance and General Life Insurance Co.	249
Showing Death Rate of 12 classes of people	253
" Value of Land Interests in Canada	282
" Value and Earnings of Railways in Canada	283
" " " " " Canals " "	284
" " of Shipping Interests " "	284
Capital invested in Canadian Industries	285
" " " Productions of Canadians Forest	285
" " " Animals and their produce	286
" " " Export Trade " "	287
" " " Industries " "	287
" " " Fisheries " "	287

"He who knows what is good and chooses it, who knows what is bad and avoids it, is learned and temperate."—*Socrates.*

"All the crimes on earth do not destroy so many of the human race, nor alienate so much property as drunkenness."—*Lord Bacon.*

"If the advocates of Freedom had put down Slavery and the Slave-trade together, fifty years ago, half a century might have been saved; and, with the requisite degree of virtue and courage, it would have been quite as easy then as now. If the friends of Temperance will lay the axe to the root of the Upas Tree of drunkenness, it too will fall, and the deluded victims awakening from their dreams will be the first to sing hymns of thanksgiving for their deliverance. But if a few spare leaves only are stripped off here and there, and the removal of a branch or two excites apprehension and alarm, the tree will still flourish in rank and luxurious growth, and its outspreading boughs cover a still wider and wider space till its poison, diffusing itself all around shall corrupt the whole atmosphere—and make England a land of disease, of crime, of desolation and of death."—*James Silk Buckingham, M. P., 1834.*

"But Censure profits little: vain the attempt
To advertise in verse a public pest
   *   *   *   *
Th' excise is fattened with the rich result
Of all this riot. The ten thousand casks,
For ever dribbling out their base contents,
Touched by the Midas finger of the State
Bleed gold, for Parliament to vote away.
Drink and be mad then; 'tis your country bids
Gloriously drunk—obey the important call;
Her cause demands the assistance of your throats
Ye all can swallow, and she asks no more.
                    —*Cowper, 1780.*

CHAPTER I

OUR NATIONAL RESOURCES.

THE extent and capacities of Canadian territory and resources are surpassingly great. No country in the world offers greater promise to coming generations. Its possibilities are beyond the dreams of the most sanguine of Canada's young sons. A great American statesman (Wm. H. Seward) has well said "Canada is destined to become the seat of a great Empire, the Russia of North America, but a Russia with civilization more advanced than the Russia of Europe."

The territory of the Dominion comprises an area of 3,470,392 square miles, or about 2,229,106,447 acres besides a great lake and river surface estimated at about 700,000 square miles. What dreams of affluence! What visions of wealth and greatness are conceivable in the contemplation of a territory so vast! Everything in the country, when considered in relation to the future, is calculated to fill the mind with the highest expectation. Lord Dufferin did not exaggerate, when speaking of Canada, he said "in a thousand localities the earth is bursting with mineral wealth, which only requires improved transportation to develop." Already that statement made about eight years ago, has been abundantly verified.

The great waters of Canada are a source of wonder in proportion as their vastness, beauty and utility are realized; and they are destined to become the joy and pride of countless thousands, who, in the not very far distant future, shall dwell upon their shores.

The forests of the country—at one time regarded as hindrances to be destroyed with ruthless hand, like the wild beasts which inhabited them,—are now treated with conservative care, as a valuable part of our great natural resources. The eagerness with which pioneer settlers fired and wrecked millions of noble trees, often unnecessarily, and without regard to the future, in order to make easy way to the surface of the land, is now deeply deplored by those who take pride in the country's growth. Immense tracts of land have been bereft of every vestige of shady trees or leafy foliage, with which to attract the rain showers, or afford shelter, shade or ornament. But, so vast and abundant was the supply in this expansive land, that there yet remains immense fields of timber land, which now constitute a most important factor in the nations fortune. Lord Dufferin said, a few years ago, that "Canada has timber enough of various kinds to set up the world in building material."

The minerals and springs already discovered in our territory have proved to be of enormous extent and value, and they are the assurance of an abundant storehouse of hidden treasury which awaits the enterprize of capital, and the operation of labor.

The surface of the land is of more than average fertility and richness. In some enormous tracts of country it is wonderfully adapted to rapid and prolific growth. In the soil of the entire domain there has been stored the rich results of Nature's chemistry which, for countless ages has steadily operated with but little disturbance. This land surface is so vast that its measure appears incredible. From east to west it stretches across a distance of 3000 miles, and from north to south it stretches from the Atlantic Ocean to a latitude about equal to that of France in Europe, a distance of about 1500 miles. It is nearly as large as the whole of Europe and is rather larger than the territory of the United States, exclusive of Alaska.

Allowing more than one-half of the entire land surface of Canada for public roads, railways, town and city buildings, and for rocky and uncultivatible soil *there is a square acre of land for every one of more than one billion of persons.* To present this in another form *there are possible farms of 100 acres of land each, for ten millions of farmers.* If five persons are allotted to each farm on an average, we may have farms for fifty millions (50,000,000) of people. If five persons live upon trade, mechanical employments and the professions, for every one living upon farms, we have ample ROOM IN CANADA FOR THE INCONCEIVABLE NUMBER OF THREE HUNDRED MILLIONS OF PERSONS.

CHAPTER II.

OUR NATIONAL WEALTH.

THE whole of this vast territory with all its variety and abundance of treasure, are nature's endowments—God's free gifts to man.

But in estimating our wealth we must distinguish between natural advantages and acquired riches. Wealth is property acquired, and is therefore attached to personal ownership. Nature's resources are man's heritage, without distinction, or respect of persons, and belong to all equally. They are not the exclusive property of any one man, or class, or race. Every human being possesses equally an inherent right to them. The late Mr. Fawcett, M.P., the eminent Professor of Political Economy, and late Post-Master General of England, said:—"Wealth may be defined to consist of every commodity which has an exchange value" while Henry George, says:—"Nothing which nature supplies to man without labor is wealth."

When we speak of wealth we do not refer to the supplies of nature. Sunlight, heat, air, water, electricity, etc. are not wealth. Rivers, lakes and seas; wild beasts, fowl or fish are not property, and do not constitute a nation's wealth. These are essential factors to its production, but until they are adapted, utilized or acquired by human effort, for the use of man they are not property. They are the raw material which lie ever ready, prolific of rich reward to man, only through labor. Every ray of sunshine, and every shower of rain, every particle of air, and every changing season, are of incalculable value as contributors to human needs and desires, but, as they come to us without effort on our part, they are not wealth, and cannot be accounted and calculated as such. Place a man alone, under the most favorable natural circumstances; let him, like Robinson Crusoe, have an Island where are in the highest degree, all the facilities of light, air, heat, water, land, forest, wild fruit, fowl, eggs and fish. All these will be absolutely useless to him unless he exerts himself. If he does not work he must starve, he must gather the fruit, catch the fish, snare the fowl and provide against storms and cold and heat. In proportion only as he labors will he have abundance.

So likewise, a nation's wealth is not measured by the extent of its territory, its forests and springs, or mineral deposits. A single province of Canada is vastly greater in these respects than the whole of the United Kingdom, yet the latter is incomparably richer than all Canada.

Nature's supplies cost man nothing. Rich treasures of raw material lie ever ready at his feet, to adapt, utilize and enjoy; but only in proportion as he converts them into articles of utility, and bring them within reach for human service do they become wealth. Thus:—A brickmaker's wealth is not measured by the quantity or quality of the clay in his pit, but by the quantity and quality of bricks produced. The value of these bricks for the purposes for which they were made is the extent of his created wealth. He has capital invested in machinery or tools, and if he has purchased the right to the exclusive use of the clay in the pit he has capital also in it, but if the clay remains in the pit unused, that portion of his invested capital will be lost to him.*

But although the elements of nature are not exchange value, and are therefore not wealth, they are essential factors in its production. They are the raw material, supplied to us, untaxed and free, by the great Creator. They are the springs from whence all wealth must be drawn. These springs are perpetual in their supply, and will continue to flow on, whether man labor or not. No effort of ours can dam them. Yet man cannot enjoy them without effort.

Our natural resources are of primary importance. The extensive and richly endowed Bank of Nature, in which for ages have been deposited, at compound interest, the inestimable treasure of this fair Dominion, is our heritage. Here we have room and supplies for countless millions of people. We but begin to see "as through a glass darkly" the vastness of our prize. It is to us, as to him, were those mighty discoveries of Sir Isaac Newton when he said, "*I do not know what I may appear to the world, but to myself I seem to have been only like a boy playing on the sea shore, and diverting myself in now and then finding a smoother pebble or a prettier shell than ordinary, whilst the great ocean of truth lay all undiscovered before me.*"

Wealth then consists of that portion of actual produce which we possess in excess of present needs, such as clothing, food, houses, cattle, ships, machinery, tools, &c., or the equivalent in money for the purchase

---

*Prof. Fawcett gives the following simple illustration:—"The seams of coal were deposited without any human agency, but the coal is not available to satisfy any of the wants of life until man's labor has dug the coal from the mine and placed it in those situations in which it is required."

of these things; and also the value which labor has given to land, water or other of nature's resources. Prof. Fawcett defines wealth as consisting "of every commodity which has an exchange value." Adam Smith says:

"Money in common language frequently signifies wealth; and this ambiguity of expression has rendered the popular notion so familiar to us that even they who are convinced of its absurdity are very apt to forget their own principles. Some of the best English writers upon commerce set out with observing that the wealth of a country, consists not in its gold and silver only, but in its lands, houses and consumable goods of all different kinds." *

Henry George says:

"Wealth consists of natural products that have been secured, moved, combined, separated or in other ways modified by human exertion so as to fit them for the gratification of human desires. It is in other words labor impressed upon matter in such a way as to store up, as the heat of the sun is stored in coals, the power of human labor to administer to human desire." †

With these definitions before me I proceed to notice the growth of wealth in this Dominion, and in doing so, desire to avoid that "ambiguity of expression" which Adam Smith refers to. It will be observed that the definitions of the able writers here quoted are not accepted as final and conclusive. Some commodities are regarded as "exchange value" which do not contribute to our wealth, and do not form any part of a nation's stock. There is a class of modern political economists who deny that land is property, and this conflicts with a portion of Adam Smith's definition. Mr. Henry George, the foremost of this class of think-

---

*Wealth of Nations, by Dr. Adam Smith.
†Progress and Poverty, by Henry George.

ers, however, in his definition of wealth, includes the increased value in land which labor has given to it. I shall have occasion to refer again to Mr. George's theory that "human desire" is the standard of wealth.

The development or improvement of the soil—the increased utility of parcels of land, whether by reason of the growth of villages into towns, and towns into cities, or through increased facilities for transportation, is the result of labor impressed upon matter in such a way as to store up the power of human labor to minister to "human desires." An acre of land upon which city buildings are erected administers more to human desires than a hundred acres of North-West prairie land. It is true that the land of the prairie might be as good for building city houses upon, as is city land, but a prairie cannot be transported to the city, and if a city is built upon a prairie it is human labor that has invested the land with greater value.

In estimating our national wealth, therefore, whether land be regarded as private property or not, we must recognise the increased value which is stored up in it, by means of labor, and to that extent at least must regard it as part of the aggregate wealth of the country.

It must be admitted that under the present system of land ownership, the holder of a plot of land may have done nothing to increase its value. He may have even kept back its real value by withholding it from use when needed. If the present selling price of certain plots of land is above the value which labor has vested in them, it is because they have been withheld from use while desire, or demand, has been growing. In such a case the price has been inflated by greed and monopoly, not advanced steadily in proportion as labor and capital have been expended.

Our cultivated lands and town lots are not value because of any natural right in any person to own land, but because labor has enhanced its utility, either directly, by improving the soil, or indirectly, by changing its surroundings.

The value of our national wealth can only be approximated. For the most part we have to depend upon the census returns of 1881 for our statistics. Half a decade has passed away since then—a period of more rapid and solid progress in material prosperity than perhaps any period of double the time in the world's history.

Appendix A to this volume contains tables showing an approximate estimate of the accumulated wealth of Canada, and also a glance at the value of our annual products. The result of the first set of tables shows that without reckoning the smaller machines, household goods, carriages, horses, cattle, &c., our accumulated property in this country including land interests, railways and canals, shipping interests, and capital invested in industries is not less than $1,500,000,000 or about $330 to every man, woman, and child in the Dominion. That this average may be greatly increased, and that every person living upon our soil may realize the advantage of his share in the common property, is the aim of all true patriotic Canadians. To this end it is our duty to enquire into the drawbacks upon our resources, and the causes which disturb our social and material progress.

CHAPTER III.

LABOR.

WE have seen that the key which unlocks the cabinet of nature is labor. It is also the distributing power which makes their contents availrble to man.

Political economists agree in dividing labor into two distinct classes, viz: PRODUCTIVE and UNPRODUCTIVE.

Adam Smith says "there is one sort of labor which adds to the value of the subject upon which it is bestowed, there is another which has no such effect." In illustrating this definition, he draws the line between the two classes so as to place among the unproductive workers all "statesmen, orators, teachers, clergymen, servants," etc. He does not mention "authors." although they are of course naturally classed with those named. But no great stretch of thought is needed to observe that the author of the "Wealth of Nations" was himself one of the greatest of the world's producers.

John Stuart Mill says :

"In a national point of view, the labor of the servant or speculative thinker, is as much a part of production in the very narrowest sense, as that of an inventor of a practical art. . . No limit can be set to the importance, even in a purely productive and material point of view, of mere thought. . . Speculative thinkers are generally classed as the producers of books, or saleable articles which directly emanate from them. But when (as in political economy one should always be prepared to do) we shift our point of view, and consider, not individual acts, and the motives by which they are determined, but national and universal results, intellectual speculation must be looked upon as a most influential part of the productive labor of society, and the portion of its resources employed in carrying on, and renumerating such labor, as a highly productive part of its expenditure."

Political Economy. Vol. I, Chap. II, pp. 50, 51.

"Knowledge is power" and it is a motive force in all production. It is to productive agencies what steam is to a locomotive engine. Without intelligence the world's work would be all drudgery, limited to the crudest ideas and the most primitive provisions of savage life. A house is the creation of a brain before its walls are erected or its foundation is laid. A bricklayer is necessary to the building of a brick house, but before one brick is laid the architect has seen the completed building. By his designs and plans he contributes more to the building than any one of the mechanics, while the mechanics themselves will produce more effective work in proportion as they can intelligently follow out the plans. An engineer sets going a hundred workmen by his designs and plans in the construction of a bridge. An inventor augments the value of labor and stimulates demand for its products.

Thus, productive power rises with intelligence, and intelligence is promoted by educative agencies. An intelligent mechanic is worth more and ranks higher in the workshop than an unskilled laborer. Moreover the educated or skilled workman is more independent, and, other things being equal, will command a higher position, and better pay than the mere mechanical worker.

The higher the training of the human mind the

greater its capacity and power for production. A piece of canvas and a few colors of paint are of small value. An unskilled house painter could quickly transfer the paint to the canvas, and at his best would add but little to their value. An artist mixes the paints with brains and produces a picture of value, not merely in proportion to the cost of the materials, and the time expended upon it, but to the measure of intellectual power expended in his work of art. Washington Gladden in his excellent little book has well said;

"All work is art. There are artists in dirt at whose feet I would fain sit in these days of garden-making; rude men, who with shovel and rake will slope a bank or trace a winding walk in a manner wholly beyond my power of imitation. There are artists in dry-goods: look at the pictures they make for you in show-windows. There are artists in wood, whom men commonly call carpenters, and artists in iron generally known as blacksmiths—men whose handiwork is always shapely, symmetrical, beautiful. There are artists in household work; indeed the finest and most delicate art is all the while displaying itself in the arrangement and adornment of our houses."—"*Working People and Their Employers.*" *Page 25, Funk & Wagnalls cheap edition.*

Dr. W. E. Channing in his lecture on the elevation of the working classes says :

"Labor becomes a new thing when thought is thrown into it, when the mind keeps pace with the hands. . . What a charm and new value might the farmer add to his grounds and cottage were he a man of taste! The product of the mechanic, be it great or small, a house or a shoe, is worth more, sometimes much more, if he can succeed in giving it the grace of proportion. . . Without a habit of thought a man works more like a brute, or machine, than a man. With it his soul is kept alive amidst his toils. He learns to fix an observing eye on the processes of his trade, catches hints which abridge labor, gets glimpses of important discoveries, and is sometimes able to perfect his art. Even now, after all the miracles of invention which honor our age we little suspect what improvements of machinery are to spring from spreading intelligence and natural science among workmen. (Channing's works, page 46.)

It is in preparing these artists for their work that the educator increases the world's power to produce. He who developes mental faculties and quickens intelligence is surely a productive worker of the first order.

We may claim also that whoever helps in the aggregate production of the world's wealth is a producer. A servant who cooks a dinner and prepares a bed is as really a producer as a baker who makes a loaf, or the upholsterer who manufactures the bed. It is true that the cook who only prepares the dinner for immediate consumption does not add directly to the capital, or the surplus wealth of the world; but as Henry George would say her "labor is impressed upon matter so as to administer to human desire;" she does more than this however; she administers to human needs. Moreover as the surplus wealth of the world is not acquired single handed, but by the co-operative labor of many, he or she who prepares the meals, or bakes the bread, is as necessary to the production of that wealth as the hands who work, or the capitalist who owns the mill.

But "man does not live by bread alone." We are gradually rising to a higher plane. We "have life more abundantly" with every advancing tide of knowledge. Corn and cattle, houses and lands are not all of wealth. What are termed luxuries, are becoming, to our more abundant life, absolute necessaries. Books and pictures and musical instruments are essential to every home in which education has prepared the way for their appreciation, and these things are no less the products of labor than are our chairs and tables, or our clothing and shoes.

Our possibilities never appeared so great as they do now; with increasing demands our supplies multiply. The child of to-day has a wealth of knowledge, and a capacity for enjoyment, which were never dreamed of by his grandfather. Labor is asserting itself. Work is taking its true rank as a crown of rejoicing, a source of joy, and a fountain of good.

But to the end that the workingman may be free and independent, labor must be enfranchised. It must be unyoked from the juggernaut of vices, it must be freed from the degrading and pauperising effects of a chain of evils which is coiled around it.

CHAPTER IV.

PRODUCTIVE AND NON-PRODUCTIVE LABOR.

THE glory of labor is production. Only slaves work for mere wages. Labor is shorn of its dignity when it has no other aim than a stipulated wage. A slave does as he is bidden and asks no questions, but a free man has an interest in his work for its own sake. He wants to know what he is accomplishing, as well as how much wages he is to get for his work. Mere wages do not make labor profitable. If taken out of capital without giving back an equivalent it decreases wealth. It is waste—not produce. Let a man be employed for the sake of a "job" in digging a hole one day, and filling it up the next, the result of his two days work is less than nothing. If he receive, say three dollars for the "job" with which he purchases the necessaries of life, that amount is taken out of capital or surplus wealth, and the nation is poorer by that much.

An independant man will feel himself degraded by such work. But, suppose a man to have dug a hole, a certain size and shape, which is to be converted into the cellar of a house, he will feel that he is a producer and he will be conscious of having done something for his wages. There is dignity in such labor, and although it may weary the man, it does not degrade him. A good carpenter would not be content to cut up timber into fragments, or convert it into sawdust, even if he were paid his regular wages for doing it.

Set him to whittle sticks without a productive object, and he will quickly become dissatisfied and disgusted. A true workman detests "a job" which progresses slowly, much more one that shows no result.

To be compelled to work without interest in the object or aim of the work is degrading. In the British army,* formerly, one of the punishments of court martial was to inflict upon the offending soldier a penalty of a given number of days or hours of unproductive toil, by compelling him to carry cannon balls a certain measured distance, lay them down in a certain spot, and then proceed to carry them back again. One of the most detested of punishments under the "hard labor" service of the British prisons is the treadmill, which the prisoners describe as "grinding wind." The sting of the penalty is not in the heaviness of the task, but in the fact of working hard and yet doing nothing. As prison punishments take the form of useful employments, much of the sting of compulsory labor is removed by the conscious sense of "doing something" as distinguished from "doing nothing" or "grinding wind." The training is a healthy one and tends to beget a respect for labor instead of an utter disgust and contempt for it. There is no surer method of manufacturing confirmed criminals and idle paupers, than to degrade labor in the eyes of any class of people.

Productive labor not only enhances value but stimulates the desire for increased intelligence, supplies motive to the operator, and in a hundred ways contributes to the advancement of material wealth and progress. Such labor is no degradation. On the contrary it is the greatest blessing to the human family.

---

*This system of punishment under court martial may be still in operation for anything I know to the contrary.

Sanctified and hallowed by its purpose and aim it is God's ordained agency through which comes every good, and every needful thing.

But labor which does not directly or indirectly contribute to human good is degrading. It gets without giving; it consumes without paying; it begets indifference and idleness; it is the parent of paupers and criminals. If the ordained law of God in relation to labor be set aside it will become as a "whip of scorpions" to afflict society.

UNPRODUCTIVE LABOR.—WHAT IT IS.

It is "that which adds nothing to the value of the subject upon which it is bestowed." So says the author of the "Wealth of Nations." Examine this definition closely, and apply it, and it will be found that the unproductive agencies are chiefly those which are associated with, or grow out of the excesses, follies, and vices of society.

In a public billiard room we see capital and labor expended in expensive tables, ivory balls and general furnishings. The subject upon which this expenditure operates are "our boys." If we follow up the effects of the billiard room training upon the boys we shall find that *"nothing is added to the value of the subject,"* but that in every sense the moral and material worth of the boy is discounted, if not ruined by the process.*

---

*The moral evil of these institutions to our young men is second nly to the bar-room of the saloon. The writer knows of parents who for months and even years were unable to account for the demoralization which they saw working in the character of their boys. They saw them loose candour, truthfulness and honor. They were made painfully conscious of the loss of reputation for faithfulness and it has cost considerable sums of money and much humiliating trouble to meet certain deficiences which would have involved the youths' in ruinous exposure. The history of the first theft of petty

Honest toil must be a vigorous giant to withstand the numerous sweating processes to which he is subject. Not the least of these are the swindling of the gambler, at the race-course, on 'change, at the regatta and even in the gymnastic contests of our boys at the lacrosse grounds or the base ball club.

It is admitted that speed may be accelerated and the quality of stock improved by competition at the agricultural show, &c.,* but what a costly curse is the race-course with its attendant gangs of professional bookmakers, gamblers and blacklegs—the spawn of the saloon! Such places established with capital, drained from honest labor, are the gambling dens of thieves, rogues and lazy vagabonds.

I am not contending against amusement. I plead for recreation. Let a man work! work! work! and never stop except to sleep, and never sleep except to rise to work again, such a man may have muscle and fibre, but he will soon lack vital energy.

"All work and no play, makes Jack a dull boy."

There must be play in order to recreate. The body and mind must sometimes unharness and be free for sport or pleasure. The tight belts which bind us to the machinery of duty must now and then slacken so that we may expand our chests—take in a longer breath, and play, in order that we may rest, and that our rest may be healthful, fitting us for work again.

---

cash or postage stamps, the first false entry in accounts, the first forged cheque, the loss of character and position are traceable in hundreds of instances to the elaborate and seductively furnished billiard rooms which exists by grace of law in our cities, towns and villages.

*The tendency of the promoters of Industrial and Agricultural Fairs to depart from their real purpose and substitute as leading attractions the race-course and various sideshows marks their coming downfall.

A friendly boating contest upon the lake or river, or a race upon the village green, will give pleasurable recreation and excite to efforts of strength and speed, but of what practical benefit to the world are professional pugilism, running or sculling? According to newspaper reports Hanlan netted about $60,000 in money and its equivalent by his Australian trip. Beech, his opponent, probably made as much more. These sums are only a small per centage of the money which on this one occasion the ringleaders, managers and betting men drained out of the produce of honest labor. Besides which, every man so employed is diverted from honest work, and by the gilded successes of a few, thousands are seduced from the field of labor to become burdens or paupers upon society. They are as a swarm of drones feeding upon the honey gathered by the toil of the bees. Worse than that, they continue to drive the bees to destitution and death, while they take up the warm winter quarters and feast upon the gathered riches of their victims.

CHAPTER V

DESTRUCTIVE LABOR.

TO speak of destructive labor may seem somewhat fanciful and heterodox, since political economists have not made, or recognized, such a classification. It seems indeed, at first sight, paradoxical to speak of labor as destructive.

But if we look below the surface of things we shall discover that labor may be so expended as to be positively destructive both directly and indirectly. To quote Adam Smith once more, productive labor is that which "adds to the value of the subject upon which it is bestowed." Reverse this and we have destructive labor defined, viz.: *that which destroys the value of the subject,* etc.

It is necessary for us to have clear ideas of what we mean by value or wealth. If Henry George's definition of wealth is correct, (see previous article on "Our National Wealth") then indeed, there can be no such thing as destruction in any labor so long as it contributes to the gratification of human desire."

But if we understand value as that which contributes to the wants—material, physical, intellectual, or moral, as well as to our desires, we preceive that much of the labor of the world is expended in the opposite direction, *i.e.,* destruction.

Of course all labor has an object in view. No one engages voluntarily in any kind of work without some expectation of reward. The workman looks for wages, the employer for profit. These are attainable up to a certain point, in proportion as desire is gratified, but all men cannot be gainers unless those desires only are gratified which contribute to human good.

Our enquiry therefore is not whether an article will sell—not whether it will contribute to human desire, but whether it will promote the interests or good of mankind.

If human desire only be the basis of value the basest of passions may contribute to it, and he whose desires are associated with power may crush the weaker in the gratification of passion and yet contribute to the stock of wealth.

In this connection we may consider the use and abuse of an article. Dynamite may be used in the interests of science and commerce. It was so used in the shattering of the rock at Hellgate. The labor expended in producing that dynamite was a contribution to the removal of that great obstruction, and therefore was in the interests of human progress and good.

But the labor expended in manufacturing dynamite to be used by a league of Nihilists in the destruction of property and life is obviously a contribution to destruction. The latter however gratifies human desire as well is the former, but there is a wide difference in their respective effects. Every man who helped to make the explosives used in the scientific triumph at Hellgate was a contributor to human good as well as to human desires.

The men who make dynamite for Nihilists or Anarchists to employ in a work of destruction, respond also to the call of human desire, but not to human good. They are contributors in a work which produces nothing but disaster and death.

Whether they do so knowingly or not, so as to share the moral guilt is beside the question, and does not affect the argument.

It is often alleged that war contributes to trade by promoting industry in certain departments. The ship builder, the manufacturer of ammunition and soldier's supplies, all receive impetus at the first dread sound of the war bugle, and large classes of people in old countries regard a European war as a most desirable event.

Yet who will deny that all labor expended in the interests of war is a contribution to human woe and disaster. No modern political economist would defend war as a means to increase the wealth of the world, simply because 'it gives temporary impulse to certain trades and excites human desires.

War is a destroyer, and all labor expended in it is destructive. It must, therefore, leave its mark upon the national exchequer as well as elsewhere. It reduces the common fund because it destroys the common wealth, and the result is that productive labor is taxed on account of it.

The power of production is enormous. The extent to which the human family can augment the world's wealth is beyond calculation. But great as it is, it comes far short of man's power to destroy. If but a few men are engaged in a work of destruction, how fearfully prolific of evil results is their labor.

Some idea of the enormity of the evils produced by war and towards which all the labor employed in making war materials contributes, may be gathered from the following facts. :

The war debt for every man, woman and child in Europe is in round figures as follows :—

Austrian Empire	$57
Belgium	62
France	26
German States	31
Gt. Britain and Ireland	109
Italy	63
Holland	84
Portugal	87
Russia	26
Spain	150
Turkey in Europe	50

The cost of the American civil war is estimated at $5,342,237,000.

The Franco-German war cost France about $1,857,000,000. These enormous and inconceivable sums of money represent only a part of the awful devastation and ruin effected, and do not take into account the value of the human lives lost in these wars.

Mulhall gives the loss of life by war between 1793 to 1877 as 4,470,000.

In the war between England and France 1793 to 1815 the loss was 1,900,000 lives.

In the Crimean war the loss was 485,000.

In the American civil war 656,000.

In the Franco-German war 290,000.

In the Russo-Turkish war 180,000.

Thus, millions of men who ought to have contributed to the world's wealth were slain in the very prime of life and productive labor is taxed to support their widows and orphans as well as to carry the whole of the burden of cost of war itself. Washington Gladden speaking of the American war says:

" Hundred's of millions of wealth were obliterated utterly: burnt up, demolished, shot away in iron, lead and gunpowder. Of course such a destruction of property must impoverish the land. A nation may tide over the shoal of debt, heaped up in such a time, on a flood of paper money; but the due bills of the government must be settled bye and bye. When that time comes it will be seen that paper is poor stuff with which to patch up the breaches that war has made in the national capital." *Working People and their Employers.*

The chief cause of war, between civilized countries at least, is the maintenance of the professional soldier. Standing armies are standing menaces between nations. They are national pugilists in constant training for a "coming event" and the ever active training and preparations for war,—the anxiety of military pugilists for promotion and for opportunity to display their fighting talents, are among the most powerful incentives to war between nations.

The standing armies of Europe number 3,388,864 men, or if the reserves, militia, &c., are counted they number 19,355,461. So that in the 20 different nations of Europe we have 20 conflicting armies with nearly twenty millions of men trained to wholesale murder.

The seven principal nationalities of Europe have the following standing armies and reserves respectively:

	St'g Army.	Total with Reserves.
Austria	290,000	1,026,130
France	519,000	3,750,000
German States	445,000	5,670,000
Gt. Britain & Ireland	220,000	545,385
Italy	480,000	2,785,000
Russia	770,000	3,200,000
Turkey and Bulgaria	150,000	500,000

In addition to these, Austria has 56 Warships, France 302, German States 77, Gt. Britain and Ireland 360,

Italy 89, Russia 250, Turkey 32, while Holland has 135 and Sweden 133.

Think of all these agencies of destruction in perpetual training, and by their very existence offering a constant menace to each other, all of them ever ready for a conflict of human butchery.

When Adam Smith said that it is only by means of a standing army that the civilization of any country can be perpetuated or even preserved, he spoke according to the light of history up to his time, but not according to the science of political economy or of wiser councils of later times. There had been no demonstration of the possible settlement of international disputes by arbitration. There had never been a Geneva arbitration court. There had never been a proposal to submit an international dispute to a court of two great European nations.

The world had not seen a great nation like America marching its thousands and tens of thousands from industry to battle and back again from war to industry. There had never been great countries like Australia and Canada governed and keeping peace practically without any army at all, except such as may be called from the workshop or the merchant's desk at the call of the country to suppress an untutored and half savage uprising. The machinery of a standing army is essentially opposed to the good of society. It induces idleness and contempt for honest toil; it promotes waste and whether in time of peace or war all its machinery and labor is destructive. Henry George remarks:

"The destruction of wealth involved in a general illumination or the firing of a salute is equivalent to the burning up of so much food; the keeping of a regiment of soldiers, or of a warship and her crew is the diversion to unproductive uses of labor that could produce subsistence for many thousands of people."—*Social Problems.*

Mr. George might have gone further to show that the business and training of a regiment of soldiers or a war ship is part of an engine of destruction which when in operation speedily destroys many times more than the same number of persons could have produced.

Sir J. W. Pease, Bart, M.P., recently remarked at a public meeting in England:

"If you will go down, as I have gone down, to Chatham, and see the millions of pounds which have been wasted there, in consequence of panic cries at one time and another, you will hesitate before calling out for an increase in our warlike maritime power. I found a number of warships lying rotting at Chatham—the offspring of panic cries in the past—most of which cost the nation fifty, sixty, eighty, or even a hundred thousand pounds. Yet, for all the amount of money spent on them, they have never been to sea, and never will go. I asked one officer why those ships were lying rotting there. He said they were not fit to go to sea. After so many thousand pounds had been spent on the engines, they were not compound engines, and would not drive up to the present rates of speed. I asked why they were not sold, and the officer said they were not fit for any other purpose, and would not pay for pulling to pieces; so there they lie, side by side, monuments of panics in the past, and warnings against panics in the future. The United States have hardly any navy at all. One of the American Ministers told me that America could not bring 10,000 men together within six weeks. Yet does anyone think they are in danger, or need to be afraid of their neighbors.

Mr. Wm. Hoyle says:—

"There is a very common but erroneous popular belief, that destruction of property is good for trade, inasmuch as it is thought to create a demand for material, to replace that which has been destroyed. I can best s   the fallacy of this notion by giving an illustration. I will assume that a certain person, A., is worth £50,000; of this he has £20,000 invested in a mill. The rest of his money he has partly in the bank, and partly in sundry other investments. He, however, finds that the £20,000 he has invested in the mill pays him the best interest, and therefore he is contemplating doubling the size of the mill, so as to find employment for another £20,000. Whilst revolving these schemes in his mind a fire occurs, and his mill is burnt to the ground. People say, "It's a bad job, but its good for trade." Is this so? Those who talk thus should not forget that the money which will re-build the burnt mill would have built the second mill. In that case there would have heen two mills instead of one; and instead of 250 workpeople being needed there would have been 500; there would have been a double demand for labour, and a double production of goods; or, in other words, a double creation of wealth.

"It might, however, possibly be the case that trade was bad, and that owing to food being dear, and there being no demand for manufactured goods, A. could hardly sell the products of his first mill. Under such circumstances, therefore, he would not think of building a second. In that case, what would he do? Burn his mill down in order that he would find use for his money? No; but look out for some other investment. Very likely he might see it most profitable to invest his £20,000 in an estate, and set men to work to drain and improve it, so as to secure better and larger crops. By so doing, he would find additional labour for the workmen, increase the supply of food, and thereby reduce its price; and so, by lowering the cost of food, he would secure increased means by which to purchase manufactured goods, and thereby augment the general trade and commerce of the country.—*Our National Resources and How They are Wasted*

We shall see in succeeding chapters illustrations of this truth as related to the liquor traffic. We shall see that this traffic produces nothing but disaster, ruin and death; that it is a robber of production and a thief of capital. That instead of employing labor proportionate to the volume of capital and trade, as a productive business would do—labor is robbed of her due share of marked values by the manufacture of this destructive agent which is everywhere attended with evils, "greater than the combined evils of war pestilence and famine." Vide W. E. Gladstone.

LABOR AND LIQUOR.

What is the relation of the liquor traffic to labor?

1. *The labor expended in the manufacture of liquor is not productive.*

It does not "add to the value of the subject upon which it is bestowed." It may be objected that the work of the distiller and the brewer is productive because it augments the selling price of the article upon which the labor is expended. That is to say, whiskey or beer will sell readily for much more money than the grain from which they are manufactured.

This is another way of saying, with Henry George, that value is that which alters or modifies natural agents so as to gratify human desires.

It is strange that so logical and observant a student of social problems as Henry George should see, in human desire, the only standard of value. With him human good and utility have no place as a quality of value. He says:

"Value, it must be remembered, is a totally different thing from utility * * no matter how useful it may be, nothing has a value until some one is willing to give labor, or the production of labor, for it."

Would it not be equally correct to say that *value* is a totally different thing from *desire*? Of course desire has much to do with the price which a man will be willing to pay for a thing, and utility would not bring value without desire. But does not that which is useful create desire, while that which is desired is of no value unless it is useful in some way or other? Men are daily spending "money for that which is not bread, and their labor for that which satisfieth not."

Natural products may be "secured, moved, combined, separated or in other ways modified by human exertion so as to fit them for the gratification of human desire" and yet they may operate against human good. They may even be made so as to *create desire* and produce human woe. The cultivation and exposure for sale in our public markets of a poisonous berry might contribute to human desire and bring a considerable return in money. But the exchange of money for poison would not be producing wealth, although it might contribute to desire.

Market prices are doubtless regulated by human desires, but desires are sometimes created by supply, and demand is thereby increased for articles which give an inadequate, or possibly no return at all for the price paid. Men pay away their labor, or the produce of their labor, for comparatively, or wholly useless, and sometimes for decidedly injurious things. There is no intrinsic value in a cigar, yet cigars sell readily at a profit varying from 50 to 500 per cent. above the combined cost of the material from which they are made and the labor expended in making them.

A great proportion of the quack medicines are valueless, and their selling price is out of all proportion to their cost, yet they often find a ready sale.

A gambling saloon gratifies the desire for gambling, but it also creates desire; but there is no value or wealth produced by gambling.

A lottery contributes to human desire, but no lottery business has ever been conducted which increases value or even give a dollar's worth of chance for a dollar.*

But the traffic in intoxicating liquors has not even the small merit of the lottery and gambling business. *It is "all blanks and no prizes"* to the buyer. It is true that human desire is gratified by it, but it is also created by it, and although gratified it is not satisfied or rewarded. Once in a while we hear of a lottery ticket drawing a valuable prize (of course at the expense of the other ticket holders) but who ever heard of a man spending money for liquor and securing thereby any kind of substantial gain? Who ever heard of an acquired appetite for strong drink bringing a picture, or a house, or any other advantage, material, physical or moral?

Again, productive labor does not destroy the subject upon which it is expended, but it develops, adapts or prepares it for the better service of mankind. Raw material such as wool, cotton, iron, clay, etc., are developed by labor into cloth, steel, bricks, etc. These again are further developed by labor into garments, houses, implements, furniture.

But in the production of alcoholic drinks the subject is destroyed. Alcohol is not the outcome of a development or adaptation of food properties; it is the creature of destruction, obtainable only by the destruction of the natural properties of the subject. A log of

---

*"The world never saw, nor ever will see, a perfectly fair lottery; or one in which the whole gain compensated the whole loss; because the undertaker could make nothing by it. There is not a more certain proposition in mathematics than that the more (lottery) tickets you adventure upon the more likely you are to be a loser. Adventure upon all the tickets and you lose for certain; and the greater the number of your tickets the nearer you approach to this certainty."*Adam Smith in Wealth of Nations.*

wood may be developed, altered or adapted so as to produce a table or a case for an organ or piano. Put the log into the fire, and all that will be left of it is ashes. So likewise alcohol is the ashes of the fruit, barley, or corn, and it is of no more value as food or as a beverage than is the ashes of a burnt tree for furniture.

What then is the conversion of food into alcohol but destruction. It is certainly not production. The mission of labor in relation to food is to increase its utility, and this increases its real value. The productions of the distiller and the brewer supply no wants, satisfy no needs, and only gratify desire by creating unnatural ones.

The labor expended, therefore, in the manufacture of alcoholic liquor for beverage purposes is absolutely unproductive. The sum total of this labor forms no part of a nation's wealth, and must be deducted from the annual returns of industries, since it produces nothing of value.

The census returns of 1881 show that there were employed in the distilleries 285, and in breweries 1411 men. This gives a total of 1,696. These 1,696 persons are supposed to be classed as engaged in productive labor in the first degree, as they are not merely distributors but workers in the factory. Yet they all live upon the proceeds of other men's productive labor. That is to say, the architect, teacher, painter, carpenter and all other producers combined, have to support these men just as they have to support gamblers, or the quacks who sell soap pills to cure all the ills of man.

To illustrate this, the working brewer takes his wages for his labor and lives upon it, but his labor has produced—what? Not food—for his business is to destroy the nutritive properties of the grain he uses;

not a beverage, for all that is beverage in beer is water and that he has no hand in making. He has added to the water alcohol, and a little coloring matter, neither of which is either food or drink. He has produced ashes. He has made nothing on which to support himself or any other creature, or which will give an equivalent in value for what he consumes. Therefore, whatever of food, clothing, furniture, books or other necessaries or luxuries which he consumes must be produced by others, while his labor produces no equivalent.

On the other hand, a working carpenter for instance, takes wages for labor and lives upon it, and his labor produces—what? He does not take the raw material and destroy it, but converts it into articles of actual utility and value; he produces a chair, a table, a window frame, or some other equivalent for the food which he consumes. His very wages depend upon his making something of more value than ashes or sawdust, and of more substantial value than the material upon which he works. Both the brewer and the carpenter are supported by productive labor, but the one destroys material wealth, the fruits of labor, and contributes nothing in its place—the other develops raw material into articles of utility and value.

CHAPTER VI.

THE LABOR EXPENDED IN THE PRODUCTION OF ALCOHOLIC LIQUORS IS DESTRUCTIVE.

THE natural proprieties of grain or fruit are destroyed in the manufacture of alcoholic liquors. Brewing is not a process of cooking, preparing or developing food, but of absolute destruction of its nutritive properties. It does not make a beverage, but poisons the only beverage provided by nature. It does not prepare or adapt an article of diet, but it destroys food. The labor expended in converting food into alcoholic drinks does not promote the good or enhance the utility of the subject upon which it is expended, but renders it worse than useless.

Labor expended in destroying grain, spoiling water, and producing poision is surely a destructive agent. But circumstances may exist which justify the employment of such an agent. It is necessary at times to employ unproductive labor for the sake of securing or preserving values already produced. Thus, we employ a fire brigade or a police force to protect the interests of all, while the producer is too busily engaged in enhancing values, to be always ready himself to extinguish a fire, or detect a thief.

For similar reasons even destructive labor may be occasionally employed with advantage to the country. To save a city from the ravages of a raging and spreading fire it is sometimes necessary to destroy a block of houses so that the continuity of material for conflagration may be cut off.

War, although an unmerciful and pitiless destroyer is sometimes justified as the only means of quelling rebellion and securing the general peace and safety.

It may be urged that the manufacture of alcohol is of value for a similar reason. Alcohol is a useful agent in mechanical science and manufacture. There are many medical men who claim that it is of value as a medicine, although the number of these is rapidly decreasing. That, in certain carefully prepared doses, it may be used to neutralize the effects of some other poison is believed by a great many people.

If this be admitted it offers no solution of the economical problem at issue.

No violence is done to society in destroying one agent for the production of another which will promote human good. To the extent that alcohol supplies the chemist and the mechanic with a needed commodity, or the physician with a remedial agent, its manufacture is in harmony with economic law, just as it is economy to destroy timber when necessary to produce ashes or charcoal, if ashes or charcoal are needed.

But these considerations have no relation to the common manufacture and sale of intoxicants for beverage purposes. As well might we attempt to justify common arson, because the best way to break the continuity of the prairie conflagration is to meet fire with fire.

Thus, the use of an article has to do with its value. Suppose a factory, for the manufacture of arsenic, to supply the laboratory and the drug store for medical and scientific purposes. Utility is served thereby and the "value of the subject" is increased by that utility. But if that factory, for the sake of increasing its volume of trade, supplied arsenic for the production of an attractive looking candy, which, while it gratified human desire at the same time destroyed human good by its poisonous effects, it would be regarded as a destructive agent and would be condemned as such.

If there were no other call for alcohol than that which science and medicine demands its manufacture would be limited to the still of the laboratory. But the business of distillers and brewers is based upon the supply of an unnatural desire created by that upon which it feeds. John Wesley was in advance of his age, but not in advance of economic truth when he said:—

"All who sell spirituous liquors in the common way to any that will buy are poisoners-general. They murder His Majesty's subjects by wholesale, neither does their eye pity or spare. They drive them to hell like sheep; and what is their gain? Is it not the blood of these men? Who, then, would envy their large estates and sumptuous palaces? A curse is in the midst of them. Blood, blood is there, the foundation, the floor, the walls, the roof are stained with blood. And canst thou hope, O, thou man of blood! Though thou are clothed in scarlet and fine linen and farest sumptuously every day, canst thou hope to deliver down the fields of blood to the third generation? Not so; for there is a God in heaven; therefore thy name shall be rooted out, like as those whom thou hast destroyed, body and soul; thy memorial shall perish with thee."—*Sermon on money by Rev. J. Wesley.*

CHAPTER VII.

CAPITAL AND LABOR.

CAPITAL may be defined as that portion of wealth which is available for producing more wealth. It is not mere surplus or accumulated property. The wealth which is locked up in any way—whether in the estate of a land-owner, or money not circulated—is not capital until it is made available for productive purposes. The works of art which adorn the home of a manufacturer are wealth, but not capital; if, however he, at any time exchanges them for machinery or,—what is the same thing—money to buy machinery with which to develop or extend his business, they represent capital. A diamond ring worn as an ornament and kept for that purpose is not capital, but as part of the stock of a jeweller it is. A piano or organ in a ladies parlor is not capital but in the stock of a piano dealer it is.

Adam Smith says:—

"That part (of a man's stock) which he expects is to afford him revenue is called capital." *Wealth of Nations*, Book 2, Chap. 1.

John Stuart Mill says:—

"Whatever things are destined to supply productive labor with the shelter, protection, tools and materials which the work requires and to feed and otherwise maintain the laborer during the process are called capital." *Political Economy*, Book 1, Chap. 4.

Edward Kellogg an American writer on political economy in making a distinction between money and capital says:—

"Money is not capital for if the real capital did not first exist in these States in sufficient amount to secure the money, it would never get into them. * * The people of every State must have money for the transaction of business, yet money is not capital, it only represents the value of capital." *Labor aud Capital, Sec. 5,*

McCulloch defines capital thus:—

"The capital of a nation really comprises all those portions of produce of industry existing in it, that *may be* directly employed either to support human existence or to facilitate production." *Notes on Wealth of Nations.*

Henry George illustrates his own definition that "Capital is wealth in course of exchange." He denies that wages is drawn from capital and claims that it is produced by labor. No doubt it is true of labor, that, as it is the source of all wealth, it must be the producer of all capital, which is a part of wealth.

But it cannot be denied that capital is the constant and necessary companion of labor in the acquirement or production of wealth. If a carpenter saves of his wages $500, that amount is unquestionably the produce of labor, but by means of that money he can employ himself in building a house, he will pay his own wages out of his capital. He will certainly expect his labor to be the ultimate source of payment of wages, and he will expect to have his capital remain intact and increased; but his labor and his capital are harnessed together and the total result can only be attained by such co-operation. If the carpenter had no capital he could not have produced the house. He must have been content to work for a capitalist, and he would then only get the profit, or wages, of labor; not the profit of capital. In either case the necessary fund, or reserve wealth, by which the laborer is supported while the work is progressing, is capital.

Mr. John Stuart Mill demonstrated that capital is essential to production, that "no productive operations beyond the rude and scanty beginnings of primitive industry are possible" without it, and that "while on the one hand industry is limited by capital, so on the other, every increase of capital gives, or is capable of giving, additional employment to industry, and this without assignable limit."

A conflict between capital and labor is a civil war, which, if carried on to its extreme end, would mean a war of extermination. The one is dependant upon the other. So much are they each dependant upon each, that it is impossible to separate them without paralysing both.

Capital is powerful, not because it is independent of labor, *for it is not;* but because it is more easily organized so as to compel labor to become its servant. Men are mostly actuated in their dealings with each other by self-interest, and there has grown up a contest between the owners of capital on the one hand, and the owners of labor on the other. So long as labor was in bondage there was no conflict. Under a system of slavery the interests of capital and labor are identical, because the owner of capital is also the owner of labor. In a condition of slavery the laborer is part of capital; there can be no dispute about wages, for there is no such thing as wages; and hours of labor are only regulated by the consideration of conserving the strength of the laborer for future work, just as a horse is not overworked in consideration of its future value.

But in free countries the wage-earners were bound to assert themselves. It was inevitable that they should demand fair play. It was inevitable too, that they should do this at first in a clumsy and inefficient manner. It was inevitable that they should at first be made the tools and victims, more or less, of demagogues and anarchists.

But as intelligence advances and leaders grow out of their own ranks, like Thos. Burt and Joseph Arch in England, and T. V. Powderly in the United States, the workmen are better able to lead their own campaigns for their own interests. They are now in a position to refuse the alliance of men whose objects are doubtful and whose aims and interests are even more antagonistic to honest labor than capitalists have ever been, or ever could be.

In the struggle, the workmen have often arrayed themselves against capital as though it were their natural enemy. Their real interests lie, not in widening the breach between capital and labor, but in promoting their mutual co-operation. The gain of either the capitalist or the workman is not necessarily the loss of the other.

Of course, labor and capital, when vested in separate classes, or individuals, have some interests which are separate. Capital goes into the market to buy labor at the lowest possible price; labor on the other hand seeks the highest possible price.

But capital is naturally the friend of labor and the great purpose of all organizations should be to make their interests as far as possible identical.

Capitalists have no right to inflict a stigma upon workmen. Honorable labor is entitled to the same respect as is claimed for capital. This is the sense in which the phrase "Jack's as good as his master" may be approved. Not justice alone is the demand; but respect and equitable treatment are the claims of both the employee and the employed.

> "The rank is but the guinea stamp
> The man's the gowd for a' that."

When a capitalist purchases labor he has no right to assume an air of superiority simply because he is buyer and the laborer the seller, Superiority there may be, arising from a greater degree of intelligence or more virtuous conduct, but these are not unfrequently found on the side of the laborer.

On the other hand workmen have no right to assume an air of braggadocia, defiance and intolerance, just because they are organized in the Knights of Labor or other trades' union. It savors of the brutality of the wolf to be impudent and tyrannical in gangs, or large numbers. Tolerance and forbearance are the needful lessons for men to learn when organized in large companies for the defence and rights of labor, quite as much as when backed by the concentrated power of capital.

The present agitation will go on, probably with varying results, until the forces on both sides shall learn that labor and capital are commodities, which, when existing apart, must bargain with each other on equal terms.

It is a grave mistake to organize labor against capital by stopping production. That is a policy more immediately destructive to workmen than to capitalists. All the burdens however inflicted, whether by anarchists, swindlers, and paupers, or by laborers combining to stop the wheels of production, fall upon productive labor as the source of all wealth. To compel producers to be idle is worse than "killing the goose that lays the golden eggs;" it prevents the production of the eggs while the bird remains to be fed.

Labor's just demand is fair wages for fair work and a contract between buyer and seller on equal terms. That, also, is the only just demand of capital.

CHAPTER VIII.

WASTED CAPITAL.

PRODUCERS are everywhere crying out for more capital. Especially is this the case in young countries like Canada. If we had more capital we could improve our lands, build new and better bridges, make our public roads solid, and utilize much of the material which now goes to waste; we could better feed our cattle, both for home and foreign markets; our agricultural interests and their productive power could be advanced; we could develop our mines and increase the value of our industries in every department. All this would mean more labor and more wealth, and therefore, more demand for the productions of labor. It would mean also, better openings for our young men in every branch of industry, and in all the professions. The transfusion of so much of the best of Canada's young blood into the veins of United States commerce would cease, and Canada would prove a more inviting field for immigration, and too good a country to emigrate from.

This is no dream or fancy picture. Canada has all the natural advantages for a large growing population, with constantly increasing openings for the expenditure of labor and the establishment of millions of homes within its vast domains.

It is a very common remark that what Canada needs is more capital. It would be more correct to say that what we need is, that the capital we have should be employed in developing our interests—not in destroying them; in making more wealth—not in wasting it. Older countries are not so immediately affected by the mis-application of capital and labor as we are in Canada. In the United Kingdom for instance, where there is an accumulation of wealth, acquired and piled up during the past ages, and which has been monopolized and held by a very small minority of the people*

---

* In the United Kingdom there are 72,119,961 acres included in the official returns of lands owned; it appears there were 12 owners who possessed 4,440,467 acres; 523 persons own one-fifth; 710 persons own one-fourth and 10,207 persons own two-thirds of all England and Wales. In Scotland one man owns 1,326,000 acres and has besides 32,005 acres in England. Another has 431,000 acres; another 424,000 acres and 12 persons own 4,339,722 acres. In Ireland one person owns 170,119 acres and 12 persons own 1,207,888; 3 persons own over 100,000 acres each; 14 over 50,000 each; 90 over 20,000 acres each; 292 persons own 6,458,000 acres, nearly one-fourth of the whole island, and 744 persons own 9,611,728 acres, nearly half the entire country.

Another illustration of the concentration of wealth in old countries may be seen in the following facts: In the United Kingdom during 20 years, from 1864 to 1884; 398 fortunes of £250,000 and upwards were assessed to the probate duties, (which fortunes do not include land, as land is free from probate duty). Among these were one fortune of £3,000,000; one at £2,800,000; one at £2,700,000; seven at £1,500,000 or upwards, and sixteen at £1,000,000 or upwards.

In the United States also there is enormous capital in the hands of a few men as will be seen by the following facts:—The capital represented by the big operators of Wall-street is as follows:—J. J. Astor, $125,000,000; Jay Gould, $100,000,000; Cornelius Vanderbilt, $80,000,000; W. K. Vanderbilt, $75,000,000; Russell Sage, $50,000,000; Huntington, $25,000,000; Winslow, Lanier & Co., $20,000,000; D. O. Mills, $15,000,000; Pierpont Morgan, $15,000,000; Bob Garret, $15,000,000; Armour, $15,000,000; Fred. Vanderbilt, $12,000,000; Sidney Dillion, $10,000,000; Woerishoffer, $10,000,000; J. R. Hoxie, $8,000,000; Addison Cammack, $5,000,000; John Rockafellar, $5,000,000; Alexander Mitchell, $5,000,000; Cyrus W. Field, $4,000,000, S. V. White, $3,000,000; W. R. Travers, $3,000,000; R. P. Flower, $3,000,000; John Shaw, 2,500,000; W. E. Connor, 2,000,000; Slayback, $1,500,000; Gen. Dodge, $1,500,000; Victor Newcomb, $1,000,000; Sam Sloan, $1,000,000.

there is ample capital unemployed and always waiting the opportunity of investment. If a portion of this is diverted into distructive channels, it does not appear immediately to affect the general supply of capital for the development of legitimate industries.

In this sense therefore the employment of capital in any direction which is opposed to the general wealth, is more disastrous in a young country where money is comparatively dear, and capital comparatively scarce, than it is in a larger and wealthier community.

But is there any important percentage of our limited capital so employed as to become a weapon of destruction against our commercial interests?

In order to answer this enquiry we must keep in mind what we mean by capital. A burglars' tools are his capital, because, as Adam Smith says, they are "that part of a man's stock which he expects to bring him a revenue." But such capital when employed by the burglar, not only makes no wealth, but is at war with the interests and security of existing wealth.

Enormous sums of money are vested in immoral traffic. Large and handsome mansions are elaborately and expensively furnished, costly and seductive pictures and decorations are employed; a perfect network of active agency is sustained, in all the principal centres of population throughout the civilized world to capture young girls to their ruin. The sums of money employed in the traffic of gambling is also fabulous.

Capital so invested, may or may not, bring a revenue to the immediate investor. But whether it does or not, it is in direct antagonism to the general wealth of a country, as well as to its moral and social peace and advancement.

War is a most disastrous destroyer of capital—that is—it destroys the wealth of a country. True, it employs some capital, but what an utter mockery it is to commend anything as a commercial agent, which employs a thousand or ten thousand dollars of some persons capital, by means of which millions of other peoples' wealth is destroyed. Of course, a few persons will make private gain by the demands which immediately attend any immoral or destructive agency, just as an order for a set of burglars tools, or a counterfeit-coiner's plant will bring gain to the individuals who make them.

In short, all capital invested in the execution of agencies antagonistic to the interests, or good of society at large is wasted. Worse! it is in direct conflict with other capital.

CAPITAL AT WAR WITH CAPITAL.

THE CAPITAL EMPLOYED IN THE MANUFACTURE AND SALE OF INTOXICATING LIQUORS IS AT WAR WITH ALL OTHER CAPITAL INVESTED IN LEGITIMATE MANUFACTURE AND TRADE, AND WITH ALL MATERIAL INTERESTS OF THE COUNTRY.

(1) Because it is Capital employed in destroying what other Capital produces without giving an equivalent to the community.

In the chapter of this essay entitled "Destruction of Food" I have shown from Government returns that the destruction of grain (which is the actual product of labor and capital) in the distillation of spirits and malt liquors amounts to nearly *one hundred and fifty millions of bushels annually.*

To the utmost extent that this use of the produce of labor and capital fails to contribute to the general wealth or needs of the country, it is absolute waste, and therefore the capital so invested is at war with the other material interests of the community.

(2) Because capital so employed is locked up from other agencies which would develop the resources of the country, if available.

According to the census report 1881, the capital returned as invested in the business of distilling and brewing was as follows:—

    Breweries....................$4,592,990
    Distilleries.................... 1,303,000

This is doubtless, for obvious reasons, a very low estimate of the actual amount of money represented in the buildings, machinery and floating cash capital of the breweries and distilleries of the Dominion. There is no return given, so far as I know, of the number of licensed liquor dealers in the Dominion, and their invested capital, but the following facts will enable us to estimate them. In Ontario, under the Crooks Act, which greatly reduced the previous number, there were in 1881 licenses granted, in the proportion of one to every 462 inhabitants. Allowing for the larger ratio in some other provinces, and smaller ratios in one or two of the provinces, and allowing also for prohibitory laws in the thinly populated North-West it may be fairly estimated that the licenses granted through the whole Dominion would not be less than one to every 500 of the population. This in a population of 4,324,810, as given in the census returns of 1881 would give a total of 8,649 licensed liquor vendors in the Dominion. Prof. Foster, M. P., *esti-

---

* Speech in the House of Commons, Ottawa, March 5, 1884.

mates them at 10,000, which is probably nearer the mark. Take the smaller figure, however, and reckon that there is a capital invested in the liquor department of all these licenses equal to an average of $1,000. (some of the saloons will have thousands of dollars invested) and we have $8,649,000 as the capital locked up in the business of retailing liquors. If another one million dollars be added for the wholesale merchants, we have a grand total of $15,554,990 buried in the manufacture and sale of intoxicating liquors—a sum of money which pays no interest to the country, brings no wealth, adds nothing to the interests of the state, but on the contrary entails upon us an incalculable amount of destruction and waste.

If this enormous capital were invested in any legitimate business of manufacture, it would be increasing the general wealth and co-operating with other capital for the public good. For example, the amount of capital invested in 1881 in the manufacture of boots and shoes is given as $6,491,042, and in distilling and brewing $5,895,990. Let the reader contemplate the difference in the effects of these two capitals upon the national wealth and commerce of the country.

The one is employed, in co-operation with labor, in converting raw material into necessaries, adding to the general wealth, developing the resources of the country, and contributing to the comfort and necessities of millions of the men, women and children of the land. The other is directed to the destruction of raw material *adding nothing* to, but *decreasing* the general stock of capital in the country, and contributing to the discomfort, poverty and ruin of tens of thousands of persons every year. The one, by increasing the aggregate wealth, reduces the public burdens ; the other decreases the wealth, and increases the burden of taxation which falls upon the productive industries of the country.

(3) Because it does not co-operate with capital employed in productive industries; but opposes it. It is so obvious that it hardly needs any demonstration, that the liquor traffic is in direct antagonism with every enterprise of productive industry. Every merchant knows too well, that in proportion as a man spends his money for liquor, he is an unprofitable customer to the tailor, the shoemaker, the landlord, and the farmer. And precisely the opposite is true of every legitimate business. In proportion as a man spends his earnings in shoes or clothing, or books, so is he, as a rule, a good and profitable customer to the landlord and the farmer. All capital, therefore, employed in prosecuting and extending the traffic in liquor is *capital at war with the capital employed in manufacturing industries.*

Besides all this, the employment of capital cannot be divested of its effects. When we speak of the advantage accruing to the country from this employment of capital, we are liable to fall into the error of treating the economic question as one thing, and the moral and social as another,—the two in no way related. The truth is, they are identical in interest, inseparably bound up in each other. We cannot invest capital to the ruin of a people, and call the investment a blessing and the consequences a curse.

If a tithe or a thousandth part of the evils which flow from the unholy trinity—the distillery, the brewery and the saloon—were to come suddenly upon the community as a result of any other invested capital, we should not hesitate to hold that capital responsible for it. If for example, a soap or chemical-manure factory, in which is invested a million dollars capital, were spreading fever and pestilence over any community, the citizens would not think for a moment of any possible benefit arising from the employment of that capital. Once let it be established beyond doubt that there was an intimate relation between such a factory and the increase of graveyard population, and we should have as little consideration for the one million dollars invested as the country had for the capital invested in the North-West rebellion by Louis Riel and his associates.

CHAPTER IX.

DESTRUCTION OF FOOD.

WHAT THEN IS THE MEASURE OF DESTRUCTION INVOLVED IN THE MANUFACTURE OF ALCOHOLIC LIQUORS? The first item to consider is the waste of food.

In the United Kingdom the facts in relation to this question have been supplied to the public in a most comprehensive manner by the late Mr. Wm. Hoyle, (author of "Our Natural Resources, and How They are Wasted,") than whom there has never lived a more devoted and painstaking patriot. His work as a statistician was of the most exhaustive character, and he was regarded as an authority second to none on this great question.

Taking twelve years from 1870 to 1881 inclusive, he states that the amount of money spent upon intoxicating liquors in the United Kingdom was £1,609,241,534, being an average of £134,103,461 per annum. He further says:

"To manufacture the £134.000,000 worth of intoxicating liquors consumed during each of the past twelve years, 80,000,000 bushels of grain, or its equivalent in produce has been destroyed each year; and, taking the bushel of barley at 53lb., it gives us 4,240,000,000lbs. of food destroyed year by year, or a total for the twelve years of 960,000,000 bushels, or 50,880,000,000lbs.

The generally accepted estimate of grain consumed as bread food by the population of the United Kingdom is 5½ bushels per head per annum; if this be so, then, the food which has been destroyed to manufacture the intoxicating liquors which have been consumed in the United Kingdom during the past twelve years would supply the entire population with bread for four years and five months; or, it would give a 4lb. loaf of bread to every family in the United Kingdom daily during the next six years.

If the grain and produce which have thus been destroyed yearly were converted into flour and baked into loaves, they would make 1,200,000,000 4lb. loaves. To bake these loaves it would require 750 bakeries producing 500 loaves each hour, and working ten hours daily during the whole year."

In the United States the amount of food destroyed in the manufacture of intoxicants is enormous. Mr. A. M. Powell, of New York, read a paper at the Crystal Palace Jubilee, (Sept. 1882,) in which he says that " there were in 1881, 5,210 distilleries. These consumed 31,291,146 bushels of grain with an aggregate production of 117,728,150 gallons of proof spirits. The total beer production for the same period as reported by the Internal Revenue Department was 16,952,085 barrels."*

Dr. Edward Young, Chief of the Bureau of Statistics, Washington, estimated the cost of liquor in the United States in 1867 at $60,000,000. Dr. Wm. Hargreaves estimates the cost in 1872 at $785,720,048. Dr. Young remarks in reference to his estimates for 1867:—

---

* "Foundation of Death" by Axel Gustafson, p. 276.

"These figures are sufficiently startling, and need no exaggeration. Six hundred million! The minds of few persons can comprehend this vast sum which is worse than wasted every year. It would pay for 100,000,000 barrels of flour, averaging $2\frac{1}{2}$ barrels of flour to every man, woman and child in the country. This flour, if placed in wagons, ten barrels in each, would require 10,000,000 teams, which, allowing eight yards to each, would extend 45,455 miles—nearly twice round the earth, or half-way to the moon. If the sum were in one-dollar notes it would take one hundred persons one year to count them. If spread on the surface of the ground, so that no spaces should be left between the notes, the area covered would be 20,466 acres, forming a parallelogram of 6 by a little over $5\frac{1}{2}$ miles, the walk round it being more than $22\frac{1}{2}$ miles." *

The quantities of food wasted in Canada in the manufacture of liquor may be approximated by the following statistics and facts in relation thereto.

TABLE

SHOWING THE QUANTITIES OF GRAIN USED IN THE MANUFACTURE OF SPIRITS AND MALT LIQUORS IN CANADA DURING ELEVEN YEARS FROM 1875 TO 1885 INCLUSIVE.

The following table is compiled from Government Returns of Spirits and Malt Liquors to the year 1882, and Inland Revenue Reports for 1884 and 1885, and also the Trade and Navigation Reports for the years 1884 and 1885:—

---

* "Our Wasted Resources," by W. Hargreaves, M.D., p. 53.

	Pounds of grain for Distillation.	Pounds of Malt for Brewing.
1875	90,094,381	30,377,039
1876	59,472,129	27,980,256
1877	68,498,295	27,471,797
1878	67,594,902	25,180,327
1879	66,749,856	25,456,803
1880	53,394,258	26,419,244
1881	53,667,108	28,395,987
1882	70,402,810	34,775,986
1883	76,796,094	36,140,545
1884	75,095,450	37,563,636
1885	63,542,708	34,566,059
Totals	745,307,991	332,215,639

Grand total of grain used 10,775,523,630 lbs.

Corn is the principal grain used for distilling purposes and weighs about 56 lbs. to the bushel. The number of pounds therefore represented in the above table as used for distillation is equal to about 13,434,071 bushels. Barley is reduced in weight about 25 per cent in the process of malting so that it takes about 415,268,552 pounds of barley to produce the quantity of malt named in the table. This at the usual rate of 48 lbs. to the bushel is equal to about 8,651,428 bushels of barley. THERE WAS THEREFORE A TOTAL QUANTITY OF GRAIN CONSUMED IN DISTILLING AND BREWING IN ELEVEN YEARS IN CANADA AMOUNTING TO 22,085,499 BUSHELS.

In addition to this there was consumed in distilling and brewing 458,697 gallons of molasses and 317,861 lbs. of sugar, &c.

If all this vast quantity of food were used in any way to promote the good or to increase the wealth of the nation it would be a matter of great congratulation and rejoicing; but when we contemplate the fact that it is, not only wasted, but infinitely worse than wasted, the magnitude of the evil strikes us as perfectly appalling.

Consider the proportion of this waste to the entire growth of grain in Canada. In 1881 the total production of all kinds of grain in the Dominion including wheat, barley, oats, rye, peas, beans, buckwheat and corn was 149,461,399 bushels.

As the years 1880-1 is nearly midway of the eleven years referred to in the above table, that year may be taken as about an average year so far as the production of grain is concerned.

Taking, then, 150 millions of bushels as an average of the grain produce per year, we discover the amazing fact that once in every seven years the entire amount of all the grain produce in the Dominion, or its equivalent, is consumed in liquor.

To put it in another way, the grain destroyed in liquor making, during the past seven years, was equal to more than one year's entire growth of all kinds of grain in the Dominion.

Think of it! ye patriots who desire that the nation's resources shall be converted into wealth for her people. Think of it! ye politicians who are in search of a cry for your next election campaign. Think of it! ye judges and magistrates, before whom comes the perpetual array of drink-made criminals, while the criminals who make the drink are made jurors and governors. Think of it! ye ministers of the gospel by the grace of God. Think of it! ye farmers of the soil; ye toilers in the workshop. Think of it, every man and woman, every boy and girl; think! that the one-seventh of all the golden grain of every Canadian harvest is—consumed in fire? burnt up in one vast mountain of flame? flung into the sea without hope of redemption? No! no! Worse! a million times a million worse than that! It is turned into the vat and the still and converted into rivers of poison by which our people are afflicted with incalculable evils, and every form of human misery attends it.

I cannot do better in closing this chapter than to quote the following words of Cardinal Manning He says:—"WE TALK OF PROFITABLE INVESTMENTS, AND THEN WASTE A HUNDRED AND THIRTY MILLIONS IN THE MOST UNPROFITABLE INVESTMENT THAT CAN BE CONCEIVED IN THE IMAGINATION OF MAN. NAY, I WILL GO FURTHER. IT IS NOT ONLY WASTE. IT HAS A HARVEST. IT IS A GREAT SOWING BROADCAST. AND WHAT SPRINGS FROM THE FURROW? DEATHS; MORTALITY IN EVERY FORM; DISEASE OF EVERY KIND; CRIME OF EVERY DYE; MADNESS OF EVERY INTENSITY; MISERY BEYOND THE IMAGINATION OF MAN; SIN, WHICH IT SURPASSES THE IMAGINATION TO CONCEIVE."

Address at Newcastle on Tyne, England, Sept. 9, 1882. Vide Foundation of Death, p. 258.

CHAPTER X.

OVER-PRODUCTION.

NOTHING is more common than to attribute hard times and low prices to over-production. The idea is that if there is a large surplus of any kind of produce—whether of the farm or the factory—that the goods become a glut upon the market, prices go down, and demand for labor is checked. With this thought in view, it is frequently claimed that the only remedy for the evil is to check production.

Stript of all rhetoric this theory simply means that the remedy for hard times is to stop, or check, the making of wealth. Its language is 'close up the mills for a time, cease making implements, stop the production of clothing, shoes, and bread stuff; let the farmer check the growth of the field and the produce of the dairy, leave the soil unploughed and without seed for a season, and then, as you reduce the volume of supply, prices for stock in hand will go up, trade will get brisk and working men can go back to their ploughing and seeding, their making and building at increased wages, and everybody will be better off.'

The fallacy of all this is so perfectly transparent that it is a marvel that any thoughtful man should endorse it. Follow out this plan and you at once check the power of demand. You stop the springs of all wages and prevent the wage-earning class from taking cash in hand to pay for various articles of produce at the merchant's store.

It would give the mechanic and laborer a holiday, and at what price? Grim want, debt, poverty and destitution would quickly follow where comparative comfort and moderate supplies had previously existed. Store-keepers would have the satisfaction of selling goods at high prices, on long and dubious credit, and manufacturers would be able to rejoice in the return of of piles of notes *unpaid*—the inevitable end; BANK- RUPTCY.

There is something contradictory in the very term over-production, when applied generally. Obviously there can be no such thing while thousands and millions of people are needing and desiring the things produced. Everybody, the world over, is more or less desirous of increasing his stock of wealth—and production is the source of wealth. No one is interested in lessening his supply of the necessaries and luxuries of life, at least we have never yet found a community which regards these as burdens.

The late Mr. Wm. Hoyle, the eminent statistician thus wrote on this question :—

"To talk of an excess of goods as the cause of want is as unreasonable as to say that darkness is caused by there being too much light. True, there may be glut in one place and want in another, but that arises from the violation of some economic law affecting either the production, distribution, or consumption of wealth, and what in such a case should be done is to find out where this violation of law is being perpetrated, and correct it. There will then be plenty for all, and no glut anywhere.

A universal glut is an impossibility, for the simple reason that when people everywhere become possessed of the comforts of life in such abundance as that all their desires are met they will cease to produce. People toil, not for the love of toil, but for its proceeds—that is, to supply their wants—and this being done, the motive to labour is gone. They will then cease to labour, and over-production will be immediately checked.

And there is another point which must not be overlooked in considering the question of glut. It is this : the wants of a community invariably increase in proportion as the means of supply grow. We see this daily; for if a man by attention to business makes money, or if he be a workman and gets a fair advance of wages, he at once adds to his comforts. Perhaps he goes into a larger and better house. He then wants more furniture, more books, and more of everything; and thus he goes on, the limit of his demand being only bound by the extent of his supply.

As is the case individually, so it is nationally—the limit of what society generally is prepared to utilise for its enjoyments and wants is only bounded by the limit of its power to produce; and therefore the discoveries in science, and the inventions of machinery which have done so much to augment our producing power, instead of causing a glut in the markets of the world, and thereby involving stagnation in trade, have but multiplied our comforts, stimulated our industries, and so increared the material, social, and domestic happiness and well-being of the people."

Mr. Henry George, remarks :—

" What, when we come to think of it, can be more preposterous than to speak in any general sense of over-production ? Over-production of wealth when there is everywhere a passionate struggle for more wealth; when so many must stint and strain and contrive, to get a living; when there is poverty and actual want among large classes ! Manifestly there cannot be over-production, in any general and absolute sense until desires for wealth are all satisfied, until no one wants more wealth." *Social Problems, Chap. XII.*

" Relative over-production, of course there may be" remarks the author just quoted. There are frequently more goods produced of certain kinds than will sell at profitable rates in the available markets.

But such an irregularity cannot be cured by stopping or checking general production. Of course you may regulate supply by checking the production of the particular article in question. But if it is found that too much wheat has been grown for this year's demand, the remedy is found in growing something else. If furniture makers produce more chairs than they can find buyers for, the remedy is not in closing the factory but in making less chairs and more of something else.

'But' replies an objector, 'the fact is, that there is too much of everything produced; turn in any direction you may, into whatever channel of business you will, and you find that the supply is greater than the demand and the markets are glutted with goods!'

Let this be admitted and it then appears marvellous that thinking men do not recognize the lessons which it teaches. Surely it must be plain, that the remedy lies, not in limiting the power of production, but in augmenting the power to purchase. Take for example, our Canadian piano and organ manufactories. It is easy to conceive of their producing more instruments than they can sell, and thus glutting the market. That is over-production in the relative sense. But in the general and absolute sense there is no overproduction of pianos and organs until every one is supplied who desires them, and until the population cease to grow in musical tastes as well as in numbers.

Some years ago the present Lord Derby delivered a speech at Liverpool, in which he attributed to the commercial depression of the times to over-production. As an illustration of his theory he referred to the enormous productive powers of the stocking looms of

Lancashire, and to the fact that the colossal warehouses in Manchester, and elsewhere, were weighted down with the goods for which no market could be found.

It did not seem to occur to the Earl that the real difficulty was not that too many stockings were made, but that too few were worn, proportionate to the reasonable wants and desires of the population.

The speech above referred to was delivered within a mile or so of a large and probably the most lucrative portion of Lord Derby's own estate. Upon that very estate were living many people who, although several degrees removed from the very poorest of the people of Liverpool, were yet too poor to purchase as many stockings for themselves and their children as they desired or needed, to meet the reasonable demands of civilized life in such a city. I believe I am within the bounds of a moderate estimate when I say that there were probably at least a thousand people—men, women and children—residing upon the leasehold property of Lord Derby's estate in West Derby Ward, Liverpool, to whom new stockings were a luxury, only to be enjoyed when pressing necessity compelled the purchase of them. In some other parts of that city there are thousands of feet to which a pair of new stockings are strangers from one year's end to another. If this single fact in the lives of large masses of the people in the United Kingdom could be accurately estimated it would doubtless be found that there are literally millions of people who never buy stockings, and millions more who only get a new pair when the presence of decency or hard weather constrains them to make a special effort. *

---

* That I may not appear to exaggerate I may mention that there were in 1884 in England and Wales alone 586,717 persons receiving

Now what would be the result to the Manchester trade, and what the effect upon the stocking looms of Lancashire if these masses of people were so far relieved of their poverty as to be able to purchase each two pairs of stockings where they now buy one; or one pairs where they now buy none? It is a simple truth to say that the cry of over-production in the stocking trade would speedily be substituted for another cry, viz.: "excessive demand and pressure of work!" And what is true of stockings is true also of other essentials and luxuries of civilized life. So long as there is desire and need for the productions of the farm and the factory, there is no such thing as over-production.

The problem to be solved is not how to limit production, but how to get the hosiery transferred from the loom and the warehouse to the bare feet,—how to get the piano and organ into the homes of persons who desire them and have not the means to purchase them.

The solution of that problem, not only opens the way to a revival of trade in one or two, but in all departments, and to a permanent up-growing of demand which shall keep the wheels of productive labor in motion for as long a time per day and as continuously as is desirable.

"outdoor relief" as paupers, a kind of relief that is not granted to persons who give any indication of being able to buy stockings when they need them. There are in addition to these, 187,593 persons who are inmates of poor-houses or "work-houses." These latter are of course supplied with their allowance of clothing from the poor fund. The more than half a million above referred to as "outdoor paupers" are but a small per centage of the whole poor of the country to whom the expenditure of a sixpence is a matter of great moment.

It has been stated in the *Fortnightly Review* on the authority of Mr. John Bright that in the city of Glasgow alone there are "30,000 families that live and eat and sleep" and each family have only one room for all these purposes.

To a very considerable extent that problem is solved when we face the issues involved in the drinking system. And this is true of Canada more than of the older and richer countries. Not that we drink more, —happily much less. But as shown in another chapter, the locking up of a large portion of our national capital in an unprofitable and destructive investment, the waste of one-seventh of our agricultural produce, the employment of thousands of men in destructive labor, the cost of crime, poverty, and accident occasioned; all these things affect a young country like this sooner, and more directly, than a richer and larger populated country, especially one lying as we do by the side of a great competitive neighbor, with its larger resources and greater capital.

CHAPTER XI.

OVER-CROWDING THE LABOR MARKET.

ALONGSIDE the fallacy of the over-production theory there is another, viz: the theory of over-crowding the labor market. The two ideas are very much akin and are the result of a similar process of reasoning. "Reduce the quantity of goods produced" say the manufacturer and the capitalist "and desire will increase proportionately and prices will be higher." "Keep fresh men from entering the field of labor and competition will not be so keen, while wages will be higher" says the mechanic.

Now just as it is true that there may be relative over-production, so there may be relative over-crowding in certain branches of work or within certain communities. It is possible to have more bricklayers in one town or city than there is demand for. But it is not possible to have too many workmen *of all kinds.*

Mutual advantage among people is no where realized in such a large degree, and with such direct results, as in a community of workmen. Beginning with the farmer who produces food for all, there is a combination of interests in all productive agencies. The farmer will need the bricklayer, the carpenter, the tailor, the shoemaker, &c. These in turn, will not only need the farmer, but will need and demand each other's labor.

It is strange that men will resist the incoming of new workmen to the community of which they form a part. A carpenter sees a new comer taking up a position in the same village with himself, and he looks on with a jealous eye, remarking "there are more carpenters here now than can find profitable work." And so all around the selfish spirit of one mechanic would close the doors to another.

For the same reason labor leagues are almost invariably jealous of workmen immigrants, and especially call out loudly against Governments granting any assistance to induce immigration.

There are, no doubt, a great many outrages committed by emigration agents; and the Government may well be criticised on account of the disgraceful misrepresentations of their agents who have induced thousands of people to come to this country under promises which were not kept, and which led often to great disappointment and suffering.

During the past seven years the following numbers, according to official reports, have arrived in Canada with the intention of settling:

Year	Number
1879	40,492
1880	38,505
1881	47,991
1882	112,458
1883	133,624
1884	103,824
1885	79,165

In addition to these, various charitable societies and individuals brought into Canada during the past five years 6750 persons, mostly children.

The Government reports show that the estimated value of money and effects brought into the country by immigrants during the seven years named above amount to $21,552,222.

The chief objection raised by labor unions against assisted immigration is that every new comer brought into the country enters into competition with those already seeking a market for their labor. It does not seem to enter the thoughts of these objectors that every new comer increases the demand for the produce of labor.

The more working people there are in any country the greater is the demand for labor. So obvious is this, that the workman in search of employment almost invariably turn towards a progessive and growing centre of population.

Indeed, (contrary to that class of philosophers who raise the alarm that the world will speedily be over-populated if it be not so already,) it may be set down as a fact that society is always interested in a progressive population, and that it is everywhere desired that the village should grow to a town, and the town to a city. In Henry George's *Progress and Poverty*, there are two chapters devoted to this over-population theory to which I very gladly refer my readers for conclusive arguments and facts upon that subject. In one of those chapters he says:—*

"I assert that in any given state of civilization a greater number of people can collectively be better provided for than a smaller. I assert that the injustice of society, not the niggardliness of nature is the cause of the want and the misery which the current theory attributes to over-population. I assert that the new mouths which an increasing population calls into existence require no more food than the old ones, while the hands they bring with them can in the natural order of things produce more. I assert that,

---

* Progress and Poverty, Chapter iii.

F

other things being equal, the greater the population the greater the comfort which an equitable distribution of wealth would give to each individual. * * *

Is there any doubt that, while England has been increasing in population at the rate of two per cent per annum, her wealth has been growing in still greater proportion? Is it not true that while the population of the United States has been doubling every twenty-nine years her wealth has been doubling at much shorter intervals? Is it not true that under similar conditions—that is to say, among the communities of similar people in a similar state of civilization, the most densely populated community is also the richest? Are not the most densely populated Eastern States richer in proportion than the more sparsely populated Western or Southern States. Is not England, whose population is even denser than the Eastern States of the Union, also richer in proportion?"

It is therefore of much greater concern to the citizens of Canada to enquire why so many of our able-bodied producing citizens emigrate to the United States and elsewhere, than to ask after the abuses of Government immigration agents.

But to the workman, as such, it is of first consequence to enquire why there is any need of rivalry for work and wages. Why should men have to compete for work? Why should they be struggling one against the other, as though in the race of life the prize was only to one? Productive labor yields her prizes without stint.

Work and wages are not limited quantities. Every productive workman finds work for another. Labor is not only the source of wealth but is also a perpetual co-operative agent.

CHAPTER XII.

CO-OPERATION.

THE principle of Co-operation is rapidly growing in favor as the most hopeful and practical solution of what is called the labor problem. Its application, either by giving to labor a share in the profits of an undertaking, in which capital is provided by one set of men and labor by another, or by the laborers themselves becoming in part, or in whole, the joint proprietors, are both under extensive trial, and the results are such as to lead to the hope that in the more general application of these means, will be found a remedy for much of the evil and contention which have been growing during the past fifty years, with greater and greater volume, until the struggle has, in some instances, assumed the dimensions and character of a social revolution.

Washington Gladden has well said that:

The subjugation of labor by capital is the first stage in the progress of industry; the second stage is the warfare between labor and capital; the third is the identification of labor and capital by some application of the principle of co-operation."—*Working People and their Employers.*

Prof. Cairnes says:—

"It appears to me, that the condition of any sustained improvement of a permanent kind in the laborer's lot is, that the separation of the industrial classes into laborers and capitalists shall *not* be maintained; and the laborer shall cease to be a laborer,—in a word, that profits shall be brought to reinforce the wage-fund * * * the first and indispensible step towards any serious amendment of the laborer's lot, that he should be, in one way or other, lifted out of the groove in which he at present works, and placed in a position compatible with his becoming a sharer, in equal proportion with others, in the general advantages arising from industrial progress."—*Political Economy.*

The principle of co-operative interest involving the abolition of the class distinction between masters and servants, or wage payers and wage earners, seems to be regarded by all the great modern political economists as an inevitable event of the future. John Stuart Mill says:—

"That the industrial economy which divides society absolutely into two positions, the payers of wages and the receivers of them, the first counted by thousands and the last counted by millions, is neither fit for nor capable of indefinite duration; and the possibility of changing this system for one of combination without dependence and unity of interest, instead of organized hostility, depends altogether upon the future developments of the partnership principle."

In Mr. Mill's time that principle was already taking root as far as distribution is concerned. Co-operative societies for the supply of goods to members of such societies, who shared the profits of distribution, existed in England more than forty years ago. Nor could any movement have a more humble or more unpretentious beginning. The Rochdale (Yorkshire) Equitable Pioneer Society was commenced 1844, and in June of that year one of its most active members said "it was believed that no man, could or would, subscribe more than twopence per week per share, and when one offered to lay down half-a-crown, and another five shillings, the offers caused great surprise, and some consternation was evident when an enthusiastic member offered to venture one pound sterling."*

But the principle took rapid hold upon the weavers of that town and in the same year twenty-eight of them invested a capital of $5 each and opened up their store. Mr. W. T. Thornton in his work "On Labor" speaking of this event, says:—

"When the day and hour for commencing business arrived the little party assembled within to take part in the ceremony, were abashed by the largeness of the crowd assembled to witness it. Some delay took place before anyone could brush up courage to take down the shutters, and when at last the store and its contents were exposed to public view, all Toad Lane was in a roar."

But ridicule soon gave place to confidence and admiration. The business expanded until in ten years the 28 members had become 900, and in 1867 the Rochdale Pioneers numbered 6,823 with a capital of over $640,000.

In another town in Yorkshire, (Rawtenstall), six workingmen commenced a society in 1850 by saving a few shillings each, with which to buy a load of meal or flour. "They then rented a cottage as a store at 1s. 3d. (31c.) per week, and met every evening to dispose of their goods. At the end of the first quarter they divided 1s. 6d. in the pound on the purchases ($7\frac{1}{2}$ per cent), after paying 5 per cent on capital." Ten years afterwards they owned the building used as a store, had a paid up capital of $15,000, and 387 members. In 1860 there were 16 co-operative stores and one co-operative mill in England, with capital united amounting to a total of nearly $470,000.

---

*See Meliora, Vol. iii., page 300.

In the seventeenth Annual Report of the Bureau of Statistics of Labor, of Boston, Massachusetts, there is given a most exhaustive and valuable history of the Co-operative movement with statistical tables involving great care and supplying a vast amount of information. The Report says of distributive co-operation of Great Britain, that "it has been of great benefit to the working classes." Summarising the results it says:

It has brought to 680,165 members, £24,084,113 in profits, and incidentally it has produced other results which no statistics can adequately portray, results moral rather than material. It has stimulated thrift, taught self-reliance, encouraged the ownership of property, prevented debt by making cash payments obligatory, and placed in the hands of its patrons goods practically free from adulteration.

The Report is of extraordinary interest, and details the progress of the co-operative principle in France, Germany, Austria, Denmark, Spain, Hungary, Italy, Sweden, Switzerland, The Netherlands, Australia, as well as in Great Britain and the United States.

In the United States the principle of co-operation was recognized at a Convention of the New England Workingmen's Union, Sept. 1845, when the following resolutions were adopted:

"*Whereas*, all means of reform heretofore offered by the friends of social reform, have failed to unite the producing classes, much less attract their attention, therefore,

Resolved, That protective charity and concert of action in the purchase of the necessaries of life are the only means to the end to obtain that union which will end in their amelioration." *

---

* The Labor Movement in America, by Dr. Ely, Page 173.

The New York Industrial Convention appointed a 'Committee on organization of Industry,' which Committee in 1849 issued a report with the following:

"Brothers, shall we content ourselves with the miserable idea of merely saving a few dollars, and say we have found enough? Future generations, aye, the uprising generation, is looking to us for nobler deeds. Shall we disappoint them? No! by all that is great and good, let us trust in the truth of organized industry. Time, undoubtedly, must intervene before great results can be expected to accrue from a work of this character. We must proceed from combined stores to combined shops, from combined shops to combined houses, to joint ownership in God's earth, the foundation that our edifice must stand upon."

As in England so in the United States, the first efforts of these co-operators appeared insignificant, and out of all proportion to the pretensions of their resolutions. But as we learn from Dr. Ely, they began their work "with faith in God and the right," (to use their own words) "and the purchase of a box of soap and one half box of tea." Dr. Ely gives a most interesting account of the uprising and growth and draw-backs of the various co-operative efforts, both for the distribution and production of wealth. He says that an estimate of the total business transacted by co-operative distribution in the United States is scarcely possible, but he ventures to guess it at twenty millions of dollars per annum.

Speaking of the application of co-operative principles to production, Dr. Ely gives an account of one large Company * which has adopted a novel method of establishing mutual relations between capital and labor. The employees are paid "weekly wages, in cash and in full, and these wages to be fully up to the prices paid

---

* The Kentucky Railroad Tobacco Company.

for corresponding labor in any factory in the vicinity." The wages are regarded as a dividend of six per cent interest on the labor capital represented by the workman. Thus, if a workman's wages averages $12 pei week, his labor stock is estimated at $10,000, for at six per cent that would yield $600 or about $12 per week. "In other words, wages are capitalized and added to money capital. As labor has already received six per cent in wages, capital must first receive six per cent out of any profits. The surplus is a dividend on labor stock, and on cash capital. Thus, if eight per cent on the entire capital is realized, the laborer whose earnings are $600 per annum will receive an additional $200, or two per cent on his labor stock of $10,000." Dr. Ely quotes the following lines from the circular of the Company, which he says are under scored:

"Every stockholder in this concern must be a worker. No one is allowed to hold any stock who does not work in the factory. Every worker in the factory must be a Knight of Labor. The only factory in the United States that recognizes the equality of labor and capital."

The President of the Company, J. R. Ledyard, says that "so much does every one in the factory feel interested that it requires no watching, no ordering, no admonitions, but all are alert to do and keep everything the best." *

From the same authority I take the following paragraphs:

"The most remarkable success of co-operative production is found among the coopers of Minneapolis. Their first co-operative barrel factory was started in 1874 and there are now seven of them doing a business of one million dollars yearly. Interest is paid on money invested, and surplus profits are divided among the coopers in proportion to earnings. Nearly all the millers of Minneapolis are supplied by them, and are well satisfied with their work." †

---

* See Labor, etc., by Dr. Ely, Page 187.
† The Labor Movement, page 188.

Dr. Albert Shaw of the Minneapolis *Tribune* writing to Dr. Ely, says of the co-operative coopers :—
"So far as I am aware these cooper-shops form the most successful examples of productive co-operation in the world; and yet if anybody has ever alluded to them in a scientific way, I have never found it out. When I state that the flour mills of this city, far surpass those of any other milling point in the world, and that they have a daily capacity of 30,000 barrels of flour, you will perceive the necessity for coopers. Not far from half the flour is shipped in barrels. There are some 700 coopers at work on flour barrels. About 250 of these are 'journeymen' working for 'boss' coopers in three different shops. The remaining 450 (more or less) are grouped in seven co-operative shops, which they own and manage themselves. The system is indigenous. It has been developed by laboring men, without any patronage, or preaching, or persuasive literature. It began a dozen years ago in the feeblest way without friends or capital, and in the face of suspicion and distrust. It has won its way until two-thirds of the coopers have gone into the co-operative movement. It has secured such State laws as it required, and it has credit and standing. Its moral effects are more marked and gratifying than its financial and industrial success. It develops manhood, responsibility, self-direction, and independance. * * * Co-operative building associations have had some degree of success here, still greater in St. Paul. A good many of the co-operative coopers own houses which they were able to build by virtue of membership in co-operative building associations." ‡

Profit sharing is another application of the co-operative principle which is rapidly growing in favor. A course of six essays has been published by Mr. Sedley Taylor, M. A., of Trinity College, Cambridge, England,* in which he gives a great deal of information on this subject. He says that upwards of fifty

‡ Labor Movement in America page 189.
* See Humbolt Library Edition.

industrial establishments in France, Alsace and Switzerland alone, are now working upon the principle of participation by workmen in the profits. Extremely interesting is his account of the Mutual Aid Society founded by that truly patriotic frenchman M. Leclaire, whose successes as an individual, were phenomenal, and whose still greater successes, in applying this principle, in spite of suspicion and police espionage, were truly wonderful.

Mr. Taylor after relating the difficulties and suspicions with which both workmen, and police regarded and watched Leclaires' movements, says:

"When however Leclaire, after collecting his participants, forty-four in number, threw upon the table a bag of gold containing 11,886 francs (£475), and then and there distributed to each his share, averaging over £10 per man, it was found impossible to withstand the 'object-lesson' thus given. All hesitation vanished and was replaced by unbounded confidence."

Mr. Taylor also gives a table of bonuses to labor, paid in each year from 1872 to 1882, commencing with 768 participants, wages paid £16,257; bonuses paid £2,331, being 14 per cent of bonus to wages; and in the last year 1882, there were 42,799 participants who received £9,630 bonuses, being 22 per cent. of bonus to wages.

From the same authority we learn the details of the system of profit-sharing in the Paris and Orleans Railway Company which shows that in 1882, no less than 16,935 employees participated in the profits of the concern, to the extent of a ten per cent. bonus upon the wages, which wages, were fully on a level with other companies.

The same application of the co-operative principle has been made to agriculture, for illustrations of which, as well as for much other interesting data I must refer my readers to the authorities here quoted. Even in the matter of credit, co-operation seems to be asserting its claim to notice, and banking institutions are beginning to recognise this claim. Dr. Ely remarks on this subject:

"Why banking institutions for working people should meet with remarkable success in Germany doing an annual business which is estimated in hundreds of millions, while they have elsewhere attained no considerable proportions is not quite clear. . . It is, however, noteworthy, that each of the four countries where co-operation has attained immense proportions, should be specially distinguished for success along one particular line, viz:—England for vast achievements in distributive co-operation, France for productive co-operation, Germany for banking through the co-operative credit unions, and the United States for the building associations.*

I might go on to quote illustrations far beyond the limits of this volume, proving the value, and great possibilities of the co-operative system. To my mind this principle in its various methods of application offers a magnificent field for the expenditure of the force of such combinations as the Knights of Labor; and it is a most hopeful sign, that the leaders of that great body are giving special attention to this subject. They have had, and still have, doubtless, much preliminary work to go through, as well as much to learn, but they have already set on foot several large co-operative concerns, which give promise of important social and moral, as well as financial advantages to all concerned.

* Labor Movement in America page 196.

If, however, as Prof. Cairnes says, "the laborer is to emerge from his present position and become the sharer in the gains of capital he must first learn to save." Whether the principle of co-operation be applied by workmen gradually acquiring capital out of their savings, or whether it be by labor receiving interest in the profits of business concerns, as illustrated so practically by Leclaire, it can only be very partially effective so long as the great social cancer of drunkenness remains upon the body politic.

Even if capital were to become dependant upon labor, instead of labor upon capital, it would still be true that labor—*productive labor*—would have to bear the financial burdens which waste, destruction, social corruption, and other disorders entail upon society.

Co-operation is a grand agency, if it co-operates with every other agency, for the removal of those evils which degrade workmen, rendering them slaves—not only to capitalists—but to base appetite and degrading passions far more tyrannical, and more cruel than, ever a capitalist could be.

One of the most successful illustrations of co-operation quoted in this chapter is that of a tobacco factory. The illustration is good for the principle illustrated, from one side only. The economic interests of a country as a whole—and therefore of workmen as a whole—cannot be served by a tobacco interest, since it trades entirely upon the baser habits and vices of the people—almost exclusively too, the able-bodied male population.

So far as the application of co-operative principles are concerned the illustration might have come with equal force from a distillery or brewery.

In such a case the combination of workmen-capitalists would have been working the ruin of their own class just as effectually as any capitalist brewer or distiller is now doing.

A co-operative society is like a chain. It is as strong only as its weakest link. The weak link in the chain of co-operative effort at present, is, that a large proportion of the money earned in productive industry, instead of being added to capital is sunk in liquor.

Moreover, if all workmen were combined into one great community of interest, they would still have to support the thriftless—they would still have to maintain the army of men (and their families) who are engaged in the destructive business of converting produce into poison, together with the still greater army, who profit by the distribution of the miscalled beverage.

In addition to these, they would still have to support the untold number of drink-made paupers, the workmen who drop out of the ranks of workmen into that of beggars and vagrants, or criminals, with all the other progeny of the traffic. They would still have to contend against the unequal competition of the liquor shop against the produce of industry.

What is needed is, not only a re-adjustment of the division of labor's choice fruit, but a war of extermination against the worms which eat and decay the very heart of that fruit, the most destructive and disastrous of all of which is the worm of the still.

Prof. Cairnes, remarking upon the means by which workmen might save with a view to become their own capitalists, says of the expenditure in liquor:

'In what proportion the working classes take part in this expenditure we have no means of accurately determining;

but I imagine it will not be disputed that by much the larger proportion must be set down to their account; and I am certainly within the mark in assuming that, of the money so spent, I am sure I might say three-fourths of the whole, so far from conducing in any way to the well-being of those who spend it, is both physically and morally injurious to them. Here, then, is a sum of, let us say, sixty million pounds sterling, (the Professor refers here to the United Kingdom) which might annually be saved without trenching upon any expenditure, which really contributes to the laborers' well-being. The obstacles to this saving are not physical, but moral obstacles; and supposing laborers had the virtue to overcome them the first step toward what might be called their industrial emancipation would already have been accomplished."

If Prof. Cairnes' estimate be a correct one, (and it must be remembered that he is no teetotal fanatic—but a calm, logical thinker and political economist) and if a similar proportion of the drink-bill of Canada is chargeable to the workingmen, as he attributes to those of the United Kingdom, what an enormous leverage of capital is lost to the laborers of this country.

Our Liquor bill, as we have seen, averages over thirty-seven and a half millions of dollars. Prof. Cairnes' estimate is, that much the larger portion must be set down to workingmen. Suppose we estimate it at one half—say eighteen and a half millions.

Now suppose we take it, that not the whole, but three-fourths only, of this amount is wastefully and uselessly expended. Apart altogether from the evil results, direct and indirect, see what a capital fund is thrown away by the workmen of Canada, which might lead them by a direct road, and by rapid strides to their own emancipation.

We have here a total sum of $12,775,000, which the workmen of Canada might either spend more productively, or save it and put it into capital for their own employment and enrichment.

If the reader will turn to the chapter on "Wages and Whiskey" in this volume, he will find a table which shows from Government Blue Books. that under the present system the average amount of capital required to support each man in ordinary employments in Canada is $632; but it would be easy to show that under a wider application of the principle of co-operation between labor and capital much less would suffice.

If we assume that the amount needed would be, say, $500, then we have the serious fact that the workmen of Canada throw to the winds, *and worse*, sufficient to make 25,550 workmen into their own capitalists, and therefore their own masters and employers.

Thus it matters not which way we turn, we find this gigantic drink-curse blocking the way of progress, and overshadowing every good. The great leading newspaper of England has well said of it:

"Drink baffles us, confounds us, shames us, and mocks us at every point. It outwits alike the teacher, the man of business, the patriot, and the legislator. Every other institution flounders in hopeless difficulties; the public house holds on its triumphant course. The administrators of public and private charity are told that alms and oblations go with rates, doles, and pensions to the all-absorbing bar of the public house."
—London (Eng.) *Times.*

Let working men and working women everywhere combine. 'Tis their right and duty so to do. But let their private acts and combined power be first employed to suppress the greatest of all their social enemies, the most potent of all their foes, the most enslaving of all capital-controlled interests—*the Distillery, the Brewery, and the Saloon.*

CHAPTER XIII.

THE KNIGHTS OF LABOR.

PROFOUND secresy characterized the initiatory movement of the "Noble Order of the Knights of Labor."

It was commenced at a meeting of eight friends called together by U. S. Stephens, a tailor of Philadelphia, in 1869. Its very name was not published or even mentioned. It was known to its adherents by the marks of five stars— * * * * * —and its meetings were called by means of secret signs. Dr. Ely says that "Philadelphians noticed with trepidation that a few cabalistic chalk-marks in front of Independence Hall could bring several thousand men together. Alarm spread, newspapers circulated absurd fictions in regard to its designs, in which accusations of communism and incendiarism were prominent, and Catholic and Protestant clergymen hastened to denounce the unknown monster."

The heads of the new order therefore determined to reveal their character and object, and in June 1878 a meeting was held in Philadelphia. The founder of the Order, Uriah Stevens, signed the call as Grand Master Workmen. From "*The Labor Movement in America,*" I copy the heading of the circular calling that meeting.

G

"N. AND H. O.

OF

* * * * *

OF NORTH AMERICA.

PEACE AND PROSPERITY TO THE FAITHFUL.

To the Fraternity wherever found, greeting :—

SPECIAL CALL.

The reason for this special call is stated to be on "account of what is believed by many of our most influential members to be an emergency of vast and vital importance to the stability, usefulness, and influence of the Order." The business to come before the meeting as further stated " is to consider the expediency of making the name of the Order public for the purpose of defending it from the fierce assaults and defamation made upon it by press, clergy, and corporate capital, and to take such further action as shall effectually meet the *Grave Emergency.*"

The first general assembly of the Order was held in Reading, Pa., in 1878, when its membership was reported as numbering eighty thousand. If this estimate was a correct one, it appears that on the announcement of its name and purposes many of its members seceded or left. Probably it was a beneficent purging of some of the less worthy spirits from the Order—for as men "love darkness rather than light because their deeds were evil," mere conspirators are unable to work with a body whose name, purpose and objects are open to the light of day.

Certain it is however, that the numbers were not so great for a time afterwards, as were reported before the departure from the policy of secresy.

But this re-action did not last long. The membership of the Order grew rapidly. In 1883 there were in round numbers 62,000 members; in 1884, 71,000; in 1885, 111,000, these numbers being reported each year on the first of July.

During the past year the growth of the Order has been unprecedented. In a circular issued by Grand Master Workman Powderly, in March 1885, he says, "out of sixty millions of people in the United States and Canada, our Order has possibly three millions."

A most important advance has been made by the "Knights" over the older and less successful labor unions. It was a fatal weakness, involving serious and frequent abuses, in the old Trades Unions, that they based their operations and rules on the assumption that the way to benefit themselves was to separate their interests from all others. They arraigned themselves in opposition to everything which did not avow itself in favor of conserving mechanical labor, and securing the largest amount of wages, for the shortest hours of labor, for themselves.

In short their very weakness consisted in the fact, that they too closely copied the narrow and selfish spirit and policy which they complained of in capitalists. They organised with one idea, viz:—how to damage their opponents and enhance their own interests. Too often they never thought of others less privileged even than themselves, except as so many additional hindrances in the way of their own immediate selfish purposes. Hence, they steadfastly opposed the employment of women, in any branch of work which men had been accustomed to do. They were even violent in their opposition to apprentices, and to labor saving machines. Mr. Powderly mentions in an article published in the *New York Sun*, March 29th, 1886, that his greatest difficulty in inducing machinists and blacksmiths to join the Knights of Labor lay in the contempt with which they looked upon other workers.

Thus, the Unionists, while making haste to travel were on the wrong track. Their whole interests lay in the abolition of all class distinctions. But they did not observe this rule in their conduct. The workmen who, because he is a mechanic, earning higher wages, and having greater advantages looks down, or frowns upon his brother worker, is imbued with precisely the spirit which he complains of in the lordling, or the capitalist.

But a new era seems to have set in with the advent of the Knights. That great organisation owes its very successes to its broad and Catholic spirit, and in its grasp of the real needs of the vast body of workers of every grade lies its value and power.

Its constitution recognises only one mark of distinction between men, viz:—Moral worth, and for this it aims as directly as for the material advancement of its members.

In this the sagacity as well as the moral character of its leaders is manifest. For it must be ever remembered, that true prosperity involves true principles and virtuous life. The vicious man is never truly prosperous, however rich in land or money, or stocks, he may be. He but owns that which helps him down to lower depths of degradation.

To quote W. E. Channing: " Let the working man learn to regard truth as more precious than his daily bread; and the spring of true and perpetual elevation is touched within him. He has begun to be a man; he becomes one of the elect of his race."

This principle is avowed in the very first clause of the declaration of principles issued by the Knights of Labor; and, so far as I can see, is never lost sight of in any of the twenty-one clauses which follow. (*See full text of the Preamble and principles of the Knights of Labor in Appendix of this volume.*)

That first clause reads thus: "We declare to the world that our aims are: *First, to make industrial and moral worth, not wealth, the true standard of individual and national greatness.*"

They pledge themselves also that, while demanding from the State and the National Government, certain changes as set forth, that they "will endeavor to associate their labor" to establish co-operative institutions—to secure for both sexes equal pay for equal work, &c., &c.

Another of the aims of this organizations is to prevent strikes as expressed in the last clause of the statement of their principles.

Indeed the leaders of the Knights have even been charged with "excessive zeal to prevent strikes" so evidently anxious were they in this direction.

Mr. Powderly addressing the Order, says: "I must have the assistance of the Order or my most earnest efforts will fail. Will, I have it? If so strikes must be avoided. Boycotts must be avoided. Those who boast must be checked by their assemblies. No move must be made until the court of last resort be appealed to. Threats of violence must be hushed up or driven out. * * If you do not desire to assist me in this way then select a man better qualified to obey your will and I will retire in his favor."

To this noble and manly appeal the Order responded at the last annual meeting by re-electing Mr. Powderly as the head of the Order.

Hapily the moral tone of the Knights is not now a singular circumstance. Other Unions have accepted an equally high standard. Whether this is due to the influence of the Knights, or whether it is because the various Unions are being purged of the leadership of mere demagogues, agitators, and anarchists, or because of the general improvevent in the moral tone of all workmen it is difficult to say.

But it is an unmistakable "bow in the cloud" of social problems when almost every labor organization is declaring itself on the side of morality, or at least demanding of its members, conditions of moral conduct which are not demanded in the social clubs of the "gentlemen" of society. Dr. Ely quotes abundant testimony on this point, not of course in proof that all members of the various orders are consistent moral men, but that their meetings are conducted in such a manner as to inculcate moral principles, and to encourage the education of the members. As remarked by a distinguished clergymen of New England referring to this Order "the actual is doubtless below the ideal. The two differ however, not so much as the ideal church of Christ, and the church as actually realized among men." Or, as Rev. T. K. Beecher of Elmira said in concluding a sermon:

"The Knights of Labor, having gathered if you please one hundred or five thousand names on their lists, must of necessity have gathered in ignorance, passion, lawlessness, and insubordination. Members of that church have misbehaved and will misbehave. I doubt not that there is great mortification and travail of spirit over these disgraceful infidelities to the principles of the Order. Now as a 'peacemaker' I affirm that if any man is a good Mason he will never be a drunkard or a fornicator. Yet I have known Masons of high degree who were infamous because of those vices. Nevertheless I will speak of a good Mason. I know that if a man is a good Methodist he will be a man of prayer, enthusiasm, generosity, and hope of sanctification, yet I have known Methodists of high degree that were none of those things. I know that a minister of the gospel, if he will fulfil his ordination vows will be a truly reverend man; trustworthy by day or by night, bearing about him the dying of the Lord Jesus. Yet I have known ministers, first and last, that have fallen in every vice of the criminal calendar. Nevertheless I believe in ministers."

Is it not a sign bright with hope and cheerful prospect which we may gladly set against the dismal but too faithful pictures of social anarchism, and the muttering of revolution which we hear in many large cities, that the masses—the bread-winners—the workmen—are organizing, not merely for conquest against others, but for triumph over their own weaknesses and vices?

It is yet too soon to look for any definite result of these organizations upon politics, but surely if anything can purify the muddy pools of political life, it shall be the intellectual and moral emancipation of the millions of electors who may be classed as workmen.

Let any politician read over those twenty-two propositions contained in the statement of principles of the Order of Knights, and then say whether or not such principles will not inevitably demand and secure a higher character of our legislators.

And that these declarations are not mere sentiment, let us enquire into the way in which all meetings of laborers are now conducted, as compared with a very few years ago, whether in the United States, or Canada.

"Last summer," says Dr. Ely, "I visited the Central Labor Union of New York, and was pleased to observe that when one of the members allowed himself the use of the word 'damned' to express his indignation, there instantly arose from various parts of the hall cries of ' I object to that language !' The speaker was called to order by the chairman and told that profanity was against the rules." Dr. Ely further says that the " bricklayers of Philadelphia impose a fine of fifty cents for using profane language," and he asks " how many rich mens' clubs exclude the use of intoxicants and impose fines for profanity ?"

May we not also regard these institutions as tending to promote peace among nations.

The war spirit is begotten of selfishness and base passions. The "jingo cry" in the past has depended much upon exciting the people. Get them to sing "war songs," the more of doggerel, and the less of poetry there is in them the better for the purpose, and any "jingo" Minister may then venture to declare that the country demands that its "honor shall be satisfied."

But the intelligent working men of the world have always been the most conservative brakes upon the war chariot. In the emancipation from sensualism and ignorance which awaits all laborers, through the various agencies, among which, is not the least, their own co-operative agency, their will be a greater check than ever upon the demon of war.

"The laborers "says Dr. Ely" are the most thoroughgoing peace-men to be found, and I am often inclined to think that they are the only large class who really and truly desire peace between nations, the abandonment of armies, the conversion of spears into pruninghooks and swords into plough-shares. At the time of the Franco-German war, German laborers alone protested against the slaughter of their French brothers.

At the beginning of our late war, American laborers met in convention to protest against hostilities between the sections; and in the fall of 1885, the veterans of the Union and Confederate armies among the Knights of Labor formed an organization called the Gray and the Blue of the Knights of Labor, and took the motto "Capital divided, Labor unites us."

John Swinton's Paper says, the object of this organization "is to teach the toilers who make up the armies of the world, that in peace, not in war, is the workers emancipation." And Dr. Ely further says:—

"I sincerely believe that the time is not so far distant as one might think, when organized labor will force the governments of earth to substitute arbitration for war, will compel them to live peaceably, each with the other, to devote their forces to the fruitful business of art, industry and science, and in a vast international parliament to lay the foundations of a federated world state. But even this is not the whole of their high mission of peace; for they are, in our South bringing about an amicable understanding between black and white * * Strange, is it not? that the despised trades-union and labor organizations should have been chosen to perform this high duty of conciliation. But hath not God ever called the lowly to the most exalted missions, and hath he not ever called the foolish to confound the wise?"‡

---
‡Labor Movement in America, page 139.

CHAPTER XIV.

LABOR UNIONS AND THE LIQUOR TRAFFIC.

THERE is no feature of the Labor Unions of the present day so full of promise to the laborers first, and through them the whole civilized world, as their growing antagonism to the drinking usages and the liquor traffic.

The Locomotive Fireman of North America provides in its constitution as follows: "Any member dealing in, or in any way connected with the sale of intoxicating liquors shall, unless he withdraws, be expelled. Any member found guilty of drunkenness shall be suspended for first offence. A repetition shall be punished by expulsion; and under no circumstances shall a member so expelled be re-instated before the lapse of one year." A similar rule is found in the constitution of the Brotherhood of Railway Brakeman.

The Windsor Glass Assembly No. 300, has this rule: "Any member causing this place to be idle on account of drink, shall be fined as follows: First offence, $5, each subsequent offence $10. Any member losing work through drink shall, for the first offence be fined $1 and reprimanded in open meeting of the Preceptory; for the second offence $2.50, and for each subsequent offence shall be fined $5.

The journeymen bricklayers of Philadelphia have the following fines imposed:—For attending a meeting in intoxicated condition $1, and for attending a funeral in such a condition $5. . . . Dr. Ely says: "A first floor in their hall was vacant when I visited the place. A liquor dealer had offered them a large rental for it, but they declared that they would under no circumstances allow intoxicating drinks to be sold in the building."

This action is highly creditable, and is a fitting reminder to some of the branches of Trades Unions in Canada who have yet to advance before they reach the sterling independance of their brothers in Philadelphia. It is not creditable to the Trades Unions of Toronto to be meeting in a hall over a liquor shop for the sake of saving a trifling sum, which it might cost them extra to meet in another hall. Liquor dealers have no other interest in workmen, when they offer them their premises free of rent than *self interest*. It is the story of the "spider and the fly" over again.

Mr. Powderly and Mr. Trevellick have each done grand service to their order, and to the cause of temperance by their unflinching denunciations of drinking.

"If a man given to the use of strong drink, and a serpent applied for admission to the order, I would vote for the serpent in preference to the drunkard." So said Mr. Powderly at the General Assembly of the Knights of Labor in 1885.

The General Assembly of the Knights of Labor was held in Hamilton, Ontario, October 1885, and the words of Mr. Powderly in his address on that occasion ought to be scattered broadcast over the land:

"If there is a time when men should conduct themselves with manly dignity and decorum, it is when they are in trouble. I have observed that when a strike is in progress, there are some men who insist on making exhibitions of themselves at the price of their good name, and of the good name of the Order that is held responsible for their actions.

It should be made an offence punishable with expulsion from the Order, for any member to be intoxicated while the good name of the Order is hanging in the balance. It is a criminal offence, and the severest penalty known to the laws of the Order should be visited upon the head of the offender.

We legislate against the admission of the man who sells rum, and make a member of the man who supports him; this does not seem just nor fair. The character of the society is judged by the character of its members. If a member is seen upon the streets in a state of intoxication, the society of which he is a member is blamed for his conduct. We must, therefore, look after the character of our members with a jealous eye. If a travelling member is discovered to be drunk while carrying a travelling card of the Knights of Labor, it should be made a punishable offence. We have been altogether too lenient with offenders of this character, and we must adopt suitable legislation for the regulation of the evil I have pointed out. If a man given to the use of strong drink and a serpent applied for admission to the Order, I would vote for the serpent in preference to the drunkard; for if the viper transgressed the laws by disgracing us, we could crush the life out of his worthless carcass by stepping on his head; but we must let the other and worse transgressor live to continue his villainous work.

I do not ask of those who join us to be saints, but I have a right to expect, and I do ask of them, to be men. We cannot shut our eyes to this matter any longer; the crime must be punished, and a law for the government of the offence must be framed at this General Assembly."

Again in concluding his address Mr. Powderly referred to the necessity for men of good character as alone eligible for official positions in the order in the following language:

"We should make inquiry of the men who aspire to places whether they are in the habit of using strong drink. We cannot be too careful in this matter, for sometimes a good man does some very bad things when his wits creates a vacuum in his head to be filled by the fumes of rum. In our dealings with the men who control capital we are pitted against the most intelligent men in the nation, and we cannot afford to lay aside any portion of our intelligence or cunning in dealing with them."

The labor paper called the *Trades Union*, of Atcheson, Kansas, says "the most deadly blow ever given to King Alcohol is in that declaration of the Knights of Labor which proscribes any liquor dealer for membership in the Order. It is doing more to put an end to drunkenness and to bring the rum traffic under the ban than all the laws of Kansas or speeches of St. John ever did."

In Canada, many of the leaders of the labor leagues are pronounced temperance men. At the last meeting of Prohibitionists in Toronto, called by the Dominion Alliance on Sept. 14th, 1886, a deputation waited upon the Trades and Labor Congress then assembled, and were met with the most cordial expressions of co-operative sympathy. Before the Alliance Convention was concluded a deputation from the Labor Congress waited upon that body to express " earnest hope that closer connection and continued fraternal relations might exist between the Dominion Alliance and the Trades and Labor Council," and to announce that "a Committee had been appointed to co-operate with the Alliance in joint action for this great end."

At the date of my present writing, Nov. 30, 1886, a meeting of the delegates from the various Assemblies of the Knights of Labor and the Trades Unions has been held in Toronto to nominate candidates for parliamentary representation. In the platform laid down at that meeting I find this temperance plank :

" *Any effort to reduce the consumption of intoxicants has the hearty support of organized labor.*"

Let organized labor join hands with the organized forces of the temperance movement, and the most arrogant, unscrupulous and destructive of all combinations of capital will be speedily broken down.

The doom of the liquor traffic will not be long delayed when Christian and temperance sentiment becomes woven into the constitution of all organizations of men and women aiming at moral, social and material progress.

So far as I can judge from extensive reading and enquiry, there is nothing in the purposes and constitution of the Order of the Knights of Labor inconsistent with the loftiest patriotism and the true spirit of Christianity.

Its aim is "to make industrial and moral worth the true standard of individual and national greatness." *

Consistently with this aim it receives all classes of persons, whether employers, employed, or not strictly belonging to either class—so long as their character and pursuits are in harmony with its objects and purposes.

It is to the everlasting credit of the Order that it has placed a stigma upon the liquor traffic by prohibiting all persons engaged in the business from becoming members. This one fact is a significant notice to the capitalists engaged in this business. It is the handwriting on the wall, "*Mene, Mene, Tekel, Upharsin,*' "Thou art weighed in the balances, and art found wanting."

---

* See Preamble of Knights of Labor in Appendix.

CHAPTER XV.

THE ROOT OF THE EVIL.

"*AT the bottom of every social problem we will find a social wrong.*"

So says Henry George. And he is right. But the question is, what is "at the bottom" of the social problems of to day? What *are* the social wrongs?

Mr. George says:—" We cannot safely leave politics to politicians, or political economy to college professors. The people themselves must think, because the people alone can act."—*Social Problems.*

There can be no doubt that many of the worst phases of social evil are traceable to the concentration of wealth, the existence of an idle aristocracy; and the jobbery, bribery, corruption, and swindling of the rich capitalists, politicians and stock brokers.

Far be it from me to make light of the outrages and wrongs inflicted upon society by the combinations of capitalists, who have dared over and over again, to enter into conspiracies to rob the people of millions, that they might become millionaries.

The Rev. R. Heber Newton, rector of All Souls Church, New York, delivered a lecture on the labor problems a few months ago, in the course of which he said:—

"The state should hold all mineral resources hereafter as the property of the people at large. If it were not for our conventional custom how monstrous would seem the notion

that the natural resources of the earth should be mnoopolized by individuals. A few years ago in our city a coal magnate was asked what the price of coal was to be for the coming winter. He replied with a smile, "As high as Providence will permit and as low as necessity compels." During the past winter a company of estimable gentlemen over a supper table in a Murray Hill mansion settled between themselves the amount of coal that should be mined during the coming season. Do you, with childlike innocence, imagine that this quantity was determined by the needs of their fellow beings? Round them a few hundred thousand people were buying coal by the basketful, paying at the rate of from $15 to $20 a ton. But these excellent gentlemen had no eye upon this aspect of the case, but were simply considering how to gain the largest dividends for their companies. The state has thus left in the hands of a few individuals the power of imposing an oppresive taxation upon a prime necessity of life—of lowering the real wages of labor and shrinking the profits of capital through the depression thus caused in the general demand. Copper, lead, iron, oil—indispensable all to industrial life—are thus the monoplies of individuals instead of the common wealth of the people at large. The natural resources of the earth in every form need to be held in the interests of the commonwealth. Land is the prime factor in the production of wealth. Land is a limited quantity. It does not, therefore, come under the regulation of competition. As every other monopoly, it demands, therefore, the control of the State, that the monopoly may be that of the people at large and not that of individuals. It would seem that the time had already come for us to control speculative dealing in land and at least to raise the question of regulating the normal rate of rent as we now regulate the normal rate of interest."
—*The Voice.*

Henry George apparently sees the solution of all social problems in the abolition of private ownership of lands. He says:—

There is but one way to remove an evil, and that is to remove its cause. Poverty deepens as wealth increases, and wages are forced down while productive power grows, because land, which is the source of all wealth and the field of all labor is monopolized. To extirpate poverty, to make wages what justice commands they should be, the full earnings of the laborer, we must *therefore substitute for the individual ownership of land a common ownership. Nothing else will go to the cause of the evil, in nothing else is there the slightest hope.*

Progress and Poverty.

Undoubtedly, the causes of social evils are not one, but many. We suffer from a complication of disorders. But there is an organic disease which lies at the root of all other social troubles. No careful diagnoses of that disease can trace it to unequal distribution of wealth or to monopoly. These are partly an effect and partly a cause of certain aggravated symptoms.

Society is weak, not merely because there are robbers who have fattened upon her, as parasites do upon decayed meat, but because there is some corrupting agent at work at her very heart. If the people of free and civilized countries were not paralysed or poisoned at the fountain of their social life, they could and would strangle organized robbery and break up the rings of monopolists.

A straight look at the symptoms of a disease will often indicate the cause of it without conjecture or speculative enquiry. If millionaires were abolished, money brokers suppressed, land and railway speculation made impossible, and even Henry George's remedies against landocracy made supreme, would not the vast mass of social disorder, vice, poverty, crime, and the consequent burden of taxation still remain practically untouched?

It is wise and right to face *all* the problems of society—but what avails it, if we apply a remedy to the back when the seat of the disease is at the heart? Will society be healed of blood-poisoning by setting a broken limb? Let the limb be properly set and the back be wisely healed by all possible means, but above all get at the heart and the blood of social life, if you would heal the disorders which unhappily afflict us!

All Mr. George's remedies would leave the root of the diseases untouched. His remedies would not make the thriftless thrifty, or the drunken sober. And for this reason, that they would not convert the liquor shop into a business, promotive of social order and comfort. They would not reduce the proportion of criminals to the ratio of alcoholic compounds consumed; nor turn the capital invested in the traffic into a channel of productive industry; nor reduce the volume of pauperism and inefficiency which attends the use of intoxicants wherever it is consumed as a beverage.

Cardinal Manning has quite recently put into a categorical form the close relation which exists between drink and the national good. This telling and eloquent array of questions is applied by the Cardinal to the United Kingdom, but they apply, with greater or less degree, to the United States, and to our own Dominion, while the relation of the "dominant vice" to the questions here under consideration is everywhere a fact that cannot be gainsaid.

Is there, then, any one dominant vice of our nation? To answer this let us ask:—

1. Is there any vice in the United Kingdom that slays at least 60,000, or as others believe and affirm, 120,000 every year?

2. Or that lays the seed of a whole harvest of diseases of the most fatal kind, and renders all other lighter diseases more acute, and perhaps even fatal in the end?

3. Or that causes at the least one third of all the madness confined in our asylums?

4. Or that prompts directly or indirectly, 75 per cent of all crime?

5. Or that produces an unseen and secret world of all kinds of moral evil, and of personal degradation which no police court ever knows and no human eye can ever reach?

6. Or that in the midst of our immense and multiplying wealth, produces not poverty, which is honorable, but pauperism, which is a degradation to a civilized people?

7. Or that ruins men of every class and condition of life, from the highest to the lowest, men of every degree of culture and of education, of every honorable profession, public officials, military and naval officers and men, railway and household servants; and what is worse than all, that ruins women of every class, from the most rude to the most refined.

8. Or that above all other evils is the most potent cause of destruction to the domestic life of all classes?

9. Or that has already wrecked, and is continually wrecking, the homes of our agricultural and factory workmen?

10. Or that has already been found to paralyse the productiveness of our industries in comparrison with other countries, especially the United States.

11. Or. as we are officially informed, renders our commercial seamen less trustworthy on board ship.

12. Or that spreads these accumulating evils throughout the British Empire, and is blighting our fairest colonies?

13. Or that has destroyed and is destroying the indigenous races wheresoever the British Empire is in contact with them, so that from the hem of its garment there goes out, not the virtue of civilization and of Christianity, but of degradation and of death? * * *

It is not to be denied that the voice of intemperance is an heirloom which cleaves to us like the shirt of Nessus.

But these evils might perhaps have been brought by legislative and moral authority within some control were it not for two causes which have lifted it to its fatal pre-eminence. The first cause is the enormous capital of one hundred and thirty or one hundred and forty millions which is annually employed in the supply and sale and distribution of intoxicating drink; and the other the complicity of Government in raising more than thirty milllons of revenue from the same trade. * * * *

It is precisely in our great industrial cities and centres that the vice of drunkenness is most rife; and it needs little reflection to forsee what would be the condition of those centres, if, as some years ago, our great industries were to fail. When men and homes are suffering there is little reasoning. Hunger has no logic, but it has a burning thirst. The safety of the commercial world is being sacrificed to swell the profits of the drink-trade. But the safety of the Commonwealth is above both, and ought to interpose its mandate.—*Cardinal Manning in the Fortnightly Review, Sept. 1886.*

It is unreasoning and illogical to hope for improved conditions for the masses, through any means whatever, which do not take cognisance of this terrible array of facts. The material advancement of the people cannot be generally improved until the drink traffic be suppressed and the drinking habits of society are changed.

What is wanted for the bettering of the condition of the workers is—not merely a re-adjustment of finances, or a more equitable distribution of wealth, but a regular and natural stimulus to the demand for the products of labor.

This would inevitably exist if there were not some gigantic "*dominant*" agency disturbing the normal conditions of the law of supply and demand. This agency is not in the nature of a monopoly or a tax merely, but necessarily a deeper rooted evil that either. It is obviously an agent which *destroys* production—not merely *consumes* it—which paralyses the arm of the producer, perverts the moral tone and life, and which poisons supply at the fountain, and destroys demand at the spring.

In brief, if the wants and desires of civilized people had their natural sway, unchecked and free from the demoralization and crippling effects of the liquor traffic, every factory and mill would be well employed, and all produce would find a market according to its value. For the market is not slack because of the lack of desire, but for want of the very material, wealth and purchasing power which drink consumes and wastes.

CHAPTER XVI.

MORE WAGES AND LESS LABOR.

"Eight hours work, eight hours play,
Eight hours rest and eight bob a day!"

THIS was the cry of the workingmens' unions of England a quarter of a century ago. And the demand for more leisure and higher wages is the present aim of all labor leagues. Nor can any one reasonably question the right of the laborer to combine for a larger share of the fruits of their toil.

The workman is everywhere puzzled at the present condition of things. He sees on every hand the marvellous development of productive agencies. He lives in an age of mechanical miracles. Labor-saving machines are multiplied beyond count. The power to produce has advanced with inventive genius, until there is no branch of industry that is not now supplied in varieties and quantities out of all proportion to the times of our grandfathers.

But these facts are not coincident with an equal advance in the material conditions of the workman. Men have still to labor six days a week and from ten to sixteen hours daily, while the hurry-scurry of the age drive many men into the seventh day of toil in every week. On the other hand, the cost of living is proportionately higher.

LAND, LABOR AND LIQUOR.

There has undoubtedly been a considerable increase in the actual amount of wages paid to workmen as compared with a generation ago, but if allowance be made for the increased desires, dearer fuel, higher rate of house-rent, and other modern changes arising out of the growth of cities, etc., it is doubtful whether the advance has been equal to the greater demands upon the wage-earner.

Very interesting statistics are given in the valuable and able report of the Bureau of Industries for Ontario prepared by Mr. Blue, the Secretary.*

He has gathered statistics from a large number of employers, and employed, in towns and cities with a view to ascertain the relative wages and cost of living of workers, including "skilled and unskilled laborers of almost every class and occupation." As a result of this enquiry he publishes a table of the earnings and cost of living of 2,637 work people. The table gives the following among other interesting particulars.

Average yearly earnings of 1,621 workers...$431 87
Average cost of living of the same.......... 330 50

Average surplus of cost of living over earnings.$101 37

Average yearly earnings of 710 workers.....$321 50
Average cost of living of same............ 321 50

Average yearly earnings of 306 workers.....$317 16
Average cost of living of same............ 368 66

Deficit.........................$ 51 50

The cost of living referred to in this table includes rent, fuel, clothing and food of the worker and his de-

---

* See Annual Report of Bureau of Industries for Ontario, 1885.

pendents, and does not count anything for furniture, books, club or insurance fees, medicine or other necessities and occasional liabilities. Mr. Blue says "in the nineteen towns and cities from which returns have been obtained, the average cost of rent for the year is $74.41, and of fuel $40.53." The average cost of food of the worker and his dependents *per capita* is $47.67; and Mr. Blue confirms this latter item by showing that "the tables of food consumption in thirteen public institutions in the Province show that the average cost of a ration of food is $12\frac{1}{4}$ cents, or $44.71 a year *per capita*." So that the estimate of $47.67 does not admit of any extravagance, or indeed of many luxuries.

A very valuable report published by the Massachusetts Bureau of Statistics of Labor has just come to hand. In that report there is given a most carefully prepared set of tables showing the average amount of food consumed by working people. The cost of the total food, per man, per day, in the different dietaries, as given in these tables, averages:—among a miscellaneous Massachusetts community, 25 cents, or $91.25 per annum; among French Canadians in Massachusetts, 24 cents, or $87.60 per annum; among French Canadians in Canada, 14 cents, or $50.90 per annum. If it be borne in mind that these figures refer to adult men, while Mr. Blue's statistics include the men and their families, these two sets of tables may be compared with advantage.

Nor are mechanics and laborers the only workers who are driven to excessive toil or insufficient means. The alternative of one or the other faces almost every class. Farmers, store-keepers, and even professional men are subject to a strain upon the physical and mental powers which results in snapping the cords of life prematurely, or in reducing men to mere machines, driving, and straining, and toiling for existence.

Why is this? Why do both men and women have to labor incessantly? Why do we, as a rule, have to kill ourselves to live?

Carlyle says: "It is not to die, or even to die of hunger, that makes a man wretched; many men have died; all men must die. But it is to live miserable, we know not why; to work sore and yet gain nothing; to be heartworn, weary, yet isolated, unrelated, girt in with a cold, universal *laissez-faire.*"

Our riches are increasing, our productive power multiplying. Yet the millions are either in poverty or struggling on the verge of it.

John Stuart Mill remarked, "It is questionable if all the mechanical inventions yet made have lightened the day's toil of any human being."

Figures given by Mulhall show that the wealth of the United Kingdom increased about three hundred per cent. from 1810 to 1880, and the population only one hundred per cent. The average wealth per inhabitant grew from $635 in 1812, to $1,245 in 1882. According to Mr. Edward Atkinson, ten men can feed one thousand in New York with bread, two can furnish them with iron, four with cotton and woolen cloth, and one with shoes. *It has been estimated that eight million laborers, with the aid of machinery, produced as much in England in 1870, as three hundred million laborers could without such assistance.* The work done by the steam and water power of the United States has been recently estimated by a good authority as equal to 25,000,000 horses, or to that of nearly 150,000,000 men, or to a population of nearly 500,000,000.—*Ed. W. Bemis, Ph. D., in the New York Independent.*

Mr. Gladstone estimates that the amount of wealth that could be handed down to posterity, produced during the first 1800 years of the Christian era, was equalled by the production of the first fifty years of this century; and that an equal amount was produced in the twenty years from 1850 to 1870.* According to Emerson the power of machinery in the mills of Great Britain was estimated as equal to 600,000,000 men, or more than all the adults, male and female, in the world.

Surely, with development of productive agencies, and the amazing increase of power, by which the drudgery of labor may be transferred from the human worker to the machine, there ought to be some relief from incessant toil. Why should millions of people, in a land like ours, or the United Kingdom, or the States, be driven to the most harassing toil, and yet be afflicted with poverty?

Certainly the fault is not in nature. Certainly it is not through any defect in economical laws. We hear much about the laws of supply and demand, but what are these but the responses of productive labor to the wants and desires of mankind, and *vice versa?*

Evidently there is a broken link in the chain, or the relationship between the two would be perfect and complete. Let us try to get at the facts in something like consecutive order.

1. Rate of wages, proportion to labor, depends upon the demand for the produce of labor.

---

* "Our Country," by Dr. J. Strong, p. 155.

2. Every man desires to possess wealth—the product of labor.

3. Desire rises with advantage. The more of the good, or of the luxuries of life a man possesses, the more he desires, He who rents a house would own it if he could. A good book begets a desire for another. The possession of a picture educates the eye and the taste, inviting comparison with other pictures. A concertina or an accordian begets a desire for a cornet, a harp, an organ, or a piano. And desire continues to mount with every increasing advantage.

4. Desire, however, does not fix the value of any commodity, although it does regulate the market price. But, as the desire of a man may tend to his poverty and ruin, so a community will be weakened and impoverished which has no higher aim than the gratification of human desire.

5. If labor or money be expended in destructive agencies, so in proportion will the price of produce be greater than the relative power of wages to purchase it. All labor or money spent in the production or consumption of liquor, not only reduces the amount available for other commodities, but it assists in supporting a business which levys innumerable burdens upon the wages of production.

6. Whatever increases demand increases the value of supply. Whatever checks demand depreciates the value of supply. Show me any interest which is built upon the ruins of productive industry and the waste of produce, and I will show you a two-edged sword waging perpetual war against the rate of wages accruing to labor, and against the general supply of wealth.

The advocates of temperance have frequently illustrated the fact that if the money spent in liquor was turned into other channels, not only would the purchasers be that much richer, but the manufacturers and merchants would also be gainers.

Take for illustration the city of Toronto. There are at present 292 licensed taverns and shops in that city, besides shebeens. If it be estimated that the average receipts for liquor at these places is $80 per week, (a low estimate for city taverns) there will be an expenditure in Toronto of $1,214,720 per annum. This, it will be remembered, does not take into account the illicit sale, nor any of the business done by the brewers or distillers directly with consumers. If these were added the probable total would not fall short of $1,500,000, as the yearly liquor bill of the city of Toronto.

This is actually a larger amount than the entire coal trade of the city. The estimated amount of the coal business of Toronto in 1881 was $1,238,000, and this includes a large wholesale trade, much of which is transacted outside of the city.

Now let the reader reflect upon this enormous liquor expenditure in the one city of Toronto. Is it not clear to the most casual observer that if this money was turned into the legitimate channels of productive expenditure it would result in a revival of trade which, if it came suddenly, would amount to a revolution of the business of that city?

What an amount of added comfort it would bring to the city! And what a stimulus to every branch of honest industry! Let the reader contemplate the purchasing power of such a sum of money. It would be sufficient to pay for—

10,000	Men's and boy's suits, averaging....	$15 00	$150,000
10,000	Hats,	"	1 50	15,000
10,000	Womens' dresses,	"	6 00	60,000
20,000	Childrens' dresses,	"	2 00	40,000
10,000	Pairs blankets,	"	3 50	35,000
10,000	Tables,	"	3 50	35,000
10,000	Couches,	"	7 00	70,000
10,000	Bedsteads,	"	4 00	40,000
50,000	Chairs,	"	1 00	50,000
1,000	Sewing machines,	"	50 00	50,000
2,000	Washing machines,	"	15 00	30,000
It would build 500 houses at		1,000	500,000
It would allow $2.00 for books for every child in the city,			100,000
Interest at 6 per cent on $2,000,000 for Public Parks,			120,000
Interest at 6 per cent on $2,000,000 for City Public Bldgs.,			120,000
Contribution to Public Hospitals.....................			20,000
Contribution to Childrens' Homes.....................			20,000
Support Public Library at cost of.....................			25,000
It would leave for other Charities.....			20,000
			$1,500,000

But the good resulting from such a change in the expenditure of money is not visible on the surface. Not only would every factory be on full time and every merchant be reaping a harvest, but competition would not be so keen. Labor would be at a premium and wages would bear a fair relation to the cost of produce. No willing hands would need to be idle. The demand which every man's wants and desires create would be undisturbed by the multiplicity of evils associated with drinking. The tremendous burdens which attend drunkenness would be removed. The destruction of food would cease. New avenues of employment would open, house-building would be stimulated and all the numerous trades interested therein.

Let the wasted labor be diverted to productive fields and you increase the volume of supply to meet increasing demand.

The reader will see in another chapter that the quantity of grain destroyed in distilling and brewing is equal to more than one-seventh of the entire growth of Canada. So that one-seventh of the farm labor is absolutely worthless to the country.

Again all the labor of all the workmen at the brewery and the distillery, as well as all the ten thousand persons engaged in retailing liquor is wasted labor.

Honest labor toils extra hours to support the workmen thus engaged in wasted labor. It must also give extra hours to pay the taxes which the liquor traffic creates. Every idle vagrant, every drink-made criminal, every broken down drunkard, and all their families are additional burdens upon labor.

If labor wants more wages and shorter hours it must combine, and the Union must strike against the drinking system and the liquor traffic in all its phases.

Let GIANT ALCOHOL be slain and no power on earth can prevent the speedy conquest of those other giants CAPITAL and MONOPOLY.

There is reason as well as poetry in the following lines by J. G. Blanchard:

We mean to make things over; we're tired of toil for nought,
But bare enough to live on; never an hour for thought.
We want to feel the sunshine. we want to smell the flowers;
We're sure that God has willed it and we mean to have eight hours,
We're summoning our forces from the shipyard, shop, and mill
Eight hours for work, eight hours for rest, eight hours for what we will
The beasts that graze the hillside, the birds that wander free
In the life that God has meted, have a better lot than we.
Oh! hands and hearts are weary, and homes are heavy with dole;
If life's to be filled with drudgery, what need of a human soul!
Shout, shout the lusty rally from shipyard, shop, and mill
The very stones would cry out if labor's tongue were still!
The voice of God within us is calling us to stand
Erect, as is becoming the work of His right hand.

Should he to whom the Maker His glorious image gave,
Cower, the meanest of His creatures, a bread and butter slave,
Let the shout ring down the valleys, and echo from every hill
Eight hours for work, eight hours for rest, eight hours for what we will.

And why not? Why should not the aspirations of the human mind find time and opportunity. This is not to be announced as though the laws of economy— of supply and demand, had nothing to do with it. God has wonderfully harmonized all laws. The man who regards morality and economical law as opposites has yet to learn the first lesson on the equity and harmonious operation of all primary laws

CHAPTER XVII.

WAGES AND WHISKEY.

IT may be said in reply to the foregoing chapter that the distillers and brewers employ labor and pay wages, and if these establishments were closed the men employed would be turned adrift, and would enter into competition with other labor, and so lessen the chances of workmen obtaining employment at fair wages.

Now there is no better proof that the real cause of labor difficulties and low wages is not generally realised, than the fact that nothing scares the average workman so much as competition. He dreads immigration and engages in perpetual war against prison labor. If he were assured that the idlers of the country, or a gang of tramps were about to turn honest workman, and to enter his own particular trade he would instantly resist the invasion on the ground that competition reduces the chances of the workman. And it must be admitted that, as things now are, such would appear to be an immediate result.

But wages are not a limited commodity. If a sum equal to, say $10,000 were all that 100 people could possibly obtain in wages, there could only be $100 for each of the 100 persons, and if 10 others came into competition with them, there would only be a little more than $90 for each person. But wages cannot be so limited in any community where the wages fund is expended upon articles of utility produced by labor, because every producer is an employer. That is to say, every man who earns wages by productive labor, is creating a fund which will continue to employ him, and will also employ other labor besides his own. There is no fund so prolific and reproductive to wages as the wage-fund of the workman, because no other fund is so immediately distributed into the various channels of commerce.

But the wages of unproductive and destructive labor is not capable of this self-sustaining and augmenting power. Labor which produces nothing, or worse than nothing, soon exhausts the capital which is expended upon it, or else makes a continual drain upon other capital.

If $10,000 were the limit of capital available among 100 men and the whole amount of ten thousand dollars were paid in wages for unproductive work, there would be only $100 for each man, and when that was paid, the whole fund would be exhausted.

On the other hand, every person is a consumer, and if there are one hundred men and their families in a community, ten of whom are kept in idleness through any cause, the wages or earnings of the remaining ninety is all that is availale to support the hundred.

Working men make a grave mistake when they combine to keep men from working. Every idler must be supplied out of the produce of labor. It is the interest of the workmen therefore to demand that every one shall contribute something to the general weal in return for his living.

It is still more the interest of the productive workman to resist a business which lives upon destruction.

With what manifold force does this apply to the liquor business in its relation to wages. More than one-seventh of all the grain produce of Canada, or its equivalent, is destroyed in distilling and brewing. In order to see the effect of this upon wages let us suppose that all the grain of the Dominion is grown by one farmer who employs—say 10,000 men as farm workers. Now if Mr. Canada, Farmer, loses by fire or otherwise one-seventh of all his produce in any one year, it is certain that he will be, by the value of that one-seventh, less able to pay his men. If this waste or loss occurs only once or twice he might pay the normal rate of wages to all his men out of reserve wealth or capital, but if it be continued year after year the workmen would have to contribute to the loss, *i.e.* the wages of all the farm laborers must be one-seventh less.

But it will be objected that this is not the position of the farmer in relation to the brewery and distillery because he receives market value for all the grain he sells them, and is thereby enabled to pay his workmen.

This objection only drives us back to the working or wage-earning population as a whole. The annual waste of one-seventh of the grain *does* take place; the fires of the still *are* ever burning and somebody *must* pay for the waste. *That somebody* is the productive workman, including, of course, the agricultural laborer or farmer who must pay his full share on account of the waste. It must never be forgotten that the ultimate fund of all wages is production. The very wages paid to the employees of the brewer and the distiller comes from that fund.

It is frequently stated on behalf of the liquor manufacturers that they are large employers of labor. But we have already seen that the wages paid to the employees of brewers and distillers must come from the fund created and sustained by productive labor.

The claim has recently been made by the brewers of the United States that they employ 500,000 men, upon which a writer in a leading organ of labor unions in that country makes the following remarks:

"Think of this, working-men! Half a million men employed in destroying food, in rotting grain, etc., turning it into a poison that makes men fiends, wives widows, children orphans, the industrious lazy, the intelligent numbskulls, and sends women and children to work in place of men, thus filling the land with tramps and loafers, for the workers to support. If it is true that every person who produces nothing beneficial to society is no better than a pauper, . . . then all labor employed making, handling or selling such drinks is labor wasted, and people so employed are paupers and makers of paupers. . . The brewers, distillers, liquor, wine and beer-dealers, are among the worst enemies of working-men; the temperance people are their friends. The former rob them of their health, happiness and life; the latter want to see every man, woman and child well housed, clothed and fed. The objects of temperance are the abolition of poverty, crime, disease and premature death."—*John Swinton's Paper.*

But there is no phase of the liquor question more misleading than this *employment of labor* cry. Let the capital invested in the liquor business be turned into any other channel of industry and the number of workmen employed thereby would be multiplied, and the wages fund would be indefinitely enlarged. Let the money expended in the products of the brewery be expended in the products of the farm and the factory, and the impetus which would be immediately given to the demand for labor would be such as would make the wage-earners of the country independant and comparatively affluent.

Sir Wm. Collins, of Glasgow, Scotland, in his address as President of the Economic Section of the National Temperance Congress, held at Liverpool in June, 1884, made the following remarks on this point:

"It is contended that this expenditure of $126,251,359, (the estimated amount for the year spent in the United Kingdom on liquors), yields a large profit to the manufactures and the 180,000 distributors of alcoholic drinks; but this argument is worthless, as it assumes that a similar amount of expenditure on the manufacture and sale of articles of necessity and utility, would not yield a similar amount of profit. Now it is a notorious fact that no industry in the country employs a smaller number of the laboring and artisan classes, in comparison with the amount paid by the consumer for the manufactured article; indeed I believe I am within the mark when I say, that were the earnings of our industrial classes diverted from the till of the publican to the till of the grocer and provision merchant, or to the purchase of clothing, furniture, and houses, or even articles of luxury, employment would be given to at least fourfold the number of individuals that are at present engaged in connection with the drink traffic."

The reason for this is manifest to those who will examine the real character of the liquor factory. It is easy to destroy. It takes brains and muscle to develop, or to produce. Two or three men in a distillery can destroy the produce of as many score of farm workers, just as two or three men can pull down a house which required scores of men to build.

The *Scotsman* a leading newspaper of Edinburgh, Scotland, is authority for statements from which we learn that the amount of spirits produced at the Caledonian Distillery, Edinburgh, is 40,000 gallons weekly or about 2,000,000 gallons per annum. This would bring a cash turn over, (at the wholesale rate of 15s. per gallon) of £1.500,000 or $7,500,000. Now with this enormous revenue the total number of men employed is—150

Contrast this with the Atlas Iron and Steel Works at Sheffield, England. The revenue of that great Company was just about one half that of the Caledonian Distillery, and they employed 4,000 hands.

Writing to an English paper recently the Rev. J. Horsely says:—

"The other day I stood on the roof of a large factory. Near it I saw a large distillery flanked appropriately enough by a workhouse on one side and an asylum on the other. I asked my friend what is the capital of that distillery company? A million. And how many men do they employ? Three hundred. And what is the capital of the company that runs this mill? Three hundred and fifty thousand. And how many men, women, and children do you employ? Four thousand. This was a striking instance of the comparative value of the two trades as promoting the prosperity of the town.

In the *Trade Review* of 1880, published by Mr. Galbraith, the Commercial Editor of the *Globe*, it is stated that the daily production of the Gooderham & Worts distillery is "8,000 imperial gallons during the season of eight or nine months. The total production the past season was 2,000,000 gallons of spirits. * * Taking $1.50 as the average price per gallon, the produce of this distillery during the year was $3,000,-000." How many hands are employed at this establishment? I quote again from the same authority. "This firm employs 100 men, eighty of whom are in the distillery, ten in the malt-house and ten outside."

During that same year 1880 there were two large firms in Toronto engaged in the manufacture of reapers, mowers and other agricultural implements. The Toronto Reaper and Mower Co., manufactured during that year 3,500 machines, the sales amounting to $350,000. The firm employed 225 men at an average wages of $1.75 per day. The Massey Manufacturing Co., turned out during the same year 1,500 reapers and mowers, and 3,000 horse rakes, the receipts being $250,000. This Company employed from 150 to 200 men at wages varying from $1.00 to $2.50 per day, say an average of 175 men at an average of $1.75 per day wages. The joint results then of the two firms (allowing 300 working days in the year) will be:

    Machines and Implements made... 8,000
    Men employed at $1.75 per day.... 400
    Total receipts of the two firms..... $600,000
    Wages paid.................... 210,000

Rate of wages to value of Products 35 per cent.

Compare this with the great Toronto Distillery. This firm employed 100 men at an average wage of $7.95, per week let us say $8.00. At this rate the wages paid during the year will amount to $41,600. This gives the following results:

    Spirits made............... Galls. 2,000,000
    Receipts for same............... $3,000,000
    Wages paid.................... $41,600 .

Rate of wages to value of Products $1\frac{1}{4}$ per cent.

With a view to further test these striking statistics by actual example, I wrote recently to one of the largest manufacturing company's in Toronto, asking to be favored with statistics of their annual products, its value, number of men employed, amount of wages paid, &c. I received a letter in reply bearing date Nov. 1st, 1886, which says:—"*We are doing a business of from $600,000 to $800,000 a year, paying out in wages in the different departments of the works between $250,000 and $300,000 a year, for material about $200,000, and the number employed in the different departments would run from 600 to 800 men.*

Let men ponder these contrasting figures. Let them take in their full importance in relation to the wages market. The producer of implements pays $210,000 out of $600,000 for labor, the maker of whiskey pays $41,600 out of the enormous total of three million dollars.

The firm quoted above pays between 250 to 300 thousand dollars for wages, out of a business of 600 to 800 thousand dollars, and employs from 600 to 800 men.

The whiskey factory scopes in three million dollars and pays $41,600 in wages—employing only 100 men, or $1\frac{1}{4}$ per cent.

Let us now see if this is in harmony with the general results of manufacturing industry as compared with the manufacture of intoxicating liquors. The following table has been carefully prepared from the returns given under different heads in the Census Report of 1881. The object of the table is to show the rate of wages proportion to the capital invested, and to the value or cash income in return for the articles produced. Fifteen of the largest manufacturing industries have been selected to compare with the two interests of Distilling and Brewing. In order to anticipate a possible criticism as to the fairness of this table, I may remark that I have purposely omitted one or two of the interests which appear to be the largest, judging by the amount of money involved, such for instance as flour and grist mills, in which the value of raw material handled, bears such an overwhelming proportion to the value of the materials produced, that it would destroy the ratio of a table intended to give average results. To illustrate this—the value of *raw materials* used at our flour and grist mills is $34,677,414 and the value of the *produce* of the mills is $41,772,372. If, however, allowance were made for the difference, in the value of the materials used, the ratio of wages paid in proportion to value of products, and to capital invested, would average much the same in Flour Mills as in other industries.

LAND, LABOR AND LIQUOR.   137

TABLE

SHOWING THE RATIO OF WAGES TO CAPITAL AND TO PRODUCE IN FIFTEEN OF THE PRINCIPAL INDUSTRIES AS COMPARED WITH THE TWO INTERESTS OF BREWING AND DISTILLING.

Also showing number of hands employed, amount of wages paid, &c.

Name of trade.	Value of Raw Materials Used.	Capital Invested.	Value of Articles Produced.	Wages Paid	Men Employed.	Women, Boys & Girls Employed.	Rate of Wages to Capital.	Rate of Wages to Value of Produce.
	$	$	$	$			p.c.	p.c.
Ag. Implem't M'k'rs.	1,839,197	3,995,782	4,405,397	1,241,279	3489	167	31	27½
Blacksmiths	2,486,568	3,056,653	7,172,469	2,597,539	12151	300	86¼	32
Boot & Shoe Making	9,786,745	6,491,042	17,895,903	4,382,584	13825	5124	67	25
Furniture Makers	2,051,979	3,943,419	5,471,742	1,723,604	5206	651	43¾	31½
Carpenters *	1,656,395	1,242,531	3,893,910	1,307,513	5574	128	102	34
Carriage Makers	2,451,546	3,798,861	6,579,082	2,275,290	8420	293	59	34
Cotton Factories	1,979,655	3,476,500	3,759,041	714,259	975	2252	20¾	16¼
Dress M'k's & Milln'rs	2,977,575	1,601,239	4,926,871	89,242	114	7724	55¾	18¼
Fitters & Founders	1,254,588	1,797,897	2,684,631	809,309	2014	180	45	30
Foundries & Mach'ists	3,581,175	7,675,911	8,773,957	2,924,898	7476	313	35½	31
Printers	1,541,060	4,291,136	4,742,904	1,797,112	4055	1256	36	32
Saddle Harness M'k's	1,662,361	1,323,845	3,233,973	771,688	2775	136	58	23¾
Sash, Door, &c., M'k's	2,692,930	1,996,858	4,872,362	997,836	2760	118	49	20½
Saw Mills	20,798,389	25,487,233	38,569,652	8,146,996	39135	2950	13	22½
Tailors & Clothiers	8,914,131	5,719,729	15,102,963	3,165,367	5200	12829	56	32
Average Ratios							51	27
Distilleries	1,092,100	1,303,000	1,790,800	16,230	273	12	1¼	.10
Breweries	2,282,185	4,592,990	4,768,447	567,639	1359	52	12	11¾
Average Ratios							6⅛	6¼

* It is possible that the Census Returns do not include workman's tools as part of the capital invested in carpenter work. If this surmise is correct it would alter the proportion in this instance but would not materially effect the average of the table.

Thus it is seen that while the average rate of wages in proportion to capital invested in the 15 trades mentioned is 51 per cent; in the distillery it is only $1\frac{1}{4}$ per cent, and in the brewery only 11 per cent, or putting the two together only $6\frac{1}{8}$ per cent. And further; while the average of wages to production in the fifteen trades is 27 per cent, in distilling it is less than one per cent, and in distilling and brewing combined a litttle over 6 per cent.

In other words the investment of $1,000 capital in any of the above trades will result in an annual payment of $510 wages; and an expenditure of $1000 in agricultural instruments, shoes, furniture or any of the other commodities named will give a return of $270 to the wage earner. On the other hand, a capital of $1000 invested in whiskey-making will only pay $12.50 per year to wages, and an expenditure of $1000 in whiskey will only pay to wages $8.50.

Contrast 510 with $12\frac{1}{2}$ and 270 with $8\frac{1}{2}$, and you have the relative value of legitimate industries as compared with the whiskey business.

Now let us test this by enquiring into the relation of wages to the produce and capital of the whole country. It must be borne in mind that this includes all industrial interests some of which do not give an average proportion to the wages market.

TABLE.

Showing the value of all other industries in Canada and the proportionate value of these to wages, as compared with the manufacture of whiskey and beer.

CANADIAN INDUSTRIES.

Capital invested..............$161,377,783
Value of Produce..............$303,116,821
Total Wages Paid.............$ 58,845,733

Persons Employed..................253,239
Average Capital required for every
    Person Employed................$ 632
Average Rates of Wages Paid to Value
    of Produce.............(Per Cent) 19
Average Rate of Wages Paid to Capital
    Invested..............(Per Cent) 36

BREWERIES AND DISTILLERIES.

Capital required for every person em-
    ployed in Breweries and Distillieries, $3,612
Wages Paid by Distillers in proportion
    to Value of Produce......(Per cent) 00.10
Wages Paid by Distillers in proportion
    to Capital invested......(Per Cent) $1\frac{1}{4}$
Wages Paid by Distillers and Brewers
    to Capital Invested................ $6\frac{1}{8}$
Wages Paid by Distillers and Brewers
    to Value of Produce............... $6\frac{1}{4}$

Surely no further proofs are needed. It is abundantly established by unbending facts that the liquor traffic is the very worst investment of a workman's earnings, even from the wages point of view.

It is manifest that the boasted value of the liquor traffic as a factor to the labor market, and as an investment of capital, profitable to the community, has not the slightest backing of actual facts, but that, on the contrary, it is at war with the interests of all workmen, and is a monopolist of the worst and most enslaving character.

CHAPTER XVIII.

OUR NATIONAL DRINK BILL.

IT is a startling fact that, in this young country, our annual Liquor bill is twice as large as our entire expenditure for schools and churches. In other words, we spend twice as much for drink as for religious work, churches, missions and education.

It is a still more startling fact that this entire consumption of liquor is so much waste. Nay more, that in every branch and detail of the business of the manufacture and sale of intoxicating liquors, there is absolute destruction, without a single redeeming or qualifying feature. The raw material used is wasted, the labor expended upon it is wasted, the money spent by the people for the liquor is wasted.

To present a full view of this waste we must see how much of these various items are consumed, and then we must take into account the indirect losses occasioned to the nation by drinking usages.

The actual Liquor bill for direct cost of liquors consumed has been variously estimated, from $27,000,000 to $40,000,000 per annum.

The Toronto *Globe* of April 5th, 1884, published a table of statistics estimating the cost for that year at $27,627,965 : to which is added the following important comment :

This is a "larger amount than the total value of the farms, with their buildings, implements, and live stock, of the richest county among thirty-four out of the forty-five counties or districts in Ontario. This startling expenditure would appear still larger if the whole consumption of liquor could be got at. If a little may have to be deducted for the quantity of liquor used for scientific purposes—an inconsiderable quantity in this country—there would have to be much more added for the wines of Canadian vineyards, to say nothing about the "crooked" whiskey which escapes the eye of the excise-man."

Professor G. E. Foster, M. P., estimates the drink bill of 1883 at $36,769,618. (See Canadian Temperance Manual.)

The authorities for quantities are the same in both cases, and are the only reliable sources available, viz., the Inland Revenue Reports, and the Trade and Navigation Returns; but the estimates of cost to the public are not quite the same. The *Globe*, for instance, estimates the price paid for whiskey at the taverns at $4 per gallon. Mr. Foster's estimate is $5. But the *Globe* admits that its estimate is low in the following remarks:

"Whiskey drinks are cheaper in Canada than in the United States, and rarely cost more than five cents apiece. This, however, would bring the price of every gallon up to $3.20. But as the custom of watering whiskey before offering it at the bar is not uncommon; in fact, is estimated by parties in the trade as amounting to from a quarter to a third of the whiskey sold, it is reasonable to place the cost to the public at $4 per gallon."

I have been told by parties in the trade that whiskey is frequently watered to the extent of one-half, and the strength is made up by the various processes of "doctoring" known to the trade. (See Appendix.)

On the whole I think Prof. Foster's estimate of retail prices is quite within the mark. The *Globe's* estimate of the retail price of beer and that of Prof. Foster are the same, although, here again, there certainly can be no charge of exaggeration. The regular price of ales at the counter is five cents a glass, and there are from 12 to 20 glasses in a gallon, according to the size of the glass used. Sixty cents per gallon for beer, therefore, is a low estimate.

With these preliminary explanations I submit that the following table represents the expenditure of this country in liquors so far as quantities can be ascertained from official documents, and, of course, not allowing for home made Canadian wines which are not reported in government official returns, or for the "crooked" whiskey sold.

TABLE

SHOWING THE COST OF DISTILLED AND MALT LIQUORS ENTERED FOR CONSUMPTION IN 1885. THE QUANTITIES ARE TAKEN FROM THE LAST INLAND REVENUE REPORT AND THE TRADE AND NAVIGATION RETURNS. THE PRICES QUOTED ARE THE ESTIMATED COST OF THE LIQUORS TO CONSUMERS.

Spirits, (Canadian)	3,888,012	galls., at	$5 00	$19,440,060
Spirits, (American)	11,392	"	" 6 00	68,352
Spirits, (Imported)	1,191,187	"	" 6 00	7,147,122
Beer, (Canadian)	12,071,752	"	" 60	7,243,051
Ales, (Imported)	363,379	"	" 2 00	726,758
Wines, (Imported)	493,278	"	" 5 00	2,466,390
Wines, in bottles, (Imported)	27,373	"	" 6 00	164,238
	18,046,373			$37,255,971

The consumption of intoxicating liquors in Canada for the year 1885, therefore, amounts to 18,046,373 gallons. The cost of that liquor to the people at the above estimate amounts to 37,255,971 dollars.

It is necessary, however, to remark that this is probably in excess of the actual consumption during the year; that a portion of this quantity] was consumed during the year 1886, so that the next published returns should be correspondingly smaller. A "Statistical Abstract and Record," published by the Dominion Government (Oct., 1886) remarks that " *Owing to the Canada Temperance Act having been adopted in many parts of the Dominion, and more particular by the majority of Counties in Ontario, it was thought that there would be a decided falling off in the revenue derived from spirits and malt liquors; contrary, however, to expectation, the revenue from both sources showed a large increase over 1884 amounting to $734,444, though this was not brought about by increased consumption, but by large withdrawals from bond in anticipation of additional duty.*"

It will be seen from the above that in order to arrive at the actual expenditure it is essential that we should take the average of a period of years, and not any one particular year.

Taking, then, the eighteen years since Confederation, up to, and including 1885, we have the following

TABLE

SHOWING THE COST OF THE CONSUMPTION OF INTOXICATING LIQUORS IN CANADA FROM 1868 to 1885 INCLUSIVE.

Spirits, (Canadian)......	61,474,770 galls.,	at $5 00	$307,273,850
Spirits, (Imported)......	18,719,987	"	" 6 00	112,318,922
Beer, (Canadian)........	166,423,390	"	" 60	99,854,034
Ales, (Imported)........	5,153,910	"	" 2 00	10,307,820
Wines, including bottled (Imported).........	9,743,462	"	" 6 00	58,460,772
Total...........	261,515,519			$588,215,398
Average per year...	14,528,639 gallons,			$32,678,633

Thus it is apparent that while the last year's consumption is above the average of the last eighteen years, our annual liquor bill, without counting indirect losses occasioned thereby, amounts to the total of more than thirty-two and a half millions of dollars.

INDIRECT COST TO THE NATION.

Waste of Food.—We must now enquire as to the quantity of food wasted in the manufacture of these liquors. In this enquiry we will leave out of calculation the raw material used in the manufacture of imported liquors, as we are considering it now from a national point of view. But in any more general view of the question, it must not be forgotten that the materials used in Europe and elsewhere, for the manufacture of imported spirits, ales and wines are destroyed equally with our own.

TABLE.

SHOWING THE QUANTITY OF GRAIN AND OTHER MATERIALS USED IN THE MANUFACTURE OF SPIRITS AND MALT LIQUORS AT CANADIAN DISTILLERIES AND BREWERIES FROM 1868 TO 1885 INCLUSIVE.

Years.	FOR SPIRITS.			FOR BEER.	
	Grain used.	Molasses	Sugar, &c.	Malt used.	Sugar & other substances.
	Lbs.	Gallons.	Lbs.	Lbs.	Lbs.
1868	67,685,511	....	....	22,681,749	380,787
1869	52,359,505	1,085	....	21,915,137	174,449
1870	58,901,557	12,364	....	20,463,338	147,352
1871	86,788,405	23,609	....	23,707,258	21,654
1872	79,324,907	16,042	2,006,050	26,108,073	285,328
1873	91,452,901	....	5,502	30,309,789	282,375
1874	87,539,173	4,520	162,398	28,685,003	207,361
1875	90,094,381	8,642	14,992	30,377,039	215,004
1876	59,472,129	....	....	27,980,256	68,560
1877	68,498,295	....	....	27,471,797	....
1878	67,594,902	....	....	25,180,327	89
1879	66,749,856	....	....	25,456,803	2,410
1880	53,394,258	8,201	2,413	26,419,244	450
1881	53,667,108	502	9,674	28,395,987	....
1882	70,402,810	....	....	34,775,986	....
1883	76,796,094	....	392,476	36,140,545	....
1884	75,095,450	....	620,390	37,563,636	4,619
1885	63,542,708	....	3,826	34,566,059	8,682
	1,259,459,950	74,965	3,217,721	508,198,026	1,799,120

The principal grain used for distilling is corn, which weighs 56 lbs. to the bushel. Barley is rated at 48 lbs. to the bushel, and it takes 100 lbs. of barley to make 75 lbs of malt. Taking the above figures, and calculating the average value during these eighteen years at 60c. per bushel, barley at 70c, Sugar at 5c. a lb., and molasses at 30c, a gallon, (in some years the market

K

prices have been greatly above these) we have the following:

QUANTITIES OF MATERIALS USED IN THE MANUFACTURE OF INTOXICATING LIQUORS DURING EIGHTEEN YEARS, WITH AN ESTIMATE OF THEIR VALUE.

22,490,356 Bush. of Corn, Rye, &c., at 60c.	$13,494,213
14,116,617 Bush. of Barley, " 70c.	9,881,631
3,217,721 Lbs. of Sugar for Spirits at 5c.	160,886
74,965 Gall. of Molasses " " 30c.	22,489
1,799,120 Lbs. of Sugar for Beer " 5c.	89,956
	$23,629,175

Coal, &c.—In addition to these items, the coal and other fuel consumed adds greatly to the amount of waste. One firm of distillers is reported as using 8,000 tons of coal in one year.* The quantity used therefore cannot be less than 50,000 tons per year. Valued at $5 per ton, this would amount to $250,000.

Labor Wasted.—The next item to be considered is the waste of labor involved. If the men now engaged in the manufacture and distribution of intoxicants were employed in some productive work they would, at least, be producing sufficient to support themselves. As it is, the country has to support them out of the produce of other labor. The number of these so employed may be estimated as follows:

Persons engaged in breweries in 1881	1,411
Persons " distilleries	285
Persons " Malt-houses	500

---

* See Galbraith's Financial and Trade Review of Toronto for 1880.

LAND, LABOR AND LIQUOR.

Persons engaged in retailing liquor....... 8,000
Persons   "   wholesaling liquor.... 2,000
                                            ———
                                          12,196*

In a report recently issued by the Ontario Bureau of Industries, Mr. Blue the Secretary has supplied some valuable statistics in regard to labor, wages &c. He there shows that the average earnings of the work-people of the Province amounted to about $370, and the average cost of living to $318. Taking then $370 as the average value these persons should have made in productive labor, we have the sum of $4,510,720 as the sum lost to the country on this account.

It is estimated that there are 50,000 drunkards in Canada. This estimate places the ratio of drunkards to the population at a little over one per cent which may be regarded by some as an exaggeration.

In his work on the "wasted resources" of the United States, Dr. Hargreaves estimates the proportion of drunkards to every saloon or liquor shop as at least four. If we take this view of the matter, and place the whole number of licensed and unlicensed liquor shops in Canada at 10,000 (see chapter on wasted capital) we should have a total of 40,000 drunkards. This would give a proportion of about one drunkard to every 115 persons in the Dominion a proportion which I fear is below the actual facts. Let any Canadian citizen consider for a moment the number of persons resident within his own neighborhood, who are habitually or frequently drunk, and this estimate will not appear excessive. It appears also that the

---

* The Official Records do not give the number of persons employed in Malt-houses and in the retailing of liquor. These are therefore estimated and the reader will probably regard it as a low estimate.

total number of charges at our police courts for drunkenness in 1882, was 43,505 or one charge to every 101 of the population, and in 1883 the total was 47,141 or one to every 95. If it be alleged that many cases of drunkenness are charged against persons who are not habitual drunkards in the common acceptation of the term, and that there are many cases which represent the repeated offences of the same person, it must also be remembered, that there are many drunkards who are never arrested by the police and are therefore not included in these statistics.

On the whole I think my estimate of 40,000 is below the mark rather than above it. If these 40,000 persons average a loss of half their time, or productive power, through drink we have the loss of production equal to the value of the work of 20,000 persons which at the rate of $370 per annum amounts to $7,400,000.

There is the further loss to the country of the wasted time of persons who lose part of their labor through drinking and occasional drunkenness. The total male population of the Dominion in 1881 was 2,188,779, one half of whom are neither too old nor too young to work (see *Abstract and Record* page 84, published by the Dominion Government, 1886). Deducting the liquor makers and vendors, and the drunkards who have been already counted, and the police, criminals and others, yet to be considered, there are about 1,000,000 of a working male population in this country. If one-sixth of these adult males use intoxicating drinks, to an extent which results in the loss of one days work in six of their labor, we have an additional loss of nearly eight and a quarter million days work, equal in value to at least $8,500,000.

A Commission was appointed by the British Government in 1834 to enquire into the drink question, and in their report they said:

"The loss of productive labor in every department of occupation to the extent of one day in six throughout the kingdom (as testified by witnesses engaged in various manufacturing operations) by which the wealth of the country, created as it chiefly is by labor, is retarded or suppressed to the extent of one million out of every six that is produced, to say nothing of the constant derangement, imperfection and destruction in every agricultural and manufacturing process, occasioned by the intemperance and consequent unskilfulness, in attention and neglect of those afflicted by intoxication, producing great injury in our domestic and foreign trade."

If a similar proportion of our productive labor were lost to us in this country it would amount to a total of 52,500,000 days, or the full time of 175,000 men per annum, reckoning the working male population at 1,050,000 and the working days at 300 per year.

My estimate given above does not show a loss nearly so great as this, but allowing that half the time of habitual drunkards is lost to us, and one-sixth of the time of occasional drunkards, I make the loss of our labor power as equal to 14,250,000 days work per year or the full time of about 47,500 men. I have taken no account of the loss of labor power through premature deaths of workmen occassioned by drink; but simply the proportion of the actual loss to our various iudustries of the average existing working force of the country.

Nor have I estimated anything for the deterioration of the quality of work through drink, nor for the loss of productive power of our female population from this cause.

In another chapter a further estimate as to the proportion of drinking and drunkenness to the community will be found, showing that the above estimates of the loss occasioned by drink are not excessive.

Capital Wasted.—Add again the loss of the value of the capital which is extracted from the working power of the country, and which would be available for productive industry were it not absorbed in the destructive force of liquor making and vending. We have seen elsewhere that capital invested in productive industries bears an enormous interest to the wages market, besides greatly increasing its own volume and value. In another chapter I have shown that the amount of capital locked up in the liquor interests cannot be less than fifteen and a half millions of dollars.

This involves a loss to our productive industries of, at least, $3,000,000 per annum.

Cost of Crime.—There is also the cost of crime occasioned by drink, the maintenance of the criminals, the proportion of cost of police, gaolers &c., chargeable to this agency. All who have to do with criminal records agree that a very large proportion of all crimes is directly or indirectly traceable to drink; the estimates varying from 60 to 90 per cent. It will certainly be a low estimate if we reckon that one half of the cost of crime and its consequences would be saved to the country but for drink. This would amount to the sum of at least, $1,500,000. (*See chapter on Liquor and Crime.*) Add again the loss to the country of the value of the work of one half the entire staff of police, gaolers, criminals and others who would be engaged in productive labor but for drink—a sum not less than $1,000,000.

Lunacy.—In a subsequent chapter I have dealt separately with the question of drink in relation to lunacy. It is there shown that a very large proportion of the cost involved in maintaining our lunatic population is traceable to drinking. It will be seen that the cost to the country and the losses sustained on account of it are not less than two and a half millions, one-third of which is undoubtedly chargeable to alcoholic drinking,—say $800,000.

THE ANNUAL COST OF INTOXICATING DRINKS IN CANADA will therefore be about as follows so far as can be estimated:

Direct cost of drink consumed	$32,678,633
Value of food destroyed which might be turned to account of national wealth or the land upon which it is grown used for productive purposes	23,629,175
Value of fuel consumed which might be employed in productive industry, or used to supply the increased wants of Canadian homes	250,000
Value of labor wasted in brewing, distilling and retailing liquor which ought to be employed in productive service	4,510,720
Indirect loss of productive service through drunkenness	7,400,000
Indirect loss of time and service through occasional intemperance	8,500,000
Loss of the value of capital at present locked up in the liquor business and which ought to be employed in productive service	3,000,000
Loss occasioned by crime through drink	1,500,000
Loss of productive labor of criminals, police, gaolers and other officers of justice	1,000,000
Loss through insanity occasioned by drink	800,000
	$82,268,528

The reader will, of course, understand that this calculation, although carefully made, and as I have shown, based mainly upon official returns, is nevertheless only an estimate. It may therefore be reduced or enlarged according to the judgment of the reader.

But it must be borne in mind that no attempt is here made to estimate other serious losses indirectly traceable to drink and which are incalculable.

There are numerous accidents constantly occuring as a result of drinking. We can hardly take up a newspaper without reading of some such cases. The report of the Committee on Intemperance in the United Kingdom, 1834, already referred to, mentions among the consequences of drink to the National welfare.

"The extensive loss of property by sea, from shipwrecks, founderings, fires, and innumerable other accidents, many of which according to the evidence of the most experienced ship-owners, nautical men and others, examined by your Committee are clearly traceable to drunkenness in some of the parties employed in the navigation and charge of such vessels whose vigilance, had they been sober, would have been sufficient safeguard against their occurence.

While I write, the Toronto *Globe* (Jan. 6, 1887) publishes an article deploring the great losses by fire which in the United States and Canada amounted last year to the total of $116,600,000. Here is a consideration for every property owner and every Fire Insurance Company. How frequently does it happen that fires originate from some cause unknown, but in the language of newspaper reporters "presumably through a drunken vagrant sleeping on the premises" or perhaps through "the carelessness of a half drunken night-watchman or servant." Even incendiarisms are frequently the result of some drunken spree or some mad freak of revenge in which drink is an incentive.

There are losses to merchants also that are incalculable. There is hardly a store-keeper of any long standing in business, but could tell of numerous losses which he would never have experienced but for drink. The black list of bad debts is almost entirely a standing mark against Intemperance.*

Then there is the cost of vagrancy, petty theft, &c,. with the addition of the loss of labor attending them.

I am of opinion that some of the items herein given are much below the actual facts, and if these additional factors in the bill were estimated the total would certainly be immeasurably increased.

Let the reader make a mental calculation of the losses under these various heads, and it will be found that it is simply impossible to conceive the value which is annually lost to the community.

Accidents by sea and lakes through drink....... ———
Accidents by fire, in the streets, in building operations, in the running of mills and other machinery, and many other occasions......... ———
Losses to Merchants....................... ———
Bankruptcies of business men................. ———
Pauperism, vagrancy, petty theft, &c........... ———
Loss of moral worth and character............ ———
Loss of human life......................... ———
Loss of human souls....................... ———

---

* I have talked with many people in business who declare that at least 90 per cent of the bad debts on their books are occassioned by drink. The other day a store-keeper said to me, "I have lost $5,000 in bad debts through drink." It is reported on good authority that store-keepers have had debts paid to them since the Scott Act came into operation in Halton and other counties that they never expected to get and had marked *bad*.

I place no figures to these items. All of them are incalculable. The last three are beyond all measure of material value. The moral worth of a man cannot be measured by sums of money, however great.

Who will undertake to assess the value of a human soul? "For what is a man profited if he should gain the whole world, and lose his own soul? or what shall a man give in exchange for his soul?"

Looking at the financial question alone, however, there can be no doubt in the mind of any candid person, in view of all the facts stated here, that the sum total of our national drink bill including the direct cost, and the indirect losses occasioned by it, will not fall short of the amount given above.

Can there be a more startling fact presented to the economic student, or the patriotic citizen than that in this young country, with a population of four and a-half millions, we are yearly wasting our resources to the tune of *Eight-two Millions of dollars.*

When we add to this fact the terrible truth that in wasting this wealth we are also destroying our people, undermining the morals of young Canada, laying waste the homes of thousands of our people and ruining the eternal prospects of thousands of souls annually, how appalling is the picture! How stupendous the cost!

Yet there are members of Christian Churches and even ministers who vote for the traffic, there are politicians and members of government who, in face of these facts, and of the fact that no question stirs the public mind as this does, yet openly declare that this *is not yet a part of the practical politics of Canáda."* *

---

* Speeches by Hon. Mr. Thompson at Orangeville, Ont., Nov. 29, 1886, and Hon. Edward Blake at Aylmer, Ont., Dec. 7, 1886.

Our national debt is a subject of much controversy. It is attacked upon every platform of the Reformers and defended at every meeting held in the interests of the Conservatives, while not one word is said by either side dealing practically with a more gigantic financial burden, involving evils which may be described as infinitely greater.

We borrow millions of money and pay interest thereon amounting to millions per annum, while we foster, protect, and license a huge system which absorbs and destroys an immense proportion of our wealth, enough if saved to make us absolutely independant.

Our national debt has steadily increased from the first year of Confederation, with the exception of the years 1871 and 1883, when there was a decrease on the debts of the previous years amounting to $501,024 and $3,026,147 respectively. The government official abstract recently issued shows that the public debt was $93,046,051 in 1867, and in 1885 it had risen to $264,703,607. By far the largest increase was in 1884 and 1885 when the amounts added to the debt were $40,323,311 and $22,221,191 respectively, or a total increase for the two years of $62,544,502.

Yet the losses occasioned by the liquor traffic in one year would pay the whole of the sum added to the national debt in these two years of unprecedented public expenditure, and still leave twenty millions to the good.

In the year 1884 the government negotiated a loan of £5,000,000 or about $25,000,000 at $3\frac{1}{2}$ per cent interest. The rate of interest on the whole public debt according to official documents is 3·55 per cent or a total amount for last year of $9,419,482.

The two years 1884-5 were, by many millions, the heaviest years of public expenditure in the country; averaging for each of the years $82,985,191.

Large as this sum is, it is actually only a trifle more than our estimate of the annual financial loss involved in the liquor traffic. In other words while we complain of the enormous cost of our government expenditure, involving such vast burdens upon the people, we actually tax ourselves with a still greater burden, without the advantage of a single benefit, and giving us infinitely worse than nothing for our money.

We complain loudly at the increase of our national debt from ninety-three millions in 1867, to two hundred and sixty-four millions in 1885, (an enormous growth surely) involving additions, year by year, amounting in eighteen years to a total of $171,000,000. Yet during that eighteen years our total liquor bill (without reckoning indirect cost) amounts to 588 millions, or nearly three and a half times as much.

Who that looks at these facts will not preceive that although the national debt is not the direct outgrowth of the liquor traffic, yet the expenditure which created it (large and extravagant as it is) could have been met with ease had not the substance of the country been wasted in liquor ? Or if a national debt were inevitable might not our own people have furnished the funds instead of paying $10,000,000 annually out of the country for interest.

It is indeed a most startling fact that if *half the actual cost of intoxicating liquors*, (without reckoning the indirect expenditure involved) had been saved to the country during the past eighteen years, it would have more than sufficed to pay the entire amount which has accumulated to such a mountain of debt as represented by the figures $264,700,000.

Let every patriotic Canadian ponder these tremendous facts, and work, and vote, and pray accordingly !

CHAPTER XIX.

COMPARATIVE VIEWS OF OUR NATIONAL LIQUOR BILL.

COMPARED with the liquor bills of the United Kingdom and the United States, our Canadian expenditure appears greatly less. The comparison is extremely unfavorable to the older and larger countries.

In the United Kingdom the statistical picture is indeed a dark one, although happily there has been a considerable diminution in the volume, of expenditure during the past five years, and a still larger diminution when considered in proportion to the increasing population.

The most eminent Statistical enquirer and writer on the liquor question was the late Mr. Wm. Hoyle of Tottington, Lancashire, England. The statistics collected by him and arrayed in such telling manner in his work entitled *Our National Resources and how they are wasted,* and, also in the numerous books and pamphlets afterwards published, were accepted as authoritative by the most distinguished statesmen, orators and writers, both in Europe and America. In his latter years and up to 1885 he published an annual letter to the London *Times* which was always the subject of editorial comments in that paper and of all the most prominent journals, and was treated as the best authority on the question by all public men.

Mr. Hoyle tells us in one of these letters that during the twelve years from 1871 to 1883 the annual expenditure upon intoxicating liquors in the United Kingdom averaged £135,000,000. If we put this into dollars it will amount in round figures to about $675,000,000.

In a very carefully prepared paper read before the British Association, at their meeting in the City of York in 1881 Mr. Hoyle estimates the indirect cost of liquor in the United Kingdom at £138,000,000 or about $690,000,000.

Through various influences including probably a season of bad trade and hard times, and undoubtedly also partly as a result of the great activity of the United Kingdom Alliance, the Blue Ribbon Movement, the Church Temperance Associations, and the various total abstinence Orders, such as the Good Templars and and the Sons of Temperance, there has happily been a considerable reduction in the liquor bill of the United Kingdom during the latter half of the present decade.

A glance at the following statistics taken from the writings of Mr Hoyle will establish this fact. During the ten years mentioned below the direct cost of liquor was as follows; the figures given represent pounds sterling, not dollars:

DIRECT COST OF INTOXICATING LIQUORS IN THE UNITED KINGDOM FOR TEN YEARS.

1873	£140,014,712
1874	141,342,997
1875	142,876,669
1876	147,288,759
1877	142,007,231
1878	142,188,900
1879	128,143,865
1880	122,279,275
1881	127,074,460
1882	126,251,359

Taking the last year of this expenditure there was expended in intoxicating liquors for every man, woman and child in the United Kingdom the sum of £3 12s. or about $18.00; more than double the amount expended by the people of Canada, proportion to population.

In the United States the cost of liquor to the community is also alarmingly great. Dr. Wm. Hargreaves of Philadelphia, has published a work entitled "Our Wasted Resources" in which he says that "during the years 1869-70-71-72 there was expended in the United States for intoxicating drinks as follows:—

In 1869	$693,999,509
In 1870	619,425,110
In 1871	680,036,042
In 1872	735,726,048
Total for four years	$2,729,186,709
Annual average	$682,296,677

or about $16.06 for every person in the United States.

The direct cost of liquor in proportion to population therefore in the three countries are represented by the following three pillars or columns:—

United Kingdom Annual Liquor Bill. $631,258,795, or $18 for every man, woman and child.

United States Annual Liquor Bill. $682,296,677, or $16.06 for every man, woman and child.

Canada's Annual Liquor Bill. $32,678,633, or $8.16 per head.

But by far the most important consideration for Canadians from the economic point of view is that of our own expenditure in proportion to our means and our other expenditures. We must compare ourselves with ourselves.

I have already referred to the tables published by the Toronto *Globe* of April 5, 1884, comparing the expenditure on intoxicating liquors with other commodities. That table was based upon the Government Blue Books including the Census Returns of 1881. I have quoted in the following diagrams some of those statistics and added others. The reader will find the diagrams most suggestive especially in view of the relative amount of monies spent in drink as compared with the necessities of life and the work of educational and Christian effort.

My estimate of Christian Church expenditure is based upon the following : The Census of 1881 shows that there were then a total of 8,652 Churches. With the aggressive efforts and increased activity of Church work since that date, I take it that there will be now about 10,000 Churches of all sects and creeds in the Dominion. I do not think it too high to estimate that these Churches average an expenditure of $800 per year which makes a total of $8,000,000. In this estimate I take into consideration that some of the larger Churches spend very much more than $800, but others again spend very much less, especially those country Churches where one minister supplies two, three or even four pulpits, and some which have no paid ministry at all.

The population of Canada in 1871 was 3,687,024 and in 1881 it was 4,324,810. The Government estimates it now at 4,695,864. Taking the population at four millions as the average of the eighteen years we have the following appalling facts :—

The average expenditure of money for intoxicants, per head, is $8.16, or in other words there is expended in liquor more than eight dollars for every man, woman and child in the Dominion. Contrast this with other expenditure and what a sad, mournful picture is presented to our view.

From the accompanying diagrams it will appear that our comparative expenditure on various commodities, which we are accustomed to regard as among our principal items of expenditure is about as follows:

1. The direct and indirect cost of intoxicating liquors is nearly four millions more than the recent heavy expenditure of the Dominion Government in all its departments.
2. The direct and indirect cost is more than five times the total amount of our expenditure for Schools, Churches and Christian Missions.
3. The direct expenditure of money in the purchase of intoxicating liquors is more than all the income of all the railways in Canada.
4. The direct expenditure is five and a half millions upwards of the value of all our Iron and Steel Manufacturers.
5. It is more than ten millions more than for Meat.
6. It is upwards of eleven millions more than for Bread.
7. It is eleven and a half millions more than for Woolen Goods.
8. It is nearly double as much as for Boots and Shoes.
9. It is two and one third as much as for Cotton Goods.
10. It is more than three times as much as for sugar.
11. We spend four times as much for liquor as for Schools and four times as much as for Churches.
12. Finally we spend 81 times as much directly in drink as we do in Christian Missions.

DIAGRAM

Comparing the gross annual expenditure in Intoxicating Liquors in Canada with the Annual Expenditure in various other directions.

(Scale, twenty million dollars to the inch.)

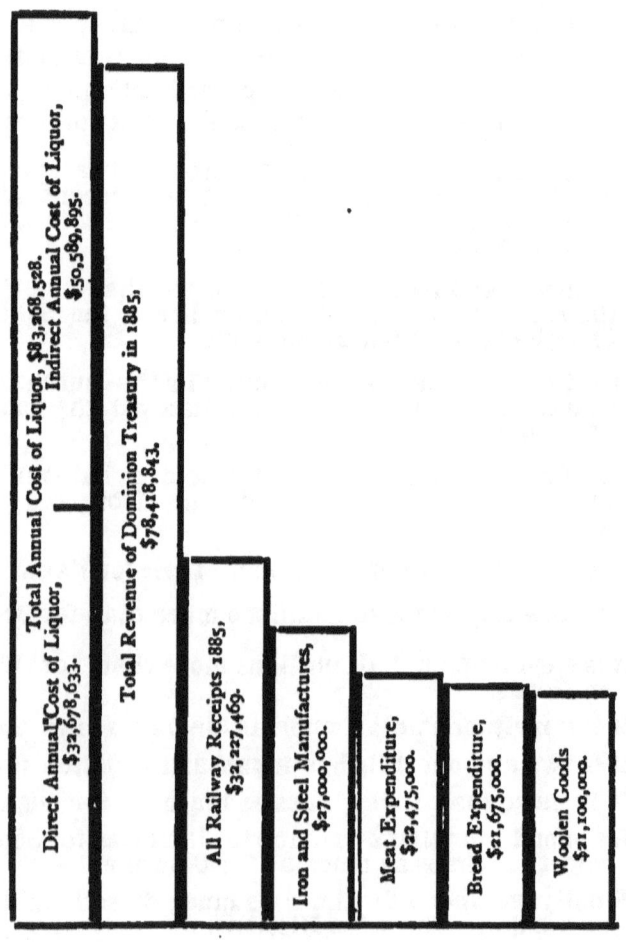

LAND, LABOR AND LIQUOR.   165

DIAGRAM—*Continued.*

Giving comparative view of expenditure in Canada in intoxicating liquors and other commodities. Also as compared with expenditure in Religious and Educational Work.

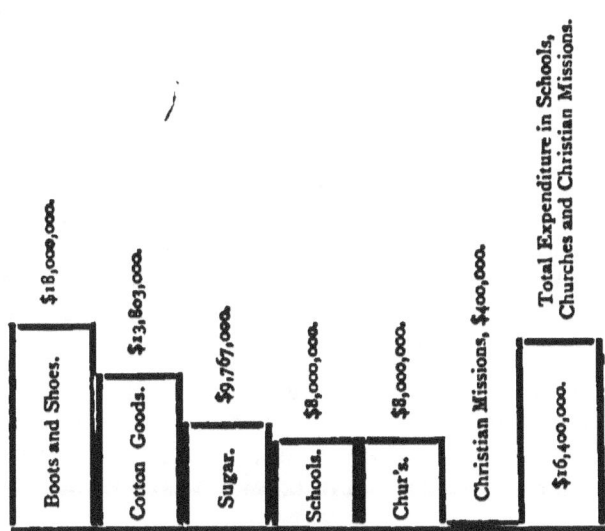

The average consumption per head of population of Spirits and Wines (not including Canadian Wines) is............1.24 galls.
Beer..............................2.38 galls.

or more than three and a half gallons per head for every man, woman and child in the Dominion, When the proportion of women and children who in this country at least, seldom drink any, and the number of men who abstain, are taken into account; it is perfectly clear that there must still be a large number of drinkers in Canada who cannot lay claim even to the dubious and indefinite term "moderate drinkers."

CHAPTER XX.

FURTHER STATISTICS AND ILLUSTRATIONS.

DURING the last eighteen years there has been consumed in the manufacture of spirits and beer in Canada no less than 36,606,973 bushels of grain of various kinds (see table) or an average of 2,033,609 bushels per year. In order the better to realise the vastness of these facts it is necessary to illustrate them so as to bring them within the reach of an ordinary reader.

A bushel of barley would give about 40 lbs of flour, and we may assume that other grain would be equal to about the same. Every 40 lbs. of flour would make 60 lbs. of bread, or about 15 four-pound loaves, for every bushel of grain. This would give a total of 30,505,135 four-pound loaves.

Many of the streets of our cities are now paved with cedar blocks. Now suppose the number of four pound loaves were filled in, end up, as in paving the streets, men do with cedar blocks, there would be sufficent four-pound loaves to pave a road 15 yards wide for the whole length of Yonge Street from the Toronto Bay to Newmarket, a distance of 34 miles.

If the loaves were designed for destruction and were conveyed from the bakers stores of Montreal or Toronto to be thrown into the river St. Lawrence or Lake Ontario, it would require 20 teams, each team carrying

500 loaves every hour for ten hours a day to complete the task in one year, allowing 305 working days in the year.

Imagine the sensation of public horror and indignation if a procession of 20 teams were driven down Yonge Street to the Toronto Bay on the morning of the first of January, each with its cargo of 500 loaves for the purpose of pitching the whole 10,000 loaves into the water.

Think of the excitement which would grow with every repetition of that procession, if indeed, the public did not rise up in rebellion against the second attempt.*

Yet this is but a faint picture of the actual waste which attends the consumption of grain in the vat and the still.

What a blessed thing it would be if we could sum up the total of our loss by simply counting up the cost of the grain destroyed! What a saving to the country it would be if the government were actually to purchase all the grain consumed in the distillery and the brewery, and deliberately destroy it by fire or water rather than permit it to be converted into alcoholic liquors to be consumed by the people.

There are not a few persons however who discredit the fact that the consumption of intoxicants in Canada is great enough to cause alarm. In order that a correct view of the facts may be given, I have prepared the following table from the various Government reports:

---

* This illustration was suggested by a similar one given by Mr. Wm. Hoyle in "*Our National Resources.*"

TABLE.

SHOWING THE QUANTITY OF LIQUORS USED FOR CONSUMPTION IN CANADA, DURING EIGHTEEN YEARS FROM 1868 TO 1885 INCLUSIVE.

YEAR.	SPIRITS.		BEER.		WINES.
	CANADIAN.	IMPORTED.	CANADIAN.	IMPORTED.	
	Imp. Gal's.	Imp. Gal's.	Imp. Gal's.	Imp. Gal's.	Imp. Gal's.
1868	3,203,830	1,290,654	6,194,738	199,704	488,098
1869	2,341,251	848,008	6,336,290	200,926	411,089
1870	3,175,857	941,479	6,075,451	188,024	562,441
1871	3,516,042	1,084,191	7,047,580	254,514	599,741
1872	3,808,292	1,320,915	7,964,441	304,734	780,820
1873	3,732,844	1,375,090	9,217,102	369,393	730,890
1874	4,560,509	1,555,907	8,976,268	415,651	860,922
1875	3,303,302	1,086,643	9,653,525	390,636	473,316
1876	3,441,225	1,251,848	9,319,190	320,324	689,304
1877	2,942,338	921,916	9,115,258	168,851	401,646
1878	3,007,870	826,046	8,578,075	294,651	382,793
1879	3,646.255	923,122	8,848,208	250,889	421,047
1880	2,290,366	636,641	9,201,213	163,266	317,421
1881	3,214,541	801,054	9,931,176	214,887	458,302
1882	3,552,818	891,467	12,036,979	248,491	553,826
1883	3,848,787	1,004,075	12,757,444	385,352	563,778
1884	3,608,021	9,609,31	13,098,700	410,435	532,968
1885	3,888,012	1,202,579	12,071,952	363,379	510,651
Totals.	61,188,100	19,722,566	166,513,590	5,174,018	9,759,663

The average consumption of spirits and wines per year is 5,037,229 gallons, and of beer 9,272,807 gallons. The consumption of spirits and wines of all kinds in 1884 was 5,101,920 gallons, and the quantity entered for consumption in 1885 was 5,601,242 gallons.

The consumption of beer rose over two million gallons in 1882 and has maintained the high rate then attained; the total of Canadian and imported beer in 1885 being 12,435,331 gallons.

Estimating the present population at 4,600,000, this means that the average consumption per head is, of spirits, 1.23 gallons, and of beer 2.75 gallons, or very nearly **Four gallons of Intoxicating Liquor for every Man, Woman and Child in the Dominion.**

If we allow for the increased quantities occasioned by the watering and mixing of spirits, and for the consumption of Canadian wines which are not included in the above table, the average quantity consumed would amount to at least five gallons per capita of the population.

It will naturally occur to the reader that there must be some people with an awfully consuming appetite for strong drink. The proportion of people who do not drink at all must be very large, probably larger in Canada than in any other American or European country.

It is worth while to make a rough estimate of the number of persons who consume all this liquor. We may best approximate this by calculating the probable number of persons who are moderate, and who abstain altogether.

The total population is now estimated at 4,600,000.

One half of these are children under fifteen years of age who, in this country at least, are (with very rare exceptions) total abstainers. Again, one half of the adult population are females. Allowing that a certain proportion of these drink, there is at least an equal proportion of the male population who are abstainers, so that it is fair to assume that half the adult population do not consume any intoxicating liquors.

If this latter be a correct estimate (and I think it is within the mark) the entire consumption of liquor in Canada is limited to about one quarter of the population: viz. 1,115,000.

Now we have seen that the annual expenditure for liquor in Canada averages a little over Eight dollars per year, *per capita*. It follows, therefore, that one quarter of the people consume on an average twenty gallons each of intoxicating liquors at a cost of $32.00 a year each.

But again, of these it may be fairly assumed that one half are what are called strictly moderate drinkers who do not consume more than the general average, costing about $8.00 per year.

If this be so, then it follows that one-eighth of the population, or 575,000 of the people of Canada, consume seven-eigths of all the vast volume of liquor, spending upon an average no less a sum than $56.00, a year each for intoxicating liquors.

We may thus obtain an approximate estimate of the number of drunkards in the community. Persons who drink to this extent cannot be classed as sober people. There are of course various stages of inebriety, and probably thousands of people who spend fifty or sixty dollars per annum, or more on liquor for their own personal use do not class themselves as immoderate drinkers. But among these 575,000 there must be a large number to whom such an expenditure is ruin, and who fall from bad to worse.

What constitutes a drunkard is a problem which is not easily solved. It is a term which is very elastic in its application according to circumstances. A laboring man who gets drunk on half a dozen drinks of spirits or beer and who becomes noisy or abusive on the streets, finds himself in the lock-up in the morning on a charge of drunkenness. The wealthy patron of the high class hotel-bar, who drinks three or four times the quantity until he is senseless or beastly, is quietly despatched home in a carriage, or sent to bed at his hotel or his club. His companions may chaff him next day about having taken a drop too much, but who would dare to call him a drunkard?

It has been said upon temperance platforms and elsewhere that there are 60,000 drunkards in Canada, and that 6,000 of these die annually. It has been established as a fact that the average life of a drunkard does not exceed ten years so that these two estimates agree. Let the reader reflect that drinking in these days is limited to about one-fourth of our people and that notwithstanding the fact that the other three fourths do not consume any, there is yet as much liquor consumed to-day according to population as there was eighteen years ago. Let him reflect again that about one-eighth of the population drink seven-eighths of all the drink consumed in Canada, and they will be driven to the unpleasant conclusion that although there are more abstainers in the country than formerly, there are also more intemperate people who must be classed as drunkards. *

But let us see whether the average consumption of intoxicants has, or has not continued at as great a rate as formerly. In order to find this out I have prepared the following table dividing the last fifteen years in three periods of five years each, beginning with 1871 and ending with 1885. I have taken the population in the first period as given in the census of 1871. In the second period I have estimated at four millions

---

* In a previous chapter I have estimated the number of drunkards at forty thousand. The above facts must convince the reader that besides the number of confirmed drunkards there must always be a much larger number in training for the places left vacant by the deaths of drunkards and it is very probable that my estimate is too low.

and in the third period I have quoted it as given in the census of 1881.

TABLE.

FIVE YEARS ENDING.	POPULATION.	SPIRITS AND WINE. Average Quantity consumed per year	SPIRITS AND WINE. Average consumption per head of Population.	BEER. Average Quantity consumed per year.	BEER. Average Consumption per head of population	Average Consumption of all intoxicants per head.
		GALLONS.	GALLONS.	GALLONS.	GALLONS.	GALLONS.
1875	36,870,24	57,646,84	1.56	89,187,68	2.05	3.61
1880	4,000,000	44,199,46	1.10	92,579,67	2.03	3.13
1885	43,248,10	51.261,82	1.18	123,035,91	2.84	4.02

It will be seen from this table that while there was a reduction in the average consumption of intoxicants in the second period as against the first; in the third period there has been an increase so large that the proportion rose considerably higher than in the first five years. This is principally accounted for by the large increased consumption of beer in the latter period, which rose 25 per cent above that of the previous five years.

But if this latter fact is used in defence of the theory that the use of the milder drinks tends to decrease the consumption of the stronger we have to face the fact that during the period of that large increase in the consumption of beer, the consumption of spirits also went up 1.10 to 1.18 gallons per head of the population.

CHAPTER XXI.

IS THE MONEY WASTED?

THE estimated expenditure in intoxicating liquors given in a previous chapter is, of course, based upon the retail cost to the consumers.

It is no uncommon remark that this expenditure is not waste because there are a number of people supported by the traffic. In other words, it is said that "as about twelve thousand persons are employed in making and distributing intoxicating liquors in this country, the expenditure in intoxicants cannot be wasted money, seeing that these people are supported out of it."

But how would this theory work in general practice. Suppose a community spent $1000 upon some well advertised quack medicine which turns out to be, not only worthless, but actually injurious, is not the whole of the thousand dollars wasted? "No!" answers some one it is not, because some persons had a profit out of it and lived upon that profit." But if the money had not been so expended it would have been available for something else, which also would have given a profit to the producers. In the latter case also it would have given value in return for the money. A dollar spent upon a worthless article is a dollar wasted, but if spent upon an article of value or utility it is not wasted.

"But" says one "the dollar spent in whiskey is not destroyed—there is not a dollar of money less in the community because I spend mine in liquor."

This is one of the mistakes common to those who take a superficial view of the relation of money to value, and to the law of trading. It must be borne in mind:—

1. That money is not wealth, but merely a representative of wealth. When a man spends a dollar, it is not a dollar that he spends. That may appear a contradiction of terms, but it is true in fact that he really spends not the money, but a dollar's worth of labor or enterprise. The piece of paper which he calls a dollar, is only the representative of that labor. In spending his labor for that which brings no value to him, it is wasted.

2. The second point is, that what is called productive expenditure, brings at least two profits, while unproductive expenditure gives one only.

Jones spends a dollar for bread, and has value for money. The bread is of more value to him than the dollar bill so that he is profited by the transaction. The dollar is but the note of exchange which represents his labor on the one hand, and the bread on the other.

Smith spends a dollar for whiskey and has no profit or value for his money. The whiskey is not an equivalent for the dollar bill, so that he is poorer by the transaction. Yet in his case also the dollar is a note of exchange which represents his labor on the one hand and the whiskey on the other.

Keeping in mind that the labor, and not the dollar, is the actual commodity which is exchanged, the case stands thus:—Jones gives his labor for bread which is value; Smith gives his labor for whiskey which is worse than valueless; Jones' dollar's worth of labor therefore has been profitable, while Smith's is wasted.

Mr. Wm. Hoyle illustrated this subject from the capitalists point of view as well as that of the laborer. He says:—

Suppose I were to engage twenty men at a pound ($5) a week each, and employ them first in digging holes, and then in filling them up again. Would the fact that twenty persons are supported by the £20 paid for hole-digging prove that the money is not wasted? Certainly not. One thing, however, is proven, namely that I have parted with my money without getting anything in return and am therefore £20 poorer.

But perhaps it will be said, are not the men who dig the the holes £20 better off. If, whilst they were digging the holes, they and their families existed without consuming food, &c., then it may be so; but if they and their families were consuming whilst the work was going on, then, by the amount by which their consumption exceeded in value what they produced, there must have been a corresponding loss. Working men and their families need to be supported, and the wages they get from week to week provide the means by which the food, clothing, &c., which is consumed in their support is supplied; but if, whilst consuming, they produce nothing, then what is paid to them must be lost. Had the men, instead of digging holes and filling them up again, spent their time in cutting drains in some unproductive land, in making a reservoir, or in digging half-a-dozen cottage cellars, then *they* would have had their wages, and *I* should have had my property increased in value.

In truth, money is but a ticket, or coupon, representing the labor and intelligence which creates wealth, So that the expenditure of money is the expenditure of labor. Even when capital or reserve wealth is expended this holds good, for the ultimate source of all wealth is labor.

Strictly speaking, there are three parties concerned in every honest business transaction: 1. The Seller.

2. The Buyer. 3. The Community generally. The business which benefits all these parties is based upon sound and fair principles. The business which gives profit or gain to one party, and fleeces either of the other two parties, is a swindle. Test the liquor traffic by this standard and what is the result.

Suppose two men, A and B, each having $1,000 the result of their savings or earnings, or of somebody else's savings and earnings.

A enters a career of waste and debauch and spends his money in whiskey. The following is the result:—

No. 1.—The Whiskey Seller gets the thousand dollars and makes a profit,

No. 2.—The Buyer has parted with his thousand dollars and got—*Nothing*—*plus* impaired health, ruined character, degraded life, and perhaps a criminal record.

No. 3.—The Community is impoverished by the amount of waste of wealth of one of its members—*plus* the poverty, disorder, accident, crime, &c., which attends his drinking and the consequent taxation involved.

B spends his money in building a house with the following results:—

No. 1.—The Seller or Builder gets the thousand dollars and makes a profit on the transaction.

No. 2.—The Buyer has parted with his thousand dollars but has now a house—an equivalent to the value of the money, *plus* the comfort, increased advantages, social standing and credit which attends a property owner.

No. 3.—The Community is enriched by the amount of a thousand dollars wisely spent by one of its members, together with the proportion of taxes which such property will pay. Every citizen is interested in every new building, and in every investment no matter who is the owner or investor.

Mr. John Stuart Mill referring to the functions of Government, observes:

"Even in the best state which society has yet reached, it is lamentable to think how great a proportion of all the efforts and talents in the world are employed in merely neutralising one another. It is the proper end of Government to reduce this wretched waste to the smallest possible amount, by taking such measures as shall cause the energies now spent by mankind in injuring one another, or in protecting themselves against injury, to be turned to the legitimate empolyment of the human faculties, that of compelling the powers of nature to be more and more subservient to physical and moral good."—*(Political Economy, Vol. II. page 552.)*

This passage in Mr. Mills' work strikes the key-note of true legislation in regard to every wasteful or ruinous traffic or business. The true object of political reform is not so much to repair the broken thread of the machinery of Government, as to improve the body politic, to elevate the social and moral conditions of the people, and to secure that the bounties of Providence shall be used for the best and highest good of the community.

The legislation which gives license to waste, and takes a revenue from it, is doing the worst that can be possibly done for the resources of any country. It is a policy of plunder and spoliation, and will inevitably work disaster and ruin in proportion as it becomes the recognized practice of the people.

CHAPTER XXII.

WHAT'S TO BE DONE WITH THE BARLEY?

THERE is another cry which is equally as fallacious as that referred to in the last chapter. Farmers and grain growers—or rather alarmists who profess to represent them—are crying out that if the liquor traffic is abolished one of the markets for grain will be consequently less and the price lower.

A good illustration of the fallacy of this cry was given in 1844 by Richard Cobden in one of his celebrated speeches on the Corn Laws. He tells of a man named James Lankester who adopted the theory that "wages rose as corn rose, and that abundance of corn made the prices of corn low, and consequently made the wages low." Mr. Cobden humorously says:—

The man was naturally of a logical mind, but it was evident that he devoted himself to the study of the *Morning Post*, and the result of that study was, that he took it into his head to carry out practically those doctrines which had been laid down in that eminent public journal. It was stated by the *Morning Post* that wages depended on the price of corn, and that when corn was dear wages were high, and of course it naturally struck James Lankester that the best way to raise the price of wages was to raise the price of corn, and the best way to raise the price of corn was to make it scarce; and, acting upon that view, he went out and set fire to Farmer Hobbs' stacks.

Baron Alderson, before whom the case was tried, stated, with his wig on, and with all the gravity of a judge, that it was a most strange and extraordinary application of the doctrines of political economy. The man had evidently drawn that deduction from the *Morning Post;* for Lankester had no malice against Farmer Hobbs, and he, therefore, did not touch his cart horses or his saddle horses, or his dairy, but he went to his stacks and set fire to them, to make corn dear, and, of course, in his opinion, to raise wages. That was the effect of carrying out practically the doctrines of the *Morning Post;* so that from such a result, they might in future call the philosophy of that journal, the logic of the lucifer match. But James Lankester was sentenced to be transported for the term of his natural life, to propagate the doctrines of the *Morning Post* in Australia.

Now, he (Mr. Cobden) wanted to know the difference in principle (for he knew there was a difference in law) between creating an artificial scarcity of that corn which the Almighty gave to all the nations of the earth—he wished to know what was the difference between making an artificial scarcity of corn by preventing us from getting a supply from abroad, and making it scarce by setting fire to the stacks of Farmer Hobbs? The plea in both cases was exactly the same, for Lankester's profession of faith was heard by the gaoler who pretended to be asleep. Lankester stated to other prisoners in gaol, that the motive which induced him to burn the stacks was in order that he might make corn dear, and so raise wages; and what then, he would ask, was the difference in principle? Where was the difference between those who made corn dear by artificial means, and Lankester, who took his own mode of making it dear?" History of the Corn Law League Vol. II., p. 224.

Poor Lankester's method of increasing the price of corn, and for which he was sentenced to imprisonment for life was not one whit more insane than making whiskey or beer with a view to raise the price of grain.

A year of plenty does not depreciate, but enhances the general good, and although market prices, *per measure*, are lower in times of plenty than in times of scarcity, even the merchants grow richer on the smaller rates when there is plenty, than on the larger rates with scarcity. The truth of this may be proved on enquiry of any class of merchants.

Suppose a man having plenty of money to spend took it into his head to buy—say 100,000 bushels of barley and make a bonfire of it. Everybody would regard such a proceeding as an act of madness or outrage, and the pulpit, press and platform would join in denouncing it as a sin against God and humanity, and a crime against the State.

But we have become so accustomed to regard the brewers and distillers as important factors in providing a market for grain, that it is difficult to remove the impression that the withdrawal of this wasted consumption would not be a disaster. It is forgotten that the closing of the distillery and the brewery would set at liberty a large amount of capital, and labor which would be diverted to other channels of business, including among other things the development of produce and its adaptation to the wants of the people. It is forgotten too, that many millions of dollars now expended in liquor would be expended in farm produce of various kinds, and that grain may be used in a number of ways to increase and improve the supply, and meet the increased and improved demand.

Take into account that there is a large proportion of our own Canadian community who do not consume as much of our farm produce as they need and desire, because of the waste of wealth in the consumption of drink and it will be easy to see that if this waste ceased, the demand for farm produce would at once increase.

Some very interesting testimony on this subject is given by Dr. F. R. Lees in his masterly *Argument for Prohibition*, for which he received the first prize of 100 guineas, given by the United Kingdom Alliance. He quoted the testimony of Mr. Colquhorn in his *Treatise on the Police of London*, who says:—

"It is a curious and important fact that during the period *when the* distilleries were stopped in 1796-7, though bread and every necessary of life were considerably higher than during the preceding year, the *poor were apparently more comfortable, paid their rents more regularly, and were better fed, than at any time for some years before.* Even though they had not the benefit of the extensive charities which were distributed in 1795. This can only be accounted for by *their being denied the indulgence of gin*, which had become, in a great measure, inaccessible from its very high price. It may fairly be concluded that the money formerly spent in this imprudent manner had been applied to the purchase of provisions and other necessaries to the amount of £100,000. The effect of their being deprived of this baneful liquor was also evident in their more orderly conduct; quarrels and assaults were less frequent, and they resorted seldomer to the pawnbroker's shop; and yet, during the chief part of this time bread was 15d. (30c.) the quartern loaf (4 lbs.); meat higher than the preceeding year," etc.

A chapter in the history of Ireland furnishes another illustration. During the years 1809-10 and 1813-14 the distilleries of Ireland were stopped because of the famine, on the ground that these distilleries wasted the grain that might otherwise be used by the people as food. Dr. Lees remarks upon this circumstance as follows:—

"We arrive at the startling anomaly, that a year of scarcity *with prohibition* is better than a year of plenty without it. The average consumption of spirits in the years 1811-12 and 1815-17 was 7½ million gallons, on the other years it was not quite 4¼. But mark how the saving of 3¼ millions reappear in the form of an increase of the following articles of comfort, which bespeak, not simply the absence of a great curse, but the presence of domestic and personal happiness, and of a thriving trade."

TABLE OF "IMPORTS."

(Extracted from the British Parliamentary Returns 1882.)

Famine Years, 1809-10, 1813-14.		Years of Plenty, 1811-12, 1815-17.	Decrease.
Haberdashery £140,936	..value..	£110,936	£30,000
Drapery or Dry Goods 3,788,514	..yards..	2,422,444	1,356,070
Iron, Hardware & Crockery £467,109	..value..	£337,458	£129,651
Blankets 60,004	.number.	26,603	33,401
Cotton Goods £179,198	..value..	£104,198	£93,000
Black Tea 3,530,643	.pounds.	3,198,132	341,511
Muscovado Sugar 381,278	..cwts..	306,954	74,324

The grain in which our Canadian farmers are most interested in this connection is barley. During the past eighteen years from 1868 to 1885 the brewers have consumed 14,116,617 bushels of barley, or an average of 784,312 bushels per year. This is about one-tenth of the entire growth of barley in the country, all the rest going to a foreign market.

It is absurd to suppose that the market which takes one-tenth of our supply regulates the price of barley. The price is regulated by the larger market rather than the smaller.

There is also a complete answer to this barley argument in the fact that the land which grows barley will grow something else; and if there is no better purpose for barley than to convert it into poison to the ruin and destruction of Canadian homes and Canadian men and women, it would be infinitely better that no barley should be grown. Indeed the farmer who perceives the mischief which it effects and still grows barley with the purpose of selling it for brewing is *particeps criminis* in the transaction of death.

But there is another important view of the matter. It is of great interest to the farmers and to the country generally to consider the development of farm industries, involving the consumption of our grain with a view to supply the markets with better provisions.

Look, for example, at the meat supply for our home markets. It is a matter of general observation and complaint among housekeepers that the meat supply is of very poor, or rather of unfed quality. It is notorious that all old country people find fault with the quality of our meat, as compared with that supplied to the English market. Yet a large quantity of the animal food of this country is shipped to England to supply the British market. But shippers of cattle know well that it is no use sending poorly fed cattle to England, and so the very best are picked out, while our own people are fed upon skinny and comparatively poor meat. Even our best cattle are not considered the best beef in the British markets unless they are put for a season upon the English system of feeding before being slaughtered.

Why should not farmers provide the very best article for our home market and also improve the supply for the foreign market? The best is always worth more money at home and abroad, and the producers of a superior class of well-fed meat would find an ample reward for their efforts. This is proven by the fact that the best meat always sells most readily even at a higher price. Toronto and Guelph markets have generally a supply of a superior class of meat, and butchers tell us that the best joints and the best meat always sell more readily than the inferior class of meat.

The same is true of fowls. There are many villages and towns where the average chicken is sold at 10c, or 12½c. at most. And this is all they are worth, so miserably poor are they of flesh fit for human food. Yet in our city markets, choice well-fed chickens are worth from 25c. to 35c. each, and in the English market from 30c. to 50c. each.

These facts have a direct bearing upon the barley question.

Barley has not yet begun to take its true place as a food. This is specially true of Canada. For some reason or other the average Canadian farmer is prejudiced against the use of barley as a grain for food. In the old country it is not so. Barley is not given to horses or other cattle where strength, bone or muscle are needed, but as a feeding or fattening commodity, it is regarded as the best that can be given.

Barley meal is as regularly sold by the millers and feed dealers as any article. In fact, in those English counties where pork is grown to perfection no one would ever think of killing a pig without first feeding it for a term upon barley meal. The result is not only that a larger and more profitable animal is produced, but the quality of the meat—both fat and lean—is of the very best. In Lincolnshire, Yorkshire, Wiltshire, Hampshire and Norfolk the farmers all feed their hogs on barley meal, and they have the reputation for the largest and best pork in the world. The hogs when thus fed weigh from 40 to 60 stone, or say from 500 to 800 pounds. What will appear more remarkable to our Canadian farmers and butchers in this connection is, that these hogs, large as they are, fetch the highest price per pound, because the bacon fed on barley meal is always preferred as the mildest and best. Mr. Harris, of Calne, Wiltshire, slaughters about 2,000 hogs per week, and all are fed on barley meal. His pork or bacon commands a ready sale at the highest market prices.

The same is true of cattle generally, and the almost universal food for fowls in England is barley in the grain, with a view to the production of larger and better eggs, with barley meal for fattening chickens, ducks, geese and turkeys.

In his invaluable works, written some years ago, on the various phases of the temperance question, Dr. F. R. Lees, of Leeds, England, gives the following interesting fact:

We have been enabled to establish the truth of our 'theories,' by a series of most conclusive and carefully conducted EXPERIMENTS—experiments instituted by Government, with the view of ascertaining the comparative value of Malt and Barley in the feeding of Cattle and the production of Milk and Butter. The experiments were made under the direction of THOMAS THOMSON, M.D., Professor of Chemistry, and R. D. THOMSON, M.D., Teacher of Practical Chemistry in the University of Glasgow, and have been published as a Parliamentary Report. The substance of them, as they bear more immediately upon the present discussion, I will now give.

Two Bullocks were selected for the purpose.

It was found, by some preliminary trials, that when the beasts were *confined* to an exclusive diet of barley or malt, they soon began to loathe and leave it thus establishing an old truth, apt to be forgotten, that in general *variety of food* is necessary to health, and that even the most nourishing food, unmixed with a coarser and more bulky sort, is unsuitable to the constitutions of both cattle and men.

The experiments for testing the relative value of malted and unmalted grain, consisted in giving the same *qnantity* and *quality* of hay, etc., each bullock, but to one a certain number of ℔s. of barley, and to the other an equal weight of malt, *both* being ground into meal and mashed.

From October 1st to 14th, the bullock fed on barley increased in weight 109℔s., that fed on malt only 90½℔s.

From November 8th to 22nd, the barley-fed bullock increased in weight 55℔s., the other only 44℔s.

From December 4th to 20th, the barley-fed beast increased 40℔s. in weight, the other only 6℔s.

Thus the Malt-fed beast soon reached its *maximum* of feeding, while the barley-fed bullock went on increasing in weight until it gained 53½℔s. over its rival.

'*These trials, continued for three months,*' says Prof. THOMSON, '*leave no doubt that Barley is superior to Malt, weight for weight, as far as fattening bullocks is concerned.*'

EXPERIMENTS AS TO MILK AND BUTTER.

The Report of Dr. R. D. THOMSON, as to the relative effect of Barley and Malt on the Milk of two excellent Ayrshire Cows, confirms all our preceding statements.

It was found that about 9℔s. of grain per day, invariably produced more Milk than a greater quantity, showing that only a certain proportion of *concentrated* or rich food should be used. *Variety of food* also contributed to increase the amount of milk.

In one case, when *entire* barley, merely steeped, was given, the milk decreased. 'This arose from a quantity of the barley being ejected without being digested;—the malt, being much more soluble, was not ejected.' Thus we perceive that the fact of which we have heard so much, 'that malt feeds faster than barley,' weight for weight, merely comes to this—that *digested* Malt feeds faster than *un*digested Barley!

'In a brown cow,' says Dr. THOMSON, '100lbs. of barley produced as much effect as 13lbs. of malt: in a white cow, 100lbs. of barley were equivalent to 119lbs. of malt.'

But as 100 parts of barley make only 80 parts of Malt, it follows, that 100lbs. of barley are *equal in use* to 125lbs. of malt; for as 80 is to 100, so is 100 to 125.

Dr. THOMSON is equally clear concerning 'the Butter yielded by the Milk in the two cases. 'The *largest amount* of butter was afforded in the brown cow by crushed BARLEY. With both animals malt is *lowest* in the scale.'
100lbs. of Barley produce 34.6lbs. dry milk: & 7.66lbs. butter.
100lbs. of Malt   "   26.2lbs.   "   & 6.35lbs.   "

Not only was the quantity of solid matter in the milk diminished, but its *quality* was deteriorated. The Soluble Salts are lessened by malting, and hence the milk cannot contain what the food has not introduced. The Casein (cheese) was also greatly lessened. The cheese principle was decreased. because it is a flesh-forming substance, containing azote, of which the average amount in barley is 2 per cent., but in malt only 1¼;—the butter was lessened, because malt contains less casein than barley.

In addition to all this, the cows were losing weight and strength daily under the Malt regimen, while they gained weight and strength when fed on the Barley. After the barley experiment they were found to be 80lbs. *heavier;* after the malt-trial, 42lbs. *lighter.*

Thus it is certain, that in every respect Malt is much inferior to crushed Barley as an article of food for cattle, giving in the first place, a less *quantity* of milk and butter; in the second, milk of an inferior *quality*, deficient in the soluble salts; and in the third place, diminishing the *live-weight* of the cattle, where the barley increases it.

Taking all items into account, therefore, we may safely affirm that 100lbs. of barley are equal in *nourishing-power*— i.e. for the full feeding of the flesh or muscle of the animal

—to 130 lbs. of Malt; or, in other words, that more than *a third* of all the malted grain in this country is criminally, because needlessly, destroyed!

And for what *end* does this machinery of mischief really work? Not, in truth, for feeding, but for *drinking* purposes! The malting-system is preliminary to that of *brewing*—the foundation of 'a manufacture of human misery' vaster and more fearful than any other which ever impeded the improvement, or blasted the prospects of our People.

These are most important facts to the farmers of Canada and they are amply sustained by many others.

Dr. Lyon Playfair, the eminent Edinburgh physician and chemist, prepared a synopsis of the relative value of different kinds of food, and he showed that barley meal is superior in this respect to the staple food of the Scotch peasant. The following is from Dr. Playfair's table:

Barley-meal contains 14 parts of albumen to 68 of unazotized matter—or fuel.

Oatmeal contains 10½ parts of albumen to 68 of unazotized matter—or fuel.

Potatoes contain 2 parts of albumen to 24½ of unazotized matter or—fuel.

Man should have the best and highest forms of food, and whether he takes it in the form of bread, or meal, or of flesh-meat, it is of the first importance that it should be the best in quality.

Dr. Lees gives the proportion of solid food in several grains, as follows:—

In 1000 parts Wheat contains 950 parts of solid food.
" " " Barley " 920 " " " "
" " " Rye " 792 " " " "
" " " Peas " 930 " " " "
" " " Potatoes " 260 " " " "

And he adds:—

It is of the greatest importance to the health and purity of the human constitution, that the food of man should be of a healthy and perfect character, after its kind. But the *flesh* of animals fed with foul or ill-assorted food, becomes diseased and unwholesome, and introduces the elements of disorder and pestilence into the blood of man. For example: it is now ascertained that cattle fed-up on oil-cake and the refuse of breweries and distilleries, or similar substances (which are deficient in several essential elements of health and nourishment) rapidly become bloated and fat, but at the expense of health, their flesh and organism being seriously diseased. Pigs, likewise fed exclusively upon potatoes or other substances deficient in nourishment will become fat while they will grow unhealthy, but let a due quantity of ground barley be mixed with unazotized food of cattle or pigs—food in other respects of a proper sort—and the animals will increase in both fat and flesh and preserve their own health at the same time. Their flesh will become *fitter* for human food.

It is a singular fact that grapes from which the wine of Europe is so largely produced also contain a very high proportion of feeding property in their natural state so as to gain for them the title which we give to wheat and maize—*staff of life*.

Yet man's ingenuity has been employed, and capital and labor is still expended—not in preserving these life germs in their natural condition but in destroying them for a narcotic and dangerous beverage.

But suppose this were not true of our grain. Suppose that the *only* use to which we could put barley, etc., so as to make it pay our farmers, is to convert into whiskey and beer—what then? Does it follow that it is for the general good that this barley shall be grown for that purpose?

Let us see:—

If the farmers of Canada took to growing opium, because they found a ready market for it—would it not be a sufficient plea against it, that men were poisoned by it—that boys and girls would be learning to use it as they now do tobacco, and that insanity and imbecility would be frightfully increasing among our rising men and women in consequence of its use? Must the temporary good of a few men—whether farmers, merchants, or wiskey vendors, be accepted as a sufficient reason why the glory of young Canada should be debauched and ruined?

Or to take another illustration :—

One of the most important branches of trade and industry is connected with the *Printing Press*. Its value is unquestionable, and to encourage it is one of the most patriotic aims of all business men. Suppose, then, a large firm of printers commenced to print and publish books of a decidedly immoral and licentious character. Such books might find a ready sale, and the firm be able to declare a handsome profit on all its transactions.

Would the interests of these printers, or the importance of encouraging the press—or the amount of weekly wage they paid—would any or all of these questions weigh for one moment with our authorities, when such a hive of vice was discovered? If they did we should blush for our country.

CHAPTER XXIII

FARMERS AND THE FOREIGN MARKETS.

I HAVE shown that the "cry" raised during the Scott Act agitation that our barley markets were threatened, was utterly fallacious. It was, in fact, a mere invention of the whiskey advocates to lead the farmers "off the scent." We were told with a great show of superior knowledge that our export trade with Great Britain was seriously in danger, and loud cries were made against the "fanaticism" and "madness" of the temperance party who would destroy the market, which the brewers of Canada created, in face of the alleged "facts" which were proclaimed as to the alarming outlook for our Canadian farmers.

What Richard Cobden facetiously called the "logic of the lucifer match" was the logic of these whiskey advocates, viz:—that if we have too much grain proportion to the demand, and therefore get a low price for it; the best way to raise the price is to reduce the quantity, and so by all means foster the traffic which wastes one tenth of all our barley, so that the other nine-tenths may sell at higher prices.

The real truth is that the public and the press of England are engaged in discussing *not the limitation of Canadian imports,* but the encouragement and increase of them.

A meeting was held in October last (1886) in the Conference Room of the Colonial and Indian Exhibition under the presidency of Sir Samuel Wilson. At that meeting a paper was read by Mr. D. Tallerman, in which he gave some important statistics on this question. A review of that paper is given in the *Christian World* of October 21, 1886, from which I take the following:—

"Last year 1,013,960 cattle (horned, sheep and lambs), of the value of £7,181,338, were landed, besides dead meat (exclusive of preserved,) of the value of £12,204,627, and £1,042,451 worth of preserved meat. Of the *whole value of £20,428,446*, only *£3,522,778* worth was received from British colonies. We received *£10,803,465* worth of foreign sugar and molasses, against *£2,965,927* worth from our colonial possessions. Other similarly striking contrasts were —foreign wheat stuffs imported, *£26,051,278*; colonial *7,685,085*. Foreign Indian corn, *£8,236,957*; colonial, *£251,728*. Surely this ought not to be. Mr. TALLERMAN rightly considers that Ireland, the richest milk-yielding country in the World, should supply us with all the butter we need. But unhappily the Irish farmer lacks enterprise, and will not by adapting himself to new circumstances, and improving his methods, grasp the opportunities which are within his reach. Mr. TALLERMAN further thinks that Ireland, with her rich grazing lands, could supply us with £8,000,000 worth more meat than she does. But apart from Ireland he considers that *Canada, Australia, and our other colonies should* have inducements offered them to further increase their exports of meat and grain foods to us."

Here than is ample room for the enterprise of Canadian Farm Industries. If so much of the British trade is done with countries having no connection with the United Kingdom, why should not Canada bid for a larger share of the business?

Look at these various items. The amounts in dollars of the value of importations of these articles of food into the United Kingdom were about as follows:

Meat..........................$100,242,200
Sugar and Mollasses............ 54,017,300
Wheat Stuffs.................. 130,256,400
Indian Corn................... 41,184,700

Of these items the whole of the British Colonies, including Canada of course, only sent about as follows:

Meat.......................... $17,613,000
Sugar and Mollasses............ 14,830,000
Wheat Stuffs.................. 38,425,000
Indian Corn................... 1,258,500

In its editorial article on this question the *Christian World* observes that "looking at the subject as a whole, it is to be desired that our Colonies and Ireland will speedily succeed in reducing the present enormous imports of food from foreign countries."

That the British markets are open to our people, and that an increased supply of our produce would be welcome into those markets there can be no doubt. The fact is that there is almost unlimited demand for the produce of this country, and the better the quality of the produce the more welcome it is into both British and American markets.

Look for example at the wonderful development of the cheese trade. In 1861 the value of our cheese exports amounted to $23,937. In 1871 it had risen to $1,109,906. In 1881 it had risen to $6,091,534. And it is still increasing as will be seen from the following returns of the value of cheese exported during the last three years which I take from the recent

Statistical Abstract and Record published by the Dominion Government. In 1883 the amount was $6,451,870; 1884, $7,251,989; 1885, $8,265,240.

Now why should not this development of our export trade go on in like measure in other directions to the advantage of people of the old land, and for the enrichment of our farmers, and through them, the whole of Canada? There appears to be but one answer to this enquiry, viz: that in proportion only as we supply quality in any kind of farm produce, will there be a ready demand for it, and more especially in the British markets.

For example there has been no increase in our export butter trade since 1871. From a Government report as to Agricultural Interests of Canada published in 1884 I take the following paragraph:—

" Let us look for the main cause of this very unsatisfactory butter trade :—At first sight, from the fact that at present, it apparently pays better to make cheese than butter, this alone, to many, seems to explain the falling off in our butter trade. A second and, in my opinion, still better reason for this decrease, is the unsteadiness of the demand for Canadian butter. Let us now look into this latter argument: Our export market for butter is undoubtedly Great Britain. Nearly 80 per cent. of our butter goes there. England wants the best brands alone; poor butter is there as elsewhere, a drug on the market."

Precisely the same may be said of other produce. The production of eggs might be enormously increasd in this country, all that is needed is to provide for the despatch of them to suitable markets. Mr. D. D. Wolson of Seaforth in the county of Huron has proved this beyond doubt. A few years ago he commenced to collect eggs and ship them to New York and other markets. The result is that the production of eggs in the neighborhood of Seaforth and the country around is twenty times greater than when he began business. Mr. Wilson now turns over about $250,000 per year, employing 30 hands and about 30 horses in the collecting and shipping of eggs. Last year the number of eggs shipped were about 1,600,000 dozen.

We might multiply illustrations of the developing power of the farm produce of this country, and the corresponding open markets which await it. But the reader can easily apply these thoughts to our general fruit and farm produce.

It is abundantly clear that we are not even temporally dependant upon such a demoralising and ruinous waste as is involved in the manufacture of intoxicating liquors.

CHAPTER XXIV.

LIQUOR AND CRIME.

THE intimate relationship between drink and crime has been assumed in the foregoing pages. The testimony in proof of this is so abundant that it would be easy to fill a volume with it. In an appendix will be found the opinions and testimony of some of the principal authorities in the world on this subject.

A perusal of these testimonies will convince any unprejudiced person that the proportion of crime to the facilities for drinking is so great that as Judge Coledrige says, referring to the Criminal Courts: "*but for the cases where offences have been brought on by the use of intoxicating liquors the Courts of Justice might be nearly shut up.*" The same eminent authority stated from the bench of the Supreme Court in 1881 that, "*Judges were weary with calling attention to drink as the principal cause of crime, but he could not refrain from saying that if they could make England sober they would shut up nine-tenths of the prisons.*"

Dr. Wm. Hargreaves in his work on "Our Wasted Resources" quotes from an article in the report of the United States Commissioner of Education for 1871 that "from 80 to 90 per cent. of our criminals connect their courses of crime with intemperance. Of the 14,315 inmates of the Massachusetts prisons 12,396 are reported to have been intemperate, or 84 per cent."

Dr. Hargreaves further says that "of 39 cases of murder and 121 cases of assault to murder in the city of Philadelphia in 1868 in almost every case it may be safely said that the murderer was intoxicated when the deed was committed."

What is true, in these respects, in the United Kingdom and the United States is true also of Canada. The measure of our National drinking is almost in direct ratio to the measure of our crime. There is abundant evidence of this fact. In 1849 a select committee of the Legislative Assembly at Montreal was appointed to enquire as to the evils of intemperance. The Report states that, "*One half of the crime annually committed, two-thirds of the cases of insanity, three-fourths of the pauperism, are ascribable to intemperance. No other form of words would have been sufficiently comprehensive to express the deliberate convictions of your Committee.*" The Report contains evidence from various officials. The Coroners for the district of Montreal testify :—

"In 530 inquests 53 of the deaths (one in every ten) were directly or immediately traced to intemperance. Many more are believed to have been ascribable to that cause ; but jurors being reluctant to return verdicts of death by intemperance, the exact number cannot be accurately ascertained."

There can be no doubt that the feeling of sympathy for the friends of deceased suicides often prevent jurors from returning a verdict which would leave the awful record upon the memory of the deceased that it was drunkenness that caused it. Hence a verdict of monomania or temporary insanity often really means intemperance. This is equally true of sudden deaths, deaths from accident, &c. If the true cause of the disease or accident which more immediately bring about these deaths were recorded, instead of a verdict of "apoplexy" or "heart disease" it would more often be " drunkenness."

The Chief of Police of Montreal gave evidence before the Select Committee and said:—

" I am convinced that crime of all kinds is ascribable to the use of spirituous liquors. It follows that the expense of the police force and other modes of repressing crime, such as courts of justice with all their officers, and gaols with all their keepers, and the loss of time entailed upon juries and witnesses, can all be traced, in a great measure, to the use of ardent spirits. It is therefore my opinion that the community at large is taxed to raise funds for defraying the expense of these establishments, which expense might be reduced two-thirds if the use of ardent spirits were not so common. Drinking thus imposes upon society a serious pecuniary burden."

The following is a tabular statement of the number of prisoners arrested by the Police of the City of Montreal in 1847 and which was put in as evidence by the Chief:

PRISONERS.		Total Prisoners.	Total Offences.	Offences arising from intemperance.
Male.	Female.			
2982	740	3772	4039	2234

In 1874 a Report of the Select Committee of the Senate was issued, which report is signed by the whole of the 15 Senators who formed that Committee. They report the reception of " 993 petitions with 349,294 signatures, and nine from other representative bodies, each acting for a considerable number of persons." These petitioners, the report says, "assert that the traffic in intoxicating liquors is shewn by the most careful inquiries to be the cause of probably not less than three-fourths of the pauperism, immorality and crime found in the country."

A Report of a Select Committee of the House of Commons published at the same time gives the following Statement furnished by the Recorder of the City of Montreal:

	1871.	1872.	1873.
Drunkenness	4,983	5,651	6,145
Offences arising out of same, about	1,306	1,350	1,608
Total	6,289	7,001	7,753
Total number of arrests of all kinds	10,584	10,942	12,085

Out of the 7,753 arrests made for drunkenness etc., in 1873, 1,017 were females.

The above statement shows an increase of 15 per cent in crime, and 23¼ per cent in that of drunkenness.

The same report contains a statement from Mr. F. W. Fenton, Chief of Police of Montreal, 1873, from which I take the following extract:

Mostly all offences are due directly or indirectly to intemperance. What is the cause of almost all larcenies?—drink! Of assaults?—drink! Disorderly conduct?—drink! Fights, furious driving, interference with the police, foul language blasphemies?—drink, drink, drink! Of cowardly wife beating?—drink! In short, intemperance is to be found as the universal, direct and indirect cause of all evils.

The Report of Capt. Prince, Chief of Toronto Police, also quoted, shows the number of all arrests and the number of arrests for drunkenness in 1871-2-3 as follows:

	1871.			1872.			1873.		
	Male.	Female.	Total.	Male.	Female.	Total.	Male.	Female.	Total.
Arrests for all crimes	3,884	1,153	4,737	3,682	1,053	4,735	4,427	1,227	5,654
Arrests for drunkenness	1,742	579	2,321	2,036	599	2,635	2,328	624	2,952

Compare this with more recent statistics, and it will be seen that not only has the volume of crime and drunkenness increased, but the rate of increase is greater than that of the population.

	1885.			1886.		
	Male.	Female.	Total.	Male.	Female.	Total.
Number of arrests	6,667	1,347	7,954	7,140	1,430	8,570
Arrests for drunkenness	3,245	619	3,864	3,630	653	4,238

In 1871 the population of Toronto was 56,091. In 1886 the population within the jurisdiction of the city police would hardly reach 100,000. Placing it at that number, however, the ratio of crime to population was in 1871 as one to 11·84, and in 1886 as one to 11·66. The ratios of arrests for drunkenness are about the same.

The Chief of Police at Ottawa, Thos. Langrell, reporting to the Select Committee of 1874 says:

The number of persons confined in the police station during the past three years has been 2282 viz:—

	1871.	1872.	1873.
Intemperate	591	631	621
Temperate	131	93	215

The report of the present Chief Constable of Ottawa, Capt. McVeity, as published in the Ottawa Free Press, Jan. 7, 1887, gives the number of arrests for drunkenness as 387, disorderly 92, vagrancy 52, keepers of houses of ill-fame 38, larceny 166, with a large number of other offences, making a total of 1007, of which 891 were males and 116 females. In a letter accompanying a copy of this report which Capt. McVeity obligingly sends me, he says:—

"The arrests for the year 1885 runs about the same. Nearly all the other crimes in the report are the offspring of drunken parents. If there was no liquor sold there would be very little use for the police. I am speaking against my own interest after an experience of 20 years in the police. I think it is the cause of 90 per cent of all crime."

In the City of Quebec the numbers given to the Superintendant of Police in 1874 were:—

	1871.	1872.	1873.
Total Arrests	2402	1900	2206
Arrests for Drunkenness	1217	889	976

Similar statistics are given with about the same average results from the cities of London, Hamilton &c., but more than sufficient is here quoted to prove that in this country as elsewhere, liquor and crime are almost interchangeable words, so far as the general results through the country are concerned.

Every newspaper contains reports of the terrible doings of drink. Take the records of a single week in the city of Toronto:—The first days police court business of this year, viz:—*Monday, January 3rd,* 1887 was opened with no less than 42 charges of drunkenness. Of these, 28 were dismissed as first offences &c. 9 were fined $1 and costs each; 2 were charged with disturbing the Salvation Army meetings while drunk, and were fined $10 each or three months imprisonment. On the same day there were three charges of vagrancy.

Turning to the *Toronto News* for five following days, I find the following records:—*Wednesday, January 5th,* 15 "drunks" 9 dismissed, 5 fined $1 and costs each; 1 drunk and assault, fined $60 and costs or 60 days hard labor. Three other cases of assault or quarrels are named, but drink is not mentioned as the cause. *Thursday, Jan. 6th,* 12 "drunks," 5 dismissed, 7 fined $1 and costs each; 2 vagrants. *Friday, Jan. 7th,* 11 "drunks," 3 dismissed, 5 fined $1 and costs, 1 fined $3 or 60 days; 2 adjourned for further enquiry on other charges; 2 vagrants fined $1 and costs each or 30 days. *Saturday, Jan. 8th,* 9 "drunks," 1 dismissed, 4 fined $1 and costs; 1 (James Jordan) "at his own request was sent down for 90 days;" 3 remanded, including Annie Warshaw, the drunken woman who was found by the police in a tumble down house in the rear of 43 Esther street. Her husband has died in the wretched place from the cold and the effects of liquor, but an inquest will not be held. The old woman seems to be scarce recovered yet from the effects of her protracted debauch. An order had been issued for the burial of the dead man, by whose side she lay so drunk that she did not even know that Death had laid him low."

The paper contains no police court report for Monday the 11th, but it is evident that there were drunken cases on that day as usual for on the 12th the *News* reports that Patrick Walsh discharged yesterday was up again this morning. He had been found drunk in the West End. The Magistrate fined him $50 and costs or 60 days. It is likely that the taxpayer will have to keep him for the 60 days, as generally happens in such cases. There were 8 other cases, 3 dismissed, 2 fined $10 or 60 days each, and 4 vagrants were each fined $1 or 3 months. Thus the number of cases of drunkenness recorded in a single newspaper for one week are 98.

Cost of Crime.—It follows then that a greater part of the cost of all crime is chargeable to the liquor traffic. In the chapter on the indirect losses occasioned by drinking, I have estimated this at one half of the whole cost, or a round sum of $1,500,000.

I think I shall be able to prove that this is a very moderate estimate of the cost of the drink-made crime of this country. As the chief of the Montreal Police remarked in his report to the select committee of 1849, "the expense of the Police Force, and other modes of repressing crime, such as courts of justice with all their officers, and gaols, with all their keepers, and the loss of time entailed upon juries and witnesses, can all be traced in a great measure" to this source. The items of cost are very varied and are defrayed by the country through various avenues. There is the Administration of justice under the Dominion Government, including payment of Judges Salaries and Dominion Police; there are also the provincial gaols, and the city, town and country police departments. Each of these have their own expenditure, and it is therefore not an easy matter to collect statistics covering the whole ground. The statistics of the Dominion Government Expenditure, and of the Province of Ontario are available and from these we may be able to get at a fair estimate of this terrible charge upon the industry of the country.

The cost of the department of administration of justice in 1884 paid by the Dominion Government was $627,252, and of Police $18,953. This latter item does not include the Mounted Police of the North-West Territories which cost $564,249. I see no reason why this item should not be included in the aggregate cost of crime, a large per centage of which is chargeable to drink. Turning to the cost of maintaining our Penitentiaries I find the total cost given in the Government abstract as $287,551, but from the Report of the Minister of Justice I have prepared the following table the total of which slightly differs from these figures.

TABLE.

SHOWING THE COST OF MAINTAINING CRIMNALS IN OUR DOMINION PENITENTIARIES DURING THE YEAR ENDING JUNE 30, 1885.

Place.	No. of staff, including Wardens Keepers, &c.	Average No. of criminals during the year.	Salaries and uniforms.	Total Expenditure.	Revenue by Convict Labor.	Nett Cost.
Kingston	68	500	$49,199	$98,183	$10,929	$77,254
St. Vt. de Paul	59	267	40,129	79,101	927	78,174
Dorchester	39	175	28,139	43,332	570	42,762
Manitoba	20	70	15,899	46,382	none.	46,382
B. Columbia	22	92	15,328	27,776	1,041	26,737
						$271,309

There was an increase of 73 criminals in the Penitentiaries of the Dominion in 1885 as compared with 1884.

The next item of the cost of crime may be classed as connected with provincial prisons and county gaols. I have not the requisite documents to give the statistics of the cost of prisons, &c. in all the provinces.

In Ontario, the cost of the Central Prison in 1885 was as follows:—

Maintenance Expenditure	$39,702
Salaries and Wages	18,975
	58,667
Less Profits on Prison Industries	20,489
Actual Cost,	$38,188

The proportion of prisoners in Ontario to the rest of Dominion is rather more than one-half. The cost of the maintenance of prisoners and the salaries of the separate staffs of officials in the other provinces will necessarily be greater in proportion than in the single provincial prison of Ontario. But, estimating it at the same, and allowing that a similar profit in prison work is made as in Ontario prisons, which however, I believe is not a fact, the cost of the other provincial prisons will be about $45,000, or a total including Ontario of $83,708.

A further item of cost is the transfer of prisoners, including travelling expenses of attendant officers &c., which in Ontario amounted in 1885 to $4,258 or in the whole Dominion about $10,000.

Consider next the cost of maintenance of common gaols. The annual report published by the Ontario Government furnishes ample statistics so far as this province is concerned. The report for 1885 shows the following as the expenditure for all the gaols of the province.

Cost of Rations, Clothing, Fuel &c.,	$54,321
Cost of Salaries, Wages, &c.	70,345
Cost of Repairs	5,081
Total,	$129,747

The Reformatory for females at Toronto cost in 1885

For Maintenance and Salaries	$27,540
Less Revenue on Earnings of Inmates	4,050
	$23,495

The Reformatory for boys at Penetanguishene cost in 1885

For Maintenance and Salaries	$40,093
Less Revenue on Farm and Garden	138
	$39,855

In all these prisons the cost would be greater but for the labor performed by the prisoners, which is entered as "unproductive," such as clothing and shoes made in the prisons for the use of prisoners.

From the above it will be seen that the cost of the various common gaols and reformatories in Ontario amount to a total of $193,473, or, (at the same proportion) for the whole Dominion, a total of about $420,000.

Next add the cost of Police. It would be difficult, if not impossible to obtain accurate statistics of the number and cost of all the police officers and constables throughout the Dominion. In some municipalities the constable is only partially employed, or is paid by the municipality for his services in other capacities besides that of constable. In some instances he receives fees according to the cases or arrests he is called upon to make.

I think, however, that the full time of police employed throughout the country may be safely put down as averaging one for every 2,000 of the population. This is very much below the proportion in cities. In Toronto, for instance, there are 172 police officers, or one to 588 of population. In Ottawa there are only 28 officers, or one to 1250 of the population.

But the proportion of one policeman to 2000 of the population is perhaps above the ratio in some country districts, especially where there is little drinking. Taking it as a whole however, it will be considered a fair estimate. This would show that our army of police in the Dominion numbers about 2,300. If the average salaries and cost of uniforms be put down at $600 each per year, the cost of police and constables in Canada will amount to $1,380,000.

In addition to all these items there is the cost of police court officials, magistrates expenses and police magistrates salaries, and the loss of time and expenses of witnesses. These are hardly within the range of a possible estimate, more especially the latter item. Sometimes the indirect cost of crime in the loss of time occasioned to the numerous witnesses, will amount to more than all the other judicial expenses, but as this is not generally reckoned as a part of the expense to the public, it is seldom estimated or even thought of.

But from the above calculations we may make the following summary of the estimated annual cost of crime in Canada.

RECAPITULATION.

Administration of Justice	$ 627,252
Dominion Police	18,953
Mounted Police, N. W. T.	564,294
Penitentiaries	271,309
Provincial Prisons	83,708
Transfer of Prisoners	10,000
Common Gaols	420,000
Police and Constables	1,380,000
Cost of Witnesses lost time, Police Court Officials, Magistrates Expenses, &c., &c.	Incalculable.
	$3,375,516

There is still another charge which falls upon the public, but of which no estimate of cost can be given, viz: the building and maintaining of lock-ups, of which there is one in almost every municipality. There are six of them in Toronto.

I have estimated the proportion of cost of drink-made crime as one and a half million dollars. This amount it will be seen is very much below the actual facts. It is certain that much more than one half of all the cost of crime is chargeable to drink. The Chief of Montreal Police, whose evidence given in 1874, is quoted on a previous page of this chapter, believed that two-thirds of the cost is traceable to drink. The present Chief of Ottawa Police says there would be very little use for police if no liquor was sold. The further evidence of eminent Judges and others given in an appendix, and the statistics of every official document of criminal records, show that at least 75 per cent of all crime is chargeable to drink. Take the reports of the Ontario prisons and reformatories, and what do we find? That more than half the committals to our common gaols are under the charges of drunkenness and vagrancy, the latter being almost entirely the product of drinking habits. Here are the actual figures:—

	1883.	1884.	1885.
Total of all Crimes	9880	12,081	11,426
Drunk and Disorderly	3895	4,650	3696
Vagrancy	1554	2130	2455

Next to these the most frequent crimes recorded for 1885 are as follows:—

Common Assaults	672
Felonious Assaults	169
Destroying and Injuring Property	112
Fraud and False Pretences	149
Housebreaking and Robbing	146
Trespass	222
Inmates and Keepers of Bad Houses	172
Abusive and obscene language	44
Breaches of the peace	117
Selling liquor without license and supplying it to Indians	60

It will be seen that these crimes, together with those of drunkenness and vagrancy constitute a very large proportion of the whole. Let any one consider how frequently such crimes as these named are associated with drunkenness. It is not surprising that those who see most of criminals should come to the opinion expressed in 1873 by Mr. Fenton, Chief of Montreal Police: "*Mostly all offences are due directly or indirectly to intemperance. What is the cause of all larcenies? drink! of assaults? drink! disorderly conduct? drink! Fights, furious driving, interference with police, foul language, blasphemies? drink! drink! drink!"*

The Prison Reports reflect further light on the proportion of drink to crime in their tables of the habits of the prisoners in the common gaols. I take the following from the last Reports of the Ontario Prisons published by the Ontario Government.

	1882	1883	1884	1885	Total 4 y'rs.
Temperate	2,942	2,378	3,080	3,315	11,715
Intemperate	6,678	7,502	9,001	8,111	31,292
Total	9,620	9,880	12,081	11,426	43,007

Thus the proportion of acknowledged intemperate persons who are committed to our common gaols is 72½ per cent as against 27½ per cent classed as temperate or moderate.

The records of the Central Prison give the following classification of the habits of its inmates:

	1883	1884	1885
Temperate	86	85	144
Intemperate	583	638	617

Only 14½ per cent of these claim to be temperate. The other 85½ per cent are classed as intemperate.

The Superintendent of the Ontario Female Reformatory gives the following classification of the habits of the inmates of that institution:

	1883	1884	1885
Temperate	22	44	48
Intemperate	95	112	94

or 27½ per cent temperate; 72½ per cent intemperate.

From this abundant accumulation of evidence, as well as from the opinions and testimony of competent judges, it is established that fully three-fourths of all the crime of Ontario is attributable to drink.

It may be alleged that many of the justices, gaols, gaol-officials and police would still be necessary for public security and order, even if there were no liquor traffic. But it is surely safe to assume that at the most one half of the present staff and fully three-fourths of the cost of maintenance of prisoners would be saved to the country were the drinking system abolished. My estimate of $1,500,000 as the cost of crime caused by drink is therefore much below the actual facts, without taking into account the last items in the bill which are "incalculable."

Moral Results of Crime.—So far the cost of crime in relation to drink has been dealt with, but this is by no means the most serious view of the matter. In fact, the mere cost to the country, serious as it is, is nothing compared with the moral and social ruin which everywhere attends the drink-made criminal. Our penitentiaries and gaols are monuments of the degradation and ruin of humanity. Let any man visit the penitentiary at Kingston and see the average 500 men marching single file from their work at six o'clock each evening, each taking from a table as he passes into his solitary cell for the night, a piece of bread and a tin mug of tea. Let the visitor observe the youthful and intelligent features of most of the prisoners, and reflect that for every one of them there is a dark shadow resting upon some home. That hundreds of Canadian hearts are broken, and hundreds of lives blighted by the crime which brought these men here. Think further that, but for drink, instead of 500, there would not have been more than a fourth or a fifth of that number, now and for all the future of their lives, branded as criminals—dead to society, to home and to love—with but little hope of a social resurrection or moral reclamation.

Extend the picture. Enter every penitentiary in Canada, and see not 500, but more than double that number of convicts. Go into the jails and reformatories of the country and see there, thousands of men, women, boys and girls, some for the first time, others the second, third, and up to the twentieth or more times, —imprisoned. Look at the sum total of our crime in this young country with little more than four and a half millions of people. In the year 1884 there were 27,045 persons sentenced in our various criminal courts, one-third of whom were actually charged directly with the crime of drunkenness; while almost every other class of offence was committed, more or less, through the agency of drink.

The following table shows the number committed for the crime of drunkenness in the five years named:—

Year.	Number Committed.				
1880	11,660,	or one to each	364	of pop.
1881	12,837,	"	"	337	"
1882	15,092,	"	"	292	"
1883	16,971,	"	"	265	"
1884	9,877,	"	"	464	"

The Criminal Statistics for 1884 are of course published in 1885. The report for 1885 is not yet published.

But what again is this in proportion to the unrecognized crime of the country? Is it too much to say that for every committal of drunkenness there are at least ten other persons who are morally and socially ruined by drink? Does not every physician and every minister of the Gospel know of many families whose heads are cursed by drink? Is not the brand of the drunkard upon the lives and character of thousands of men who manage to avoid the clutches of the police, but who, nevertheless, endanger the public safety and bring disgrace and discredit, not only upon their own families, but upon the entire community of which they are individual members.

The words of that eloquent reasoner, Dr. F. R. Lees, whose voice and pen have done so much to place the temperance movement upon a scientific, as well as a moral basis, are especially appropriate here.—"Were the great social fountain of these evils dried up, how infinite would be the gains of civilization. We would banish the traffic, because with its presence neither human nature, nor truth has fair-play. Crime, potent and prevalent as it is, is not the worst nor the greatest evil of the traffic. The noisy and obtrusive mischiefs of the traffic are as nothing in comparison with its hidden and unobtrusive influence for evil."—*Alliance Prize Essay.*

The eloquent words of the Rev. Canon Wilberforce shall close this chapter:—"It would be bad enough if this national destroyer confined himself to binding grievous burdens upon the pockets of the community; that in days when legitimate trade is depressed and honest men of business are struggling hard with impending poverty, he should annually scatter to the winds one hundred millions (of pounds,) which if circulated through useful branches of commerce would impart prosperity to all; that of the millions of rate supported paupers, who tax so sorely the resources of men of anxious toil, he should claim three out of every four as his production, the mere money tax might be endured. But from the length and breadth of the land there comes a cry of human suffering, human death; the most fearful crimes are committed every day, brutal assaults by fathers upon their children, mothers upon their infants, men upon each other; and judges, coroners, magistrates, doctors, hangmen, all give the same unvarying testimony,—strong drink is alone, they say, the cause * * the wealth, the peace, the prosperity of this great nation are slowly, but surely going down before the pestilence. The most terrible proof of the extent to which this devilish epidemic is infecting the mainspring of the life of the nation, and one which cannot too often be repeated, is found in the report of the visiting justices of the Westminster House of Correction, which exposes the appalling fact that in one year between five and six thousand women were convicted of drunkenness in this place of punishment alone."—*The Trinity of Evil, published by S. R. Briggs, Toronto.*

CHAPTER XXV

INSANITY AND ALCOHOL.

THE Census Returns of 1881 reports that there were 9,889 persons of unsound mind out of a population of 4,324,810, or one to every 437 of the population.

According to the Reports of the Ontario Asylums for the Insane, every asylum is full to its utmost capacity, there being more patients than beds, and the report for 1885 states that the number of lunatics in the asylums was 2,671, the increase of admissions "being" limited by the accommodation afforded, as is shown by the large number of insane persons in the gaols awaiting vacancies, and the number of applications for admission on the files.

The cost of insanity to the community is necessarily very heavy. In Ontario, the cost of maintenance, salaries, repairs, &c., was as follows in 1885:—

Toronto	$ 91,736
London	107,822
Kingston	65,185
Hamilton	72,815
Orillia	26,885
	$364,443

If we estimate that the other provinces do not expend more for insane asylums than the single large Province of Ontario, we have a yearly expenditure in Canada of about $730,000 on this account.

This expenditure however, represents only about half the cost of insanity to the country, as not more than half the insane are provided for in asylums, and it rarely happens that a person classed as of 'unsound mind' is self supporting. It is therefore, a very low estimate to put the cost to Canada of providing for the insane at 1,250,000. Then there is the loss of their productive labor, and also the loss of the labor of those who have to attend upon them, which together will amount to at least as much more. Thus insanity is a cost to the country of not less than $2,500,000 in money or produce.

This cost, however, large as it is, is but a trifle compared with the other losses occasioned by insanity. The community sustains a loss of mental power, the value of which is beyond calculation. Who can measure the loss to an individual of that priceless blessing—the human reason—a sound mind? And who can assess the value to a community of 10,000 minds in a country of less than five million people?

Is it not a question of the greatest concern to every moral and social reformer—nay, to every citizen—what are the principal causes of such derangement? And if any of the causes are within the reach of practical treatment, who shall dare to say that the duty is not the most urgent that can be pressed upon every statesmen and minister of the gospel and, indeed every individual citizen?

It has been said that the Official Records of this country do not show any considerable proportion of insanity as chargeable to drinking. I find on examining the Reports, that of 957 patients in the Ontario Lunatic Asylums in 1884 less than one-half of them are classified as to the "assignable causes" of the malady. Commenting upon these the Report says:—

"From the returns made by the various Asylums, the following statement of assigned causes of Insanity, both predisposing and exciting, has been compiled. It seems to be always necessary on presenting this statement, to explain that the cause as stated in each case is gathered from the so-called history of the case, which accompanies the medical certificates on the admission of each patient. The statements made as to "cause" in these cases are, to a great extent, of small value for various reasons—such as the want of knowledge of facts, carelessness in stating them, or a desire on the part of relatives to conceal important facts which should be told. Again, if a patient has been addicted to any particular vice or excess, or has recently suffered from any important accident or illness, one of these, right or wrong, is set down as the cause of the insanity; and as these histories are generally written by unskilled persons, it will be easily understood that they are, when so written, as has been said, of little value."

The following are amongst the principal of these assignable causes given in the above named Statement:

ASSIGNED CAUSES OF INSANITY, ONTARIO ASYLUM, 1884.

	PREDISPOSING CAUSE.	EXCITING CAUSE.	TOTAL.
Domestic troubles..................	1	23	24
Religious Excitement...............		31	31
Adverse circumstances, business troubles.	4	24	28
Mental anxiety "worry".............	1	31	32
Intemperance in drink.............	7	19	26
Self-abuse.........................	5	23	28
Brain disease with epilepsy...........	6	22	28
Unknown...........................	258	237	595

It is clear that no average results can be ascertained from such partial or incomplete returns. What proportion of the 595 "unknown" cases are traceable to drink we cannot tell, but it is well known that a large propertion of the other "assignable causes" are traceable to drinking, and it is probable that if the facts were known a large per centage of the whole would be found directly chargeable to alcohol.

It is worthy of note that in the Report upon Asylums of Ontario, 1884, the Inspector remarks as follows:

It is cheering to find that while in some respects in our Asylum administration we are not quite on a par with our neighbors, such as in grandeur of buildings, expense of maintenance, and so forth, there are others in which we on the whole are in no way behind, and indeed can be said to be well in the van, and this is especially so in reference to our system of treatment of lunatics, as respects the disuse of mechanical restraint, the disuse of alcohol and the employment of patients. In some of our Asylums, for instance, notably those of London and Kingston, mechanical restraint is now a thing of the past; straight jackets, muffs, crib beds, padded rooms, and all the myriad devices which ignorance and superstition in times past have invented to torture and madden afflicted humanity, are going or are gone, and it is to be hoped never to return. *Alcohol, and narcotic drugs are fast following, and we find active employment and cheerful amusements taking their places. In the Hamilton Asylum there has been no spirituous or fermented liquor used for any purpose for over five years. In the London Asylum there has been no liquor used for three or four years,* and there has not been any mechanical restraint or seclusion of any kind whatever used for eighteen months, with an average of nearly 900 patients under treatment.

Dr. Bucke of the London Asylum in the same report, gives the following valuable testimony on this subject:—

It is now three years since we have used any alcoholic stimulants, either in sickness or health, at this Asylum. The subjoined table is drawn up from the records of the institution, and embraces every whole year since the Asy-

.um was opened late in the fall of 1870. It will show better than any argument, that alcohol was of no value to us, that it neither prevented death nor assisted recovery.

The Year.	Percentage of deaths per annum calculated upon total number under treatment	Percentage of recoveries to admissions.	Alcoholic Stimulants used at the rate of—
1872............	4.72	38.17	$3 to $4 worth per patient per annum.
1873............	6.94	38.21	
1874............	4.16	41.67	
1875............	7.18	36.15	
1876............	4.53	31.24	
1877............	3.79	55.03	$1 per patient per an'm
1878............	5.10	35.40	3 to 4 cents worth per patient per annum.
1879............	4.91	37.60	
1880............	4.76	36.20	
1881............	3.92	32.22	
1882............	4.95	39.90	Absolutely none used.
1883............	5.23	43.45	
1884	4.87	44.69	

The death rate and recovery rate at an institution are liable to wide fluctuations from a great variety of causes, but the above table conclusively shows that the disuse of alcohol has not affected prejudicially either the one or the other of them.

Upon the whole, as many of our patients recover, and as few die, now that we use no alcohol as when we used that agent freely, and this is all that I ever claimed. I never supposed that three or four dollars worth per patient per annum of wine, beer, and whiskey, judiciously administered would either prevent recovery or materially shorten life. I simply said that alcohol did no good, was a useless expense, and that its use at the Asylum did harm by tending to keep alive in the country the delusion that alcohol is a valuable agent in the treatment of disease, and that therefore a little of it taken in health would probably, if wisely regulated, do good to the person taking it. These propositions I believed to be false, and I thought and still think that the right thing for me to do was to combat them in every legitimate manner.

In the report for 1885 Dr. Bucke again refers to this subject in the following terms :—

"We have passed another year without using, or seeing any necessity to use alcohol in any form or in any quantity, what I have said in former reports on this subject may be considered as reiterated here, with the added force of another year's experience.

An eminent authority on the statistics of insanity in England, Mr. W. J. Corbett, M.P., says that after many years study of the subject "under special circumstances I have reluctantly come to the conclusion that facts and figures establish clearly the progressive growth of the malady." He gives a table which shews the following as the statistics of insanity in the United Kingdom :

Date.	No. Insane.	Population.	Ratio per 1000.
1862	55,525	29,197,737	1·81
1872	77,013	31,782,522	2·41
1882	98,851	34,788,814	2·08

Commenting on these figures Mr. Corbett says:
The actual growth of numbers is continual and regular, as if influenced by some inscrutable law; there is a steady unchecked current of increase in accommodation, expenditure, numbers; and, strangest of all, in cures. * * The plain fact stands out, however others may try to disguise it in words, that in the brief course of two decades the insane in the three kingdoms have nearly doubled in number in spite of the most elaborate and costly means provided to cure them. There is, moreover, another alarming feature in that we evidently do not know the worst. The ominous words "inadequate accommodation" and "increase of provision" run through the whole series of reports from beginning to end.—*Fortnightly Review, April 1884, quoted by Axel Gustafson, in the "Foundation of Death."*

I have no means of ascertaining the proportionate increase of insanity in Canada, but it is a fact of serious importance that there is a constant steady increase of asylum population, with slight annual variations, as shown by the following admissions to the Ontario asylums: 1877-437, 1878-479, 1879-461, 1880-507, 1881-502, 1883-519, 1884-493, 1885-445. The Report for 1885 commenting on the table of admissions, from which these figures are taken, says:—

The above table, which shews what has been the yearly increase in the population of the asylums for the past nine years, exhibits a very marked decrease in 1885, as compared with any of the years which have preceded it. It must be borne in mind, however, that before the close of the official year, *all available asylum accommodation had been exhausted*, and that which was in course of preparation had not yet been completed. There was, therefore, a considerable number of applicants awaiting admission, who, if they could have been admitted earlier, would have made some change in these figures.

In other words, all the asylums are full, and the cry is still "more accommodation." It is evident that Mr. Corbett's remarks quoted above apply with equal force to this country; and apparently from the same causes.

Mr. Corbett further says:

"I hold that there is abundant evidence to prove that dissipation, drunkenness, and moral depravity, either directly or consequentially by transmission, to the next generation, is to be charged with an immense proportion of the annual increase of lunacy. No person of authority, I think, will be found to deny that evil and corrupt living in parents bears fruit in an unhealthy state of body and mind in their offspring."

He then sums up his facts in a table from which I take the following:

SOME OF THE PRINCIPAL ASSIGNED CAUSES OF INSANITY IN THE UNITED KINGDOM ASYLUMS.

	Predisposing Cause.	Exciting Cause	Not Distinguished	Total.	Proportion per cent of all patients
Intemperance in drink	168	1,268	343	1,779	13.1
Domestic Trouble	120	728	148	996	7.3
Business troubles, &c	131	638	128	897	6.6
Mental anxiety & overwork	80	552	138	770	5.6
Religious Excitement	20	343	68	431	3.1
Hereditary Influence				2,745	20.2
Unknown					21.0

What proportion of the other "assigned causes" are attributable to drink it is of course impossible to say, but it is a matter of general observation that drink is a most fruitful cause of domestic and business troubles, and all medical authorities agree that hereditary insanity is the result of alcoholism more than any other cause.

Taking the opinions and testimony of the most competent judges of the causes of insanity in the United Kingdom, the United States, and Canada, I

I find a general agreement in fixing the proportion of patients in lunatic asylums who are there directly through the use of alchohol as one-fifth of the whole, or 20 per cent, while there appears to be no doubt that the causes of the "assigned" and direct causes bring up the proportion of all insanity as chargeable to drink from one-third to two-thirds of the whole. The late Earl Shaftesbury, who was permanent chairman of the Lunacy Commission of the United Kingdom for 30 years and was a member of the Commission for over 50 years, said that "in his opinion intemperance is the cause of fully two-thirds of the insanity that prevails either in the drunkards themselves or their children" and in an address to the House of Lords he stated that *"fully six-tenths of all the cases of insanity to be found in these realms (United Kingdom) and in America arise from no other cause than intemperance."*

From an appendice to the Report of the Select Committees of the Senate and of the House of Commons, 1874, I take the following items:—

At the Binghampton Inebriate Asylum, applications for admission were made by—

   39 Clergymen,
    8 Judges,
   340 Merchants,
   226 Physicians,
   240 Gentlemen,
   1300 Rich men's daughters.

Insanity is occasioned more by this vice than by any other single influence, if we except hereditary disposition. Dr. Browne, of the Crichton Asylum, Dumfries, in a paper on the subject, declares that of 57,520 cases in thecpresent century, which he has carefully examined, and which were treated in public asylums, 10,717 were caused by intemperate habits. This does not include the numbers of the insane kept at home or in private boarding-houses. "It is enough," says this gentleman, "that while the virtuous sorrows, the inevitable misfortunes, and the physical diseases, and the many other evils to which man is exposed, produce in fifty years 40,000 lunatics; drunkenness, drinking, the pleasures of the table produce 10,000. The contrast between drunken and sober countries in relation to insanity is very striking. In Scotland there is one lunatic to 563 sane persons; in Spain, one to 7,181. In Edinburgh, every sixth lunatic owes his misfortune to intemperance; in Palermo, every twenty-first lunatic is in the same predicament. The late Dr. Blomfield, Bishop of London, from statistics of 1,271 lunatics, found that 649, or nearly one-half, were deprived of reason by intemperance. A most lamentable fact connected with this is that the children of drunkards are weak, hysterical, wayward and diseased."

The late Rev. W. J. Conybeare, in his able article on Intemperance in the *Edinburgh Review*, declares that of 300 idiots in Massachusetts, 145 were the children of drunkards.

Dr. Workman, Superintendent of the Lunatic Asylum, Toronto, says in his report for 1858, "There is abundant evidence that the children of intemperate parents are predisposed to insanity."

Dr. T. S. Clouston Physician Superintendent of the Royal Edinburgh Asylum, Scotland, says:—

We know as a statistical fact that from 15 to 20 per cent of the actual insanity of the country is produced by the excessive use of alcohol. This makes about 17,500 persons at one given time in the British Empire, who are so incapacitated by reason of mental alienation produced through use of alcohol. These people are as good as dead while they are insane; they do no work for the world or in the world, and all that makes life worth having to them they are deprived of. But you must remember that these numbers are merely of those so well known as to be available for statistics, merely the registered persons who have been so ill as to have been sent to the asylums through the excessive use of alcohol. *For every one of these numbers who had become really insane there are no doubt a large number who have become partially effected in mind through the excessive use of alcohol, and who are many of them partially insane. Lecture to the students of Edinburgh University, Dec. 19, 1883.*

Mr. Mulhall the great statistician of the world's population, &c., published a paper in the Contemporary Review in 1883. He is the only authority of any weight or position who has attempted to discredit the utterances of Lord Shaftesbury on this question. But he admits, however, that the insanity in England caused by drink amounts to nearly one-third of the total insanity of the British Kingdom; besides which, he numbers 25,800 idiots as owing their condition to drunken parentage."—*Foundation of Death, page 271.*

Dr. F. R. Lees sums up an exhaustive argument on this subject with the following :—

"Alcohol operates in a double way in producing insanity —it energizes transiently the dangerous passions, and while increasing their imperious rule, saps and weakens the moral will. The liquor traffic, then, is not simply the occasion of one insane person's insanity or idiocy out of every five we meet, *by direct temptation and participation*—but also the *exciter* of the dormant seeds, the disturber of the nicely balanced will and passions in three out of the remaining four. Savages have all our passions and are ungovernable enough. Yet they don't go mad. Turks, Arabians, Egyptians, have excitement and lusts and sufferings, but they don't go mad. Are we to believe, then, that *civilization* is the cause of our madness? That the equalizing of human destiny, the

P

spread of comfort and independence, the development of mind, has any necessary connection with insanity, or inherent tendency thereto. When we sent the Traffic to the American Indians they too went mad. * * Unfortunately also we kept the Traffic at home—and we therefore continue to go mad."

CHAPTER XXVI.

DRINK AND PAUPERISM.

AMONG the social problems demanding attention and practical treatment is the question of pauperism.

In the United Kingdom it has been, for generations past, a gigantic burden, so enormous that at one period of more than ordinary hard times, one in every ten persons where paupers. As recently as 1879, Mr. Alex. Balfour, of Liverpool, England, a distinguished social reformer in reading a paper before the National Club, London, said :—

"At the end of March this year, there were, irrespective of lunatics, 975,000 persons upon the books of the various poor law unions. But this is not a proper indication of our national poverty. The total number of persons who at one time or another came upon the books of the unions of our country during the last year, was nearly 3,000,000, or about one-eleventh of the population of the kingdom."

The system of poor relief in England enables the authorities to make returns of the number of paupers. But the evil is so vast that it has not been found easy to deal with it, and gross irregularities have crept into the system.

Undoubtedly it is the duty of the State to make some provision for the poor, even if their poverty arises from their own neglect or vices, and it is probably true that the British system, clumsy and inefficient as it is, has been a relief to large masses of people.

But the radical defect of the system is that it does not provide for that kind of assistance which will help the poor to help themselves. It puts a premium upon chronic pauperism, and does not encourage the independent humble poor. These are made to pay a price for the assistance given which makes it of questionable benefit.

There are two classes of paupers, viz: those receiving "out-door relief" and inmates of "workhouses" or asylums for the poor. The greatest possible discouragement is given to those seeking temporary or regular out-door relief. The workhouse is made as much like a prison as possible,—members of the same family separated—even to the extent of old married couples who may have lived together for a quarter of a century or more. An *"order for admission to the house"* or *nothing* is the alternative generally offered to those who seek relief, and if any out-door assistance is given at all, it is under conditions so harrassing and humiliating that it is very dearly purchased, if the recipient has any independance and respectability. The result is, that the really needy and deserving poor are frequently driven to despair, and even to starvation, rather than submit to the conditions of pauperism, or otherwise are converted into incorrigible and hopeless paupers.

In London, England, there was a Jew's Board of Guardians (established in 1859) for the relief of Jews the result of the co-operative Union of Jewish Churches. In 1868 Dr. J. H. Stallard, of London, published a work on *London Pauperism among Jews and Christians*. From this we learn that the Jew's Board make efforts to supply the poor with means of earning their own livelihood; by letting out to them sewing machines, &c., which becomes the property of the hirer who pays small weekly instalments; by loaning small sums of money to meet pressing needs or unexpected claims, such as are occassioned by sickness, loss of work, &c. Any application of this nature made to the official guardians of the poor in England from a distressed man or woman would probably be answered by a gruff intimation that the applicant could have an " order for the house."

Of course the avowed object of the poor law guardians and inspectors, is to discourage persons from becoming a burden upon society. But what is the effect of it ? While the actual number of registered paupers is not so large as formerly the cost of pauperism was never so high as at the present time. Official statistics are not given so as to cover the whole of the United Kingdom, but in England and Wales there were in 1863 (the year of the cotton famine) 1,142,624 paupers. costing the tax-payers £6,527,036 or about thirty-two and a half millions of dollars. In 1884 the number was reduced to 774,310 paupers, about 25 per cent less, while the expenditure was £8,400,000 or about forty-two millions of dollars, being an increase of 25 per cent.

In an open letter addressed to Mr. W. E. Gladstone in 1881, Mr. Wm. Hoyle says:—

Excepting the cotton famine year of 1863 the year of 1871 was the year of the highest numerical pauperism, and that from 1871 forward there was a continuous decrease especially in cases of out-door relief, This decrease arose from two causes; 1st, The great improvement in the trade of the country; and 2nd, and chiefly, the stringent action of the Boards of Guardians, in offering to paupers the alternative of no relief or of going inside the work-house.

In proof of this I may appeal to the instructions constantly issued by the Local Government Board in London, and the experience of almost every Board of Guardians throughout the country. I was a member of the Bury Board of Guardians for the ten years from 1870 to 1880, and I therefore speak from personal knowledge of the facts of the case; and though the aggregate of registered pauperism was lowered considerably, it is doubtful if real destitution was lessened. * * The question here arises, how does it come to pass that in 1880-1 the money paid in actual relief is greater than in any year during the nation's history? It cannot arise from the dearness of clothing, for during the year 1880 clothing was probably cheaper than in previous years, excepting, may be, 1879. Neither can it have arisen from the high price of food, for during 1879 and 1880 food was cheaper than during any two years of the present century.—*Our National Drink Bill, page 122.*

These words from the pen of so able and conscientious an author as Wm. Hoyle are deserving of the greatest consideration of all who find it necessary to study the treatment of pauperism. He wrote in 1881. The *decrease* of registered paupers and the *increase* of cost have still continued as will be seen from the following statistics of pauperism in England and Wales taken from official sources:

	No. of Paupers.	Cost.
1881	803,126	£8,102,136
1882	797,614	8,232,472
1883	799,296	8,353,292
1884	774,310	8,400,000

But it is of first importance to trace the source of pauperism in order that we may check it. A study of how to deal with the evil may, unfortunately, become a necessity to the legislators of Canada. But if greater wisdom and wiser measures prevail we shall face the *cause of pauperism* and stop its growth amongst us. So much has been said on the relation of pauperism to drink that it seems like repeating an oft-told-tale. Yet it appears to be necessary, as there are still able writers, and speakers on public questions, who, looking upon the dreadful pictures of poverty which exist, especially in large cities, still ignore this as the chief of all the factors in their creation.

In their invaluable report of 1869 the "Convocation of Canterbury" * said :—

From an extensive and minute enquiry prosecuted throughout the workhouses of the country—as well as from other authenticated statements,—it can be shown that an enormous proportion of Pauperism is the direct and common product of intemperance. It appears indeed that 75 per cent. of the occupants of our workhouses and a large portion of those receiving out-door pay, have become pensioners upon the public directly or indirectly through drunkenness.
* * From numerous returns submitted by the Masters of Workhouses and other officials whose information may be relied on, it appears that the recipients of parochial relief in England and Wales amount to one-twentieth of the population—and that this destitution is largely caused by intemperance."

Turning to the pages of testimony in this Report, given by various governors of workhouses, there is an uniformity of evidence as to the principal cause of poverty and pauperism, which is as startling as it is

---

* "The Convocation of Canterbury" appointed by the House of Lords and consisting of The Prolucutor, three Deans, six Archdeacons, seven Canons, two Prebendaries of the English Church, with the Archdeacon of Coventry as chairman, presented a massive report on Intemperance and its causes in 1869.

instructive. One of the questions put by the Conyocation to these governors is, "What proportion of those who have come under your cognizance as paupers have been the victims of intemperance?" 118 answers are given, and the following are a fair sample of the whole: "12 years experience—Two-thirds." "80 per cent." "Three-fourths." "18 out of every 20." "Without hesitation, I should say that 70 or 80 per cent of the paupers comes to that state through drink." "From my experience of 18 years among paupers and lunatics I consider that 9 out of 10 may attribute the cause to intemperance." These six answers are taken in the order in which they appear in the Report. Here are one or two more taken indiscriminately out of the 118. "All paupers who have come under my cognizance have more or less been victims of intemperance. I have never known a pauper who was a total abstainer." "We have had upwards of 4,000 casuals passed through the vagrant wards last year, and of that number one-half appeared to be bona-fide working men; and when in conversation with them about the degradation of coming to the vagrant wards of a workhouse, they invariably stated that it was through drink."

And so the testimony is the same, varying only a little as to proportions attributable to drink, although differing much in the form of expression.

Mr. Alex. Balfour, whose paper is quoted above says:

"All agree that three-fourths, if not nine-tenths, of this pauperism results from our habits of drinking. Change these, and our pauperism would soon almost disappear."

Mr. James Silk Buckingham, M. P., Chairman of the Parliamentary Committee on Intemperance, 1834, says:

Our parochial expenses are principally caused by excessive drinking. Of 143 inmates of a London parish workhouse 105 have been reduced to that state by intemperance; and the small remainder comprises all the blind, epileptic, and idiotic, as well as all the aged poor, some of whom would also drink to intoxication if opportunity offered. * * The proportion of this expenditure (for pauperism) occasioned by drinking may be fairly estimated at two-thirds.

Mr. Wm. Hoyle, while showing that pauperism and its cost existed in almost direct ratio to the facilities provided for drinking, and of the quantity of liquor consumed, says:

"One more fact touching pauperism, and it makes my heart sad to write it. From the forty-second annual report of the Registrar-General of England and Wales I find that of the total number of deaths in 1879 one person out of every fifteen ended his days in the workhouse, whilst in London one in nine died in the workhouse. Think of it! In the most wealthy city in the world, the capital of the foremost Christian country, one person out of every nine ends his days in the Union Workhouse!" *Our National Drink Bill, page 152.*

Turning to the United States Dr. Wm. Hargreaves says:

"There is no more difficult task than that of undertaking to find out the true cost of pauperism and crime in the United States. In truth it may be said to be impossible from the poor and irregular system, or no system, of collecting facts and statistics in the public institutions of the country."

So far as pauperism is concerned these words might be written of Canada. We have our paupers, but no poor law guardians and no poor-houses. It is certain however, that the burden of providing for the destitute poverty of this country is pressing very heavily upon some cities, towns and municipalities. Not only is their a frequent call upon the civic purse, but our magistrates are becoming very familiar with the class called "vagrants" as well as with criminals proper.

Our newspapers constantly report cases of vagrancy, and every police office finds it necessary to deal with them. Even where, as in Halton County and some others, they have no liquor-shops and *therefore* no home paupers, or very few; the travelling vagrant is a frequent source of trouble and expense.

Official statistics show that the number of vagrants committed at the Magistrates Courts of the Province of Ontario were in viz:—

1881.	1882.	1883.	1884.
1580	1449	1554	2134.

In the year 1885, the number of cases of vagrancy charged before the Magistrates Court of Toronto was 470, of which 110 were females. In addition to these, shelter was given in the city police stations to 4,034 persons.

"The number of applicants who applied to the Mayor at the City Hall for aid in 1886 was 1298. Mayor Howland says "some of these applicants were helped by fuel and food being given them, others were given passes, some sent to the Hospital, and in fact, every one helped according to the several needs and necessities."

In view of such facts as these it is evident that the question of pauperism and how to deal with it, must soon be pressed upon us for answer, unless we are wise enough to harken to the many-tongued voice of experience, and attack the *cause* before the effects overwhelm us.

Indeed there are already signs that this evil is demanding more systematic and compulsory treatment. Mr. J. E. Pell, the veteran secretary of the St. George's Society, of Toronto, was recently interviewed by a *Globe* reporter. Referring to an interview previously held with the Rev. Mr. Pearson which was reported in the same paper, Mr. Pell said:—

I attach great importance to any opinion that Mr. Pearson would express in connection with the best manner of dealing with the poor. He says, 'Our whole system of dealing with charities requires a radical change,' and I agree with him Out-door relief from the House of Industry should undoubtedly be supported by general taxation, and I might go so far as to say that Boys' Homes and Girls' Homes and institutions of that kind should be supported also by general taxation, while national societies should be on a purely voluntary system.

Mr. Pell also sees the growing necessity for a Board of Guardians. He says he agrees with Mr. Pearson that :—

"Instead of having the House of Industry dealing with the municipal grant and the Provincial grant, we sould have a Board of Guardians elected by the municipality, and responsible, like the alderman, to those who elect them. If this plan were carried out the Mayor would be relieved of all the trouble, and the difficulty which now is daily seen in the Mayor's office would be done away with. There would be only one place then to deal with applicants, and all applicants would come there to have their cases considered. I would certainly have a Home for confirmed drunkards, and have it provided that men of this kind should be looked after. I can give you a case where a man earns good wages when he works. He is a bricklayer, and earns $3 a day when he can get work. And yet his wife, and she is a most deserving, industrious, thrifty woman, came to me about Christmas time and declared that they were actually in want of food. Her husband would not work steadily through drink. What's to be done with a man like that? I often wonder what should be done in such cases, and I think a home for confirmed drunkards would be instrumental in doing such men good. I think it is only by inforced contributions that we will ever get the bulk of the people to contribute to the poor. I think each municipality should be forced to support its own poor. The Act of Parliament says that each municipality "may" provide for its own poor, not "shall." If it had read "shall" instead of "may" the poor from the county could be shipped back to their own municipality. We had a field night of it at the meeting of the St. George's Society last night. We relieved some 46 cases, and nearly 30 cases where left over for me to visit as soon as I can."—*Toronto Globe, Jan. 17, 1887.*

On the 14th of January the *Toronto News* said :—

"The city is full of vagrants just now, and a good many of them find their way to the police station."

We have seen that the uniform testimony in the old land, after a long and costly experience is, that if drinking can be abolished, pauperism will go with it. Poverty there will be. By the selfishness of humanity we shall always have the poor with us. The tyranny of might against right will provide us with much painful poverty, to say nothing of accident, disease, and unlooked for distress. But in any civilized country where productive labor has fair-play, these will be but a mere trifle to provide for—enough only to evoke the spirit of charity and teach men how "it is more blessed to give than to receive."

The chief factor in the creation of poverty is the same on the American Continent as in Europe. Dr. Hargreaves devotes a special chapter of his work to this aspect of the subject and furnishes abundant testimony that, so far as the United States is concerned, drink is the producing cause of, from two-thirds to four-fifths of all American pauperism. *See Chap, X. Our Wasted Resources.*

Dr. Howard Crosby of New York, who is not by any means a prohibitionist "crank," in his comments upon Mrs. Helen Campbell's articles on Prisoners of Poverty says:—

"The trouble is intemperance. I have been watching for 35 years, and in all my investigations among the poor I never yet found a family borne down by poverty that did not owe its fall to rum. That's it, and there's where the remedy must be applied. We must make the Legislature act; the churches can't do any more than they are doing. Make the Legislatures shut up the rum holes, so that fathers and mothers will have incomes, and there will not be so many stories of sewing girls working for starvation wages, and then being defrauded by factory owners."

The above is quoted by the writer of a letter to *The Voice* of Dec. 9th, 1886. The writer says: he has been 22 years in the administration of the Pauper Department of the city of Worcester as its executive officer and he says :—

"I charge the grog-shops with being the greatest curse with which this nation is afflicted. The proportion of paupers under my management who have come to destitution as a consequence of drink, I estimate to be 90 per cent. of the males, or 70 per cent. of both sexes. The average cost per year per pauper is, directly, $120; counting indirect cost, the average is much greater. Pauperism seems to be on the increase in this part of the country, particularly in the cities. Without doubt, the removal of the saloon would be an effective aid in the removal of pauperism.

Another executive officer, Mr. John McKenna, writes from Albany :—

Very emphatically I believe with Superintendent Murray, of the Kings County Alms-House, that liquor is the principal cause of poverty. About nine-tenths of the paupers under my control have come to their present condition through drink. This is a safe estimate. Price per pauper per year, $130. In this city and county pauperism seems to be on the increase to an alarming extent, and the cause is rum in almost every instance. To the question: "Would the removal of the saloon be an effective aid in the removal of pauperism?" I reply: Indeed it would! I go with Dr. Howard Crosby in his latest expressed views about rum's work to the extent of every word.

The Voice publishes a long series of letters from public officials with the same, practically, unvarying testimony, that drink and Pauperism are so closely allied that to remove the former would greatly reduce, if not altogether abolish the latter.

This is equally true of Canadian testimony. The Report of the Select Committee of the Legislative Assembly, Montreal, of 1849, says:—

"Intemperance leads to crime, insanity and pauperism. * * Three-fourths of the pauperism are ascribable to intemperance."

The Rev. Father Chiniquy was called in to give evidence before that committee in the course of which he said:—

In forty parishes, in which within the last year I have preached the cause of temperance, 1,415 families worth £1,378,074 (6,890,370 dollars) have been ruined, and are almost extinct from the use of intoxicating liquors. Their children, to the number of 6,229, are for the most part wanderers and vagabonds in our towns and villages, or have gone away and lost themselves in the United States.

In 1874 the Select Committee of the Senate reported that their numerous petitioners "assert that the traffic in intoxicating liquors is shown, by the most careful enquiries, to be the cause of probably not less than three-fourths of the pauperism, immorality and crime found in this country."

But it is unnecessary to multiply evidence. The facts are abundant and overwhelming. They speak in thunder tones to every social reformer, politician and Christian citizen.

But there are yet too many who do not, or will not, hear. The voices cry from ten thousand wretched men, women and children in Canada; and from that number many times multiplied in Britain and the United States, but how many there are who stuff their ears with policy and interest, and refuse to hear? There are others too who hear but heed not. As an able writer has recently said:—

"We are so accustomed to have the worship of God and the devil carried on side by side, so used to see the saloon standing cheek-by-jowl with the church, that we find it difficult to perceive things as they really are. * * * When Great Britain went to war with China to force the opium trade upon the Middle Kingdom, her neighbors were shocked, and with reason. Those, however, who perceived clearly enough, the immorality of England's policy on that occasion have failed, for the most part, to see in the national support of the saloon a betrayal of the masses bearing ugly resemblance to that involved in the opium war. * * * There are thousands of families doomed to indigence, disappointment, misery, through life, that might have lived at least in decent poverty and with self-respect, but to-day are plunged in hopeless ruin by drink, and are sinking out of sight in the quicksand." *George Frederick Parsons, in the Atlantic Monthly, January, 1887.*

CHAPTER XXVII.

THE ECONOMIC VALUE OF MAN.

THERE is a tendency to worship institutions for themselves. We construct a brotherhood, form a community, create a parliament, organise a church, and then fall down and worship the creature we have made.

But the greatest thing on earth known to man is man. Institutions exist for man, and in proportion only as they advance the interest and conserve the good of man, their existence is of value.

The progress of civilization demands that everything should be made contributory to the liberty, dignity and moral purity of manhood and womanhood. That is the meaning and object of science, that is the true evolution, and the explanation of every new discovery. Genius serves no purpose if it does not advance the human race. Literature, art and science are all handmaids of human progress; they exist for man or they are useless.

The Bible is written and given to Man for Man. Its aim and purpose is the enlightenment, redemption and exaltation of manhood. Its mission and message of mercy and love is to Man. Its appeal is always to Man, and an *appeal it is—not a command*. True it declares the law and announces the penalty of the law broken. It proclaims that "whatsoever a man soweth that shall he also reap," and in that announcement it proclaims Man's moral dignity and power.

Man therefore is responsible for the guardianship of himself for the preservation of his physical powers, as well as for the cultivation of his mind. There is in life a grand possession, a responsibility in every breath. The Rev. Dr. Cuyler has beautifully said:—

"Life is infinitely valuable, not only from the origin and the results and revenues it may reach, but from the eternal consequences flowing from it. Anyone that recklessly impairs, imperils and weakens bodily powers by bad hours, unwholesome diet, poisonous stimulants or sensualities is a suicide. * * What shall we say then of him who opens a haunt of temptation, sets out his snares and deliberately deals out death by the dram. So many pieces of silver for so many ounces of blood, and an immortal soul tossed into the balance! If I could let one ray of Eternity shine into every dram shop methinks I could frighten the poison seller back from making his living at the mouth of the pit.'"

The Economic interests of all men are in harmony with the highest moral law. The Divine proclamation that "Godliness is profitable to all things" is a scientific as well as a moral truth.

Considered as an economic fact the highest value in the world is Man; and this value reaches out beyond the range of his physical existence.

Thus the waste of human life by the use of intoxicating drink is the most tremendous of all the indictments against the system of drinking and the traffic in liquor. What the sum total of this loss is no human mind can conceive,—much less estimate it. It is an overwhelming fact that it far surpasses any other loss the world sustains.

Q

We are familiar with various estimates of the many thousands annually slain by drink, but in these calculations no allowance is made for the waste of life's forces;—for the shortening of life. Prof. Flourens of the *College de France* in his work on human longevity considers one hundred years to be the normal length of man's life. He says, "Few men indeed reach that age, but how many do what is necessary to reach it? With our way of living, our passions and worries, man no longer dies but kills himself."

Henry Ward Beecher says:—

"The proper duration of human life, I suppose to be, anywhere from eighty to a hundred years. Men are built so that they have a right to expect that. A man ought to be ashamed to die before he is seventy years old. But the average duration of human life is thirty-three years. Consider what a waste that is, when society has in itself the power of prolonging life to a hundred years, or ninety years or eighty years, and the average of the duration of life is but thirty, according to the old account, and thirty-three now according to the more modern estimate. Well, here is two-thirds wasted; one-third only does all the work that is done in human society, and if you consider the period of non-productiveness necessary to dependant childhood, and if you give to the age and outworn the liberty of some years on the other side of life and then count the productive forces I think it may be said, taking the world over, it is an insufficient estimate that one-fourth of the human family do all the work that is done, and support the other three fourths."—*Lecture on the Wastes and Burdens of Society.*

But what hope is there of any general improvement in the duration and productive power of human life so long as the highest conditions of civilization are interwoven with the drinking customs? If the human race is ever to develop towards a higer condition of physical perfection, it must begin with the advantages which civilization brings. But, if these advantages are overbalanced by an agency of death which mocks us at every turn, we preach and labor in vain to promote the advancement of our race.

What avails it that we increase our educational agencies and improve the intellectual condition of our people, if we foster and encourage and license a saloon to destroy our educated boys, and render worse than useless the refinement which education gives to our girls. The village school house does not make the boy less susceptible to the effects of the saloon. It qualifies him for the more effectual work of the liquor whether sold by permission of law or not. Education does not deaden the pain and suffering of our women who become wives of drunkards. The refined intellectual woman is the one whose heart will break soonest under the strain of drink-wrecked love and hopes.

That eminent medical authority, Sir Henry Thompson, Physician to the Queen, says:—

"I will tell you who can't take alcohol, and that is very important in the present day. Of all the people I know who cannot stand alcohol it is the brain workers; and you know it is the brain workers that are increasing in numbers, and the people who do not use their brains are going down, and that is a noteworthy incident in relation to the future."

Sir Andrew Clark, M.D., F.R.S., Physician to Mr. Gladstone, says:—

I dare say, if a man took a glass of wine, as sometimes people do to overcome their nervousness, he would succeed, and indeed I am bound to say that that sort of help alcohol sometimes can give a man, but it gives it curiously enough at the expense of blunting his sensibilities * * that is my testimony as to the effect of alcoholic liquors upon health and work, viz: that for all purposes of sustained, enduring, fruitful work, it is my experience that alcohol does not help but hinder it * * I am bound to say that for all honest work alcohol never helps a human soul. Never, Never!"

Again, Dr. Clark says :—

"If there is any honest man who really wants to get at the truth, and will not be set from his purpose by people condoling with him about his appearance, and the result of his experiment, and will try the effect of alcohol upon work, I would tell him fearlessly, and I would risk all I possess upon the back of the statement, that as certainly as he does try that experiment for a month or six weeks so certainly will he come to the conclusion that, however pleasant alcohol is for the moment, it is not a helper of work. It is not only, not a helper of work, but it is a certain hinderer of work: and every man who comes to the front of a profession in London is marked by this one characteristic, that the more busy he gets, the less in shape of alcohol he takes: and his excuse is—'I am sorry, but I cannot take it and do my work.'"

Dr. B. W. Richardson, M.D., F.R.S., in the course of an address on the action of alcohol on the mind says :—

The result of accumulated experience shows that they who, by stimulation force the growth of thought ; they who daily relax the vascular control of their centres of thought ; they who reduce that unconscious grasp which Nature, all wise and wonderful, has placed in automatic concealment, and out of the capricious control of our constantly-changing wills ; that they who defy Nature in this her imperative rule for healthy life, pay the forfeit for their temerity or ignorance. These are the men who break up at their work ; these are the men whose suns go down at noon ; these are the men dying in this day at a rate alarming to contemplate. These are the men of whom it so often is said 'whom the gods love die young.' Pernicious falsehood ! whom the gods love die old ; live out in usefulness and happiness their allotted cycle ; die without rending the hearts of any by unnatural strain of sorrow ; die as they sleep, knowing nothing of the pain and conscious bitterness of death.

For the work that comes of the mind and that comes out under pressure no taste of alcoholic stimulation is necessary. Every such taste is self-inflicted injury. The dose of alcohol which spurred the thought of to-day must be slightly increased to spur the thought of to-morrow to the same pitch. * * Of all men brain workers are the men least able to bear up against the ravages of alcohol. Of all men they are most liable to be deceived and played upon by this traitor who enters the most precious treasury, the citadel of the mind."

Shakespeare evidently understood how strong drink attacks the throne of intellectual and moral power. In *"Othello"* he makes *Cassio* say :—

"Reputation, reputation, reputation ! O, I have lost my reputation ! I have lost the immortal part of myself; and what remains is bestial."

"O thou invisible spirit of wine, if thou hast no other name to be known by, let us call thee devil!"

"O that men should put an enemy in their mouths to steal away their brains."

"To be now a sensible man, by and by a fool, and presently a beast ! O strange ! Every inordinate cup is unbless'd, and the ingredient is a devil."

Again the great dramatist gives the opposite picture in "As you like it." He makes *Adam* to say :—

"Though I look old, yet am I strong and lusty,
For in my youth I never did apply
Hot and rebellious liquors in my blood ;
Nor did not with unbashful forehead woo
The means of weakness and debility ;
Therefore my age is as a lusty winter
Frosty but kindly."

This enemy which men "put into their mouths to steal away their brains" is always antagonistic to life. It is the essential quality of the spirit alcohol to kill and the higher the form of life it attacks the more direct and ruinous are its effects. It preserves death but is ever an enemy to all form of life. As an agent of death in human society it stands at the head of all the dire catalogue of disasters and disorders.

There is unerring testimony in the facts recorded by the various Life Insurance Companies and Sick Benefit Societies. A writer in the *Alliance News* of Jan. 15, 1887, Mr. James Duthrie, has made a comparison of the sick-rate and death-rate of two societies respectively, viz:—*The Oddfellows* society which in England is not a temperance brotherhood, and the *Rechabites* who are all total abstainers and who forfeit their benefit if they fail to keep the pledge of abstinence.

	I. O. of Oddfellows.				I. O. of Rechabites.		
Year.	Average Sickness.		Death-rate.	Year.	Average Sickness.		Death-rate.
	Days	Hours			Days	Hours	
1868	11	21	1 in 53	1868	3	2	1 in 118
1869	12	4	1 in 58	1869	3	3	1 in 142
1870	14	5	1 in 48	1870	5	20	1 in 85
1871	13	19	1 in 51	1871	2	16	1 in 227
1872	13	14	1 in 47	1872	2	19	1 in 200
Average	12	22	1 in 51	Average	3	13	1 in 154

"It will be observed from the above table that the average sickness per member among the Oddfellows was 12 days 22 hours, and the death-rate one in 51 2-5th; whilst the average sickness per member among the Rechabites, which is a total abstinence society, was 3 days 13 hours, and the death-rate one in 154 2-5ths."

The Rechabites are an old Order established in August 1835, in England. In consequence of the small death-rate and the consequent low rate of demand upon their income they have a capital fund of over one million dollars. The order is also strong in Australia and on the occasion of its Jubilee celebration in August, 1885, its strength counted up to a grand total of nearly 100,000 members.

In the early days of temperance advocacy—between 40 and 50 years ago a total abstainer was regarded with disfavor by Insurance Companies and some of them refused to insure an abstainer at the ordinary premiums. The chairman of the United Kingdom Temperance Provident Society mentions that he applied to three Insurance Companies, two of which accepted him at the ordinary rates through the influence of friends but the third demanded a considerable amount extra premium. When he asked the reason the answer given was, "You are a teetotaler and the directors consider teetotal lives are worse than ordinary lives."

But in 1834 the British Government appointed the famous Parliamentary Committee of which James Silk Buckingham was chairman and among the remarkable statements in their report as to the "consequences of drinking upon the national character" was the following:—

"The diminution of the physical power and longevity of a large portion of the British population, the loss of personal beauty, the decline of health and the progressive decay of the bodily and mental powers; which evils are accumulative in the amount of injury they inflict, as intemperate parents, according to high medical testimony, give a taint to their offspring even before its birth, and the poisonous stream of ardent spirits is conveyed through the milk of the mother to the infant at the breast; so that the fountain of life through which nature supplies that pure and healthy nutriment of infancy is poisoned at its very source, and a diseased and vitiated appetite is thus created which grows with its growth and strengthens increasing weakness and decay."

In another clause the report speaks of :—

The comparative inefficiency of the Army and Navy in both of which according to the testimony of eminent officers is a canker worm that eats away its strength and discipline to the very core; it being *proved beyond all question that one-sixth of the effective strength of the Army is as much destroyed as if the men were slain in battle by that most powerful ally of death, intoxicating drinks*, and that the greater number of accidents occurring in both branches of the service, seven-eighths of the sickness, invalidings and discharges for incapacity, and nine-tenths of all the acts of insubordination and the fearful punishments and executions to which these give rise, are to be ascribed to drunkenness alone.

In 1838 the British Military authorities kept a record of a number of men belonging to temperance societies in the army in India, and who were admitted to the hospitals; and also of a number who were not temperance men, admitted during the same time. The result proved that the average daily percentage of men in the hospital who were abstainers was 3.65, and of those who were not it was 10.20, or a percentage of invalid soldiers among non-abstainers nearly three times larger than that of the abstainers.

Such facts as these began to open the eyes of the public and in 1840 the Temperance Provident Institution was established in London for insuring the lives of total abstainers only, and in 1849 the directors reported that up to that date 135 deaths might have occurred according to the lowest average calculation, and 219 according to the highest, but that the actual deaths had been 73. In 1850, an important change was affected by admitting non-abstainers (respectable moderate drinkers) into a distinct section, placing in a corresponding section abstainers only.

The result of this experiment has been to prove that while total abstainers do not die as fast as the actuary's tables declare they are expected to do, the general class or moderate drinkers do die as fast, or even faster, than the expected rate.

The following tables are sufficient to prove this beyond doubt:—

TABLE OF UNITED KINGDOM TEMPERANCE PROVIDENT INSTITUTION.

TOTAL ABSTAINERS SECTION.

Year.	Expected Deaths.	Actual Deaths.	Per cent. of Deaths.
1866-70	549	411	·74
1871	127	72	·57
1872	137	90	·66
1873	144	118	·82
1874	153	110	·72
1875	162	121	·75
1876	168	102	·60
1877	179	132	·73
1878	187	117	·63
1879	196	164	·84
1880	203	136	·67
1881	213	131	·61
Total..1866-81	2,418	1,704	·70

MODERATE DRINKERS SECTION.

Year.	Expected Deaths.	Actual Deaths.	Per cent. of Deaths.	Excess of Moderate Drinkers.
1866-70	1.008	944	·94	·20
1871	234	217	·93	·36
1872	244	282	1·16	·50
1873	253	246	·97	·15
1874	263	288	1·10	·38
1875	273	297	1·09	·34
1876	279	253	·90	·30
1877	291	280	·96	·23
1878	299	317	1·06	·43
1879	305	326	1·07	·23
1880	311	304	·98	·31
1881	320	290	·90	·29
Total..1866-81	4,080	4,044	·99	·29

Again from the Obituary record of the National Division of the Sons of Temperance of North America we have the following:—

"The average age of the members who died in the last five years is as follows:

1881	64 years	&	4	months
1882	71	"	2	"
1883	71	"	6	"
1884	72	"	0	"
1885	68	"	0	"

Forty-seven deaths in all, at an average of over 69 years. This is an extraordinary showing, as they were not selected lives, and can only be accounted for on the ground that total abstinence prolongs life."

The Sceptre Life Assurance Company, the British Empire Insurance Co., the Whittington Life Insurance Co., and others of the United Kingdom, might all be quoted in proof of these facts. In the United States the same experience has been realised and the old theory that beer as a beverage is not baneful has received a knock-down blow from the unerring testimony of the mathematics of the Insurance Company's Ledger accounts. The President of the Connecticut Mutual Life Assurance Co., Col. Green says:—

"I protest against the notion so prevalent and so industriously urged that beer is harmless and a desirable substitute for the more concentrated liquors. What beer may be, and what it may do in other countries and climates, I do not know from observation. That in this country and climate *its use is an evil only less than the use of whiskey, if less on the whole*, and that its effect is only longer delayed, not so immediately and obviously bad, its incidents not so repulsive, but destructive in the end I have seen abundant proof. In one of our largest cities, containing a great population of beer-drinkers, I had occasion to note the deaths among a large group of persons whose habits, in their own eyes and in those of their friends and physicians were temperate ; but they were habitual users of beer. When the observation began, they were, upon the average, something under middle age, and they were, of course, *selected lives.* For two or three years there was nothing very remarkable to be noted among this group. Presently death began to strike it ; and, until it had dwindled to a fraction of its original proportions, *the mortality in it was astounding in extent,* and still more remarkable in the *manifest identity of cause and mode.* There was no mistaking it ; the history was a most invariable one : robust, apparent health, full muscles, a fair outside, increasing weight, florid faces ; then a touch of cold, or a sniff of malaria, and instantly some acute disease, with almost invariably typhoid symptoms, was in violent action, and ten days or less ended it. *It was as if the system had been kept fair outside, while within it was eaten to a shell; and at the first touch of disease there was utter collapse; every fibre was poisoned and weak.* And this, in its main features, varying of course in degree, has been my observation of beer-drinking everywhere. *It is peculiarly deceptive at first; it is thoroughly destructive at the last."*

Other American Life Insurance Companies confirm this testimony in the most emphatic terms.

Following the line of the United Kingdom, a Temperance & General Life Insurance Company of North America has been organized, and commenced business a year ago with the Hon. G. W. Ross as its President, and Mr. Henry O'Hara its Managing Director. The company has published a neat little colored diagram illustrating the facts referred to above, and it will well repay the reader to send to the head office, Toronto, for a copy of it.

The Royal Templars of Temperance, an organization having a special beneficiary degree, and which is making rapid progress in Canada, as well as in the neighboring States, is a dollar and cents argument which any one may test in proof that the life of a total abstainer is worth more, and therefore costs less to insure, than that of an alcohol drinker, however moderate he may be.

I am not writing in the interests of life insurance, but in the interests of human life itself. I quote the facts which these Companies and Orders supply as experience to set by the side of the scientific testimony against the use of that terrible agent of death—which Shakespeare calls—DEVIL.

It is also a fact pregnant with meaning and solemn warning to all, that the more intimately persons are associated with the liquor traffic the greater its temptations and the shorter the average life.

The Registrar General of England publishes a report which contains tables showing the average number of deaths of men between 25 and 65 years of age, in various occupations, compared with ALL MALES and MALES IN SELECTED HEALTH DISTRICTS. The Registrar General says "*The mortality of men who are directly concerned in the liquor trade is appalling*" and *that this terrible mortality is attributable to drink might be safely assumed a priori, but the figures in the table render it incontestable.*

I give that table in the form of a diagram. It will be seen that although some other occupations, such as painters, plumbers, &c., show a rate of mortality much above the average, that among brewers it is still greater; that the mortality among hotel keepers is 50 per cent. above the average, and that among bar-tenders and public house servants the death-rate rises far above double the average.

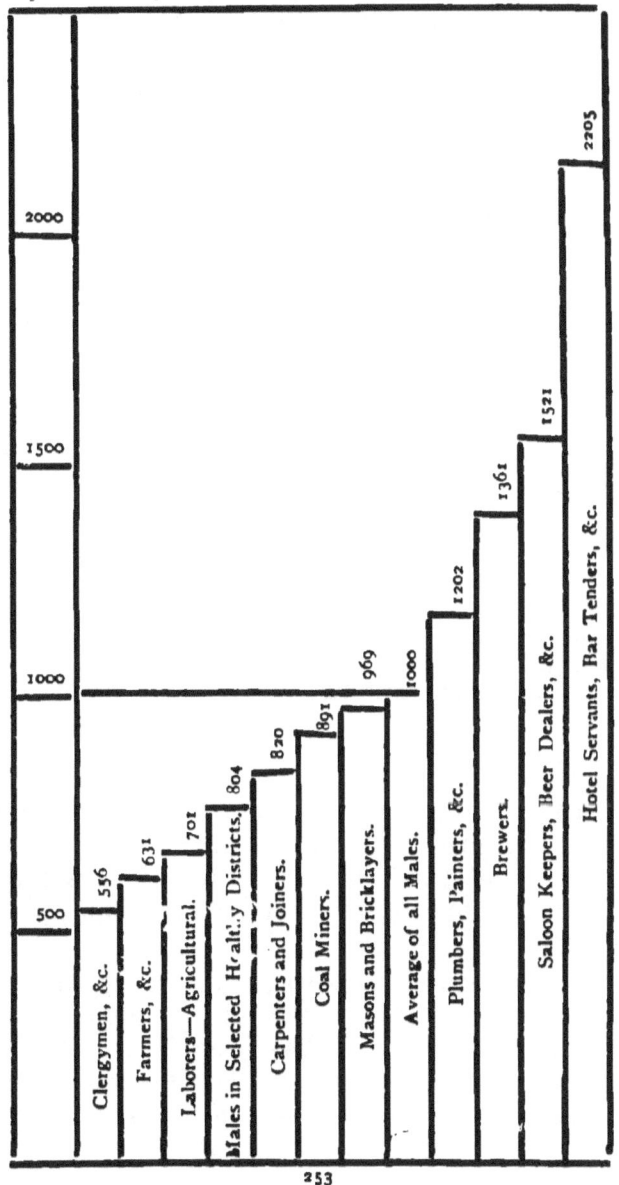

COMPARATIVE MORTALITY STATISTICS.
Compiled from the Report of the Registrar-General of England, 1880-1-2.

The *Canada Citizen* publishes the following remarkable statement of Rowland Burr, Esq., of Toronto, made before a Parliamentary Committee appointed to enquire into the subject of prohibition, as to his observations of the result of liquor-selling in a number of families. He stated that he had kept for fifty-four years a record of publicly-known evil results of intemperance in the families of one hundred liquor dealers who had resided on Yonge street, in and north of the city of Toronto, and his record made the following awful showing:—

Number of ruined drunkards in the one hundred families	214
Loss of property once owned in real estate	$234,800
Number of widows left	46
" orphans "	235
Sudden deaths	44
Suicides publicly known	13
Number of premature deaths by drunkenness	203
Murders	4
Executions	3
Number of years of human life lost by drunkenness	1,915

We have seen that the testimony of the various financial institutions which are based upon the risks of human life goes to show that more than one-third the sickness and nearly one-third the death-rate among selected insurable lives are attributed to the use of intoxicants.

The experience of medical men everywhere confirms the fact that the drinker of alcoholic liquor is more liable to disease and has less chance to recover than the abstainer. A youth who is weakly has a better chance of life *with total abstinence*, than one who is strong and robust who is the habit of taking intoxicants. Richard Cobden, writing to the late Joseph Livesey the Venerable English Pioneer of Teetotalism said :—

"I am a living tribute to the soundness of your principles. With a delicate frame and nervous temperament, I have been enabled to do the work of a strong man. . . . So you see that without beginning upon principles, I have been brought to your beverage solely by a nice observance of what is necessary to enable me to surmount an average mental labor of at least twelve hours a day." Again he says : "The moral force of the masses lies in the temperance movement, and I confess I have no faith in anything apart from that movement for the elevation of the working classes. We do not sufficiently estimate the amount of crime, vice, poverty, ignorance, and destitution which springs from the drinking habits of the people."

Sir Henry Thompson, M.D., F.R.S., with that clear perception of causes of human diseases which have made him so eminent as a Physician to the Royal Family, says :—

"I have long had the conviction that there is no greater cause of evil, moral and physical, in this country, than the use of alcoholic beverages. . . . I have no hesitation in attributing a very large proportion of some of the most painful maladies which come under my notice, as well as those which every medical man has to treat, to the ordinary and daily use of fermented drink taken in the quantity which is conventionally deemed moderate. . . . But if I venture one step further it would be to express a belief that there is no single habit in this country which so much tends to deteriorate the qualities of the race, and so much disqualifies it for endurance in that competition which in the nature of things must exist, and in which struggle the prize of superiority must fall to the best and to the strongest."

Sir. Andrew Clark, F.R.S., says :—

"As I looked at the Hospital wards to-day, and saw that seven out of ten owed their diseases to alcohol, I could but lament that the teaching about this question was not more direct, more decisive, more home-thrusting than ever it had been. . . . Can I say to you any words stronger than these of the terrible effects of the abuse of alcohol? It is when I myself think of all this that I am disposed, as I have said elsewhere, to rush to the opposite extreme, to give up my profession, to give up everything, and to go forth upon a holy crusade, preaching to all men—Beware of this enemy of the race."

Sir Wm. Gull, F.R.S., says:—

"I should say from my experience that alcohol is the most destructive agent that we are aware of in this country. . . . I would like to say that a very large number of people in society are dying day by day poisoned by alcohol, but not supposed to be poisoned by it."

Dr. B. W. Richardson, says:—

"I had learned purely by experimental observation that, in its actions on the living body, this chemical substance, alcohol, deranges the constitution of the blood; unduly excites the heart and respiration; paralyzes the minute blood-vessels; increases and decreases according to the degree of its application, the functions of the digestive organs, of the liver and of the kidneys; disturbs the regularity of nervous action; lowers the animal temperature, and lessens the muscular power. Such independently of any prejudice of party, or influence of sentiment, are the unanswerable teachings of the sternest of all evidences, the evidence of experiment, of natural fact revealed to man by experimental testing of natural phenomena. . . . It begins by destroying, it ends by destruction, and it implants organic changes which progress independently of its presence even in those who are not born."

I might go on to quote scores of medical opinions not less positive and definite than these, as to the waste of human life by drink. It would not be possible however to select four men whose eminence and weight of authority would be greater than those here quoted.

What then is the economic value of human life destroyed by alcoholic drinking. The most unquestionable testimony comes to us from financial institutions, and from medical authorities, that drink kills so many of our people that to put the numbers of the slain by drink, indirectly as well as directly, into figures, they would be so startling and stupendous that the public would receive them with incredulity and scepticism.

Yet here are the facts,—the science of the Insurance and Sick Benefit Ledgers declare that the *death-rate is about one-third less of total abstainers then of moderate drinkers and that the rate of sickness among moderate drinkers as against total abstainers is as 12 to 3, or four times greater;* while the weightiest medical authorities declare that *"men are dying day by day, poisoned by alcohol, but not supposed to be poisoned by it,* and that at the Hospital Wards *"seven out of ten owed their diseases to alcohol."*

In a little work by T. S. Brown, published in Montreal, I find the following :—

"In the old wars between England and France on this continent, while it cost each country £100 for every soldier sent out, the other side could kill him at the cost of a ball cartridge after he got here. The experiment of importing young men for the benefit of liquor-sellers might be measured by the same scale. Never in the history of the world was the value of men in a commercial sense so great as it is now. The wealth of a country is not in its houses and lands, but in its people and the strength of its people ; and the strength of the people is not in their numbers, but in their health and the number of hours of sustained labor that they can contribute for public good, which the use of alcohol sadly diminishes."

If the money value, to the nation, of lives thus wasted were put down it would far outweigh all the other statistics of our liquor bill, stupendous as they are. Think of the fact that instead of averaging as we do now about 33 years of life; but for drink the average would be increased one-third at least, or it might reach an average of 45 to 50 years.

This increased average of life would be principally added to the youth of our people. Numbers who now die young would live to a moderate old age and thus the power to produce, and the power to enjoy, would be increased beyond the dreams of the enthusiast.

"O madness! to think use of strongest wines
And strongest drinks our chief support of health,
When God, with these forbidden made choice to rear
His mighty champion, strong above compare,
Whose drink was only from the limpid brook."
—*Milton in "Samson Agonistes."*

CHAPTER XXVIII.

THE CHRISTIAN JUGGERNAUT.

CANON WILBERFORCE in that telling and eloquent little work entitled "The Trinity of Evil,"* after quoting the article from the London *Times* already referred to says:—

"Yes, drink is at the bottom of it. The fiendish epidemic prolific of suffering, suicide, murder, which is mocking every effort of every philanthropist for the well-being of the people is at the bottom of it. Utterly saddening and disgusting are the statistics of our national shame, which have been recapitulated a thousand times. Equally harassing are the details of desolate homes and broken hearts which come under the individual note of those materially engaged in the work of seeking and saving the wandering. The land is groaning under a heavy burden."

This is true of Great Britain and it is too true of Canada also. We may not too readily shelter ourselves under the plea that our liquor bill is only one half that of the United States, and less than one half that of the United Kingdom proportion to population. The dreadful fact remains that in Canada as elsewhere the one evil which overshadows every good is drink. And although our drink-bill is proportionately lower, the number of travellers or floating population to help us to consume it is proportionately less.

---

* A cheap edition of this work has been published by S. R. Briggs, Toronto, price 30 cents.

What drink is to Britain and the neighboring Republic it is to the Dominion of Canada, the one all absorbing evil, the removal of which would liberate us from the only enslavement, or enemy, we need to fear.

Archdeacon Farrar describing the effect of a speech in the British House of Commons by the Right Hon. W. E. Gladstone says:—

"I was present in the House of Commons on the fifth of March, 1880, and I saw a wave of emotion pass over the whole House upon that occasion. I saw all the members of Parliament almost visibly thrilled when he uttered those memorable words that 'the calamities inflicted upon mankind by the three great historical scourges of war, famine and pestilence were not so great, because not so continuous as those inflicted upon mankind by intemperance.'"

The human mind cannot conceive the enormity of an evil, of which so eminent an authority, without passion or prejudice, dare say it is greater than the combined evils of WAR, PESTILENCE AND FAMINE.

Were it possible to estimate the totality of these three great evils respectively, and to pile up the facts in three separate colnmns what mountains of wreck, and ruin and death would be presented to our gaze.

In another chapter I have shown that Mulhall estimates the loss of life by war during three-quarters of a century, from 1793 to 1877, amounted to 4,470,000. I will not attempt to describe what this means. What an amount of human suffering and indirect loss of life is involved. What deep, dark, overwhelming shadows have rested upon the hearts, and homes, and lives of millions more. Let the reader picture to himself three great, gaunt, grim, implacable foes to humanity spreading disease, want, misery, desolation, and death.

The first is the god of war who revels in blood, rapine, lust, outrage, violence, and ruin. Modern inventive genius has obeyed his behests and every kind of infernal machine is placed at his disposal for the purpose of human slaughter. On his breast are written in letters of blood :—FOOD FOR 100 YEARS—FIVE MILLION HUMAN SOULS.

Another bears in his right hand a two-edged scythe with which he marches unbidden into village, town and city—one by one—and, without distinction or favor, mows down men, women and children until his victims crowd the cemetery and fills the trenches, hurriedly made, whose numbers reach *ten times ten thousand souls*. His name is PESTILENCE.

A third flies on the wings of night and spreads blight, decay and death in fruit orchards and corn fields, turning the shout of "harvest home" into a wail of despair, of ruin, starvation and death. Men, women and children with skeleton forms succumb, and crowd the gates of the home of the dead. His name is FAMINE.

But there is a fourth, and by the authority of the chiefest of living statesmen he is declared greater then all the others combined. He is verily a demon incarnate. In the words of one who has endeavored to draw his picture he is thus described :—

"Could we get behind the veil that seperates the seen from the unseen, we might find that to the hidden powers these terrible pageants and dramas of life, whereof we are spectators, are things of awful consequence. I have fancied that in a vision I could see the evil that overshadows the land Embodied and Personate! A Demon Spirit—colossal—a monster truly, to make the whole world tremble! * * * Aloft upon his distended trunk behold the features, not of a smooth and laughing Bacchus, as poet and artist love to figure him, but of a brute foul aud fierce, presenting withal the features of a man. See the bloated, red and pimpled face, the pimpled cheeks, the huge swelled lips which, opening, show the cankered teeth and feverish foulness of his unhealthy mouth; matted in tough locks over the slanting forehead, red flaming hair, crowned, in mocking, with wreaths that have withered at the touch of his burning brow. See the blood-shot eyes, small and cunning, rolling with cruel ecstacy as he urges fast and furiously his fearful task.

His apparel is red with the blood of murder and crime, of rage and cruelty, of madness and sin. O look here, Christian and civilized Britons! look at these garments, red and gory, and tell me what the frightful motley means? Tunic and cloak of every fashion, velvet and ermine of King or Emperor, livery of menial, rags of beggar, chasuble of priest, geneva gown, satin and silk of noble dame, thin torn skirt of shivering milliner, gaudy petticoat of dancing columbine, peasants corderoy, and foppish coat of city clerk, the navvy's shirt and soldier's uniform—ay! and look well, ye may discern a judges gown, and not far off a gore-stained patch, the very dress wherein the criminal he condemned to death had done his sinful deed. Mark ye the great garment well for it is in itself a veritable calendar of Death! Where hath he not gathered? What hath he not won of life, of health, of power or feebleness, of fame or shame? What is there of all the varieties of life unrepresented here? It is the register of his labors, and each mark presents the fate of a human soul!

Behold him in his gaunt arms sweeping into the abyss of his lap multitudes of trembling creatures the materials of his work, for he is fashioning a chain. Draw nigh and examine it—long, living, endless it interweaves and enthrals society with a warp of death woven from out itself. His quick fingers—for the work is urgent and goes out on night and day—string together the writhing forms, and as coil upon coil rolls out, you may see again how vast is the scope of his labors! Ay! No rank is free, no family circle, no happy range of friendship. From his high seat the Demon scans the field, and, as his fingers swiftly fly, follows with greedy eyes the labors of his attendant imps. For below him, you may see them gathering in that strange spoil. In spired and pillard city, in smoky manufacturing town, in valleys resounding with the hum and clang of labor—labor blessed of God, cursed of this potent fiend!—'neath peaceful eaves of pastoral homes, amid woodbined hamlets, see those busy workers garnering in the Demon's prey. Oh! how much falls to their snares, of the best of the life and hope and promise of a goodly land! What ministers! Widespread as society, active as angels of grace, pernicious as Hell. And as they scour the world in reckless energy, for his rewards are right generous and rich, he, the Drink Demon, sweeps into his lap their shrinking spoil, and twists the living victims one by one into a great chain of life and death.

> King and courtier, priest and nun,
> Daughter, father, mother, son,
> Doctor, patient. judge and crier,
> Farmer, yokel, lord and squire.
> Weave them all in the Devil's chain,
> For ever and ever tight in the strain.
>
> Labor and sorrow, trust and truth,
> Vigor and weakness, age and youth,
> Beauty and ugliness, wealth and work,
> All the best and worst of earth.
> Poison it, kill it, kill it with drink
> Bnt bring it to me for another link.
>
> Jolly eve, ghastly morrow,
> Sorrows drowned to bring new sorrow,
> Bars thronged—prisons ciammed,
> Racy chorus—shriek of damned.
> > O drink, drink, drain, drain,
> > Another link for the Devil's chain. *

---

* The Devil's Chain. By Ed. Jenkins, author of Ginx's Baby, &c.

This picture shall suffice. The Evil is not only the greatest of the four but greater than all the others combined. Into the chain of intemperance are woven with frightful regularity and increasing industry. Every year 500,000 lives. † In ten years FIVE MILLION SOULS.

Truly War, Pestilence and Famine have each slain their thousands, but Drink, the Demon god of Christian lands, ever active by permission of state, and sanction of Christian electors slays his thousands every week. Think of five million human beings sacrificed every ten years. No ordinary mind can grasp it. Dr. J. Hudson Taylor in his wonderful book on *China's Spiritual Need and Claims* gives the following illustration of a million.

"If a railway train could go twelve hours without stopping to relieve the driver or to take water, and were to travel twelve hours at the uniform rate of thirty miles an hour it would make 360 miles a day. Seven years and a half of such travel, without a single days intermission would not accomplish *one* million miles."

Five millions—more than the entire population of Canada slain by drink every ten years. Not from heathen lands, or through the ignorance and superstition of heathen idolatry and cruelty, but from the christian homes of christian lands are the vast proportion of these victims sacrificed beneath the huge car-wheels of the licensed Juggernaut of christian lands.

---

† The estimated annual loss of life directly through intemperance in the United Kingdom is 60,000. In the United States at least 60,000 more. Then there is Canada, Australia, New Zealand, France, Germany, Switzerland, Spain, Russia, Italy, India, and even in China drink is now competing with opium in its work of death. If the total result of all the work of the drink Demon in the world be estimated it will not fall short of 500,000 human lives annually.

In an address by the Rev. D. T. Taylor on "*The increase of Crime*" delivered at Camp Hebron, Mass., Aug. 11, 1886, he quotes the returns of the U. S. Governmental census bureau on the increased use of intoxicating liquors and he says :—

This report says the total money expended for liquors in 1883 (in the United States) amounted to $900,000,000. Nine hundred millions for red-rum which spelled backwards reads *mur-der*. And murder it is. Besides the awful figures of evil the figures of good shrink into insignificance.

Nine hundred millions! Do we realize the vastness of the sum wasted yearly by our people. When Vanderbilt died he left, it is said, $200,000,000. But our liquor bill—useless and devilish—is more than four-fold greater in a single year than the wealth of the richest man on the Continent.

"In standard silver dollars, Vanderbilt's wealth would reach a heigth of 355 miles. Multiply this by four and a half and you have the dizzy heigth to which you must pile up the dollars of the liquor bill. The lofty column, a mad world's monument to crime, would stretch away from the earth into the sky 1,600 miles. It is a sin that 'reachec unto heaven.'"

Truly how insignificant are the mere figures of good compared with those of evil. The drink demon of Canada sweeps into his coffers $32,000,000 and involves us in a cost of 54 millions more, while Christian Canada subscribes $400,000 in support of Christian Missions.

Yet Drink is the God our nations worship. By the authority of the greatest governments of the world he opens his temples everywhere. Millions of men, women and children bow down daily before his altar, and there has not yet risen a statesman charged with the power and authority of a governing head who has dared to refuse license to the Demon god.

He has put into the treasury of nations, and of churches, a part of his vast revenue of blood, and Kings and Statesmen, Priests and Ministers of the Gospel of Jesus have been acquiescent. The greatest and best of living Statesmen of the present day, armed with power and political authority, backed by the parties which they lead triumphantly against other gigantic wrongs and selfish policies, stand still at the bidding of the rum power, and refuse to lead the moral forces which are demanding his extinction.

LOOK ON THIS, & ON THIS.

CANADA PAYS FOR	$
Intoxicating Liquors	32,678,633
Waste, Police, Gaols, Asylums, Penitentaries and other expenses involved by the Liquor Traffic	50,589,895
Canada's Liquor Bill	**83,268,528**

CANADA PAYS FOR	$
Support of Christian Churches	8,000,000
Maintenance of Schools	8,000,000
Christian Missions	400,000
Churches and Schools Account	**16,400,000**

Balance of Canada's contributions in favor of the Drink Institution as against the Church and the School, $66,868,528.

CHAPTER XXIX.

THE LICENSE SYSTEM IMMORAL AND DEGRADING.

"THE *struggle of the School, the Library and the Church all united, against the beer-house and the gin-palace, is but one development of the war between heaven and hell.*"

These words were written more than thirty years ago and appeared in an article entitled "How to Stop Drunkenness," published without signature in the North British Quarterly Review. It afterwards transpired that the author of the article was Chas. Buxton, M.P., well known as a coadjutor of Clarkson and Wilberforce in their philanthropic, and finally successful efforts to abolish British slavery.

Mr. Buxton was a Brewer and therefore not chargeable with any prejudice against the liquor interest. But with his philanthropic mind he could not fail to recognize in the traffic the most terrible weapon of warfare against every good and holy purpose, and against the material welfare of a nation. His article was a most instructive one. In it he advocated the adoption of the principle of prohibition by local veto, and I believe that this was the first time such a principle had been advocated in any influential quarter. It is the principle afterwards adopted by Sir Wilfrid Lawson, M.P., in his Permissive Bill for the United Kingdom and also in the Dunkin and Scott Acts for Canada. In his article, Mr. Buxton said :—

It would not be too much to say that if all drinking of fermented liquors could be done away, crime of every kind would fall to a fourth of its present amount, and the whole tone of moral feeling in the lower orders might be indefinitly raised. Not only does this vice produce all kinds of wanton mischief but it has a negative effect of great importance. *It is the mightiest of all forces that clog the progress of human good.*

It is in vain that every engine is set to work that philanthrophy can devise, when those whom we seek to benefit are habitually tampering with their faculties of reason and will—soaking their brains with beer, or inflaming them with ardent spirits. The struggle of the school, the library, and the church, all united against the beer-house and gin palace is but one development of the war between heaven and hell.

It is in short intoxication that fills our gaols—it is intoxication that fills our lunatic asylums, and it is intoxication that fills our workhouses with poor. Were it not for this one cause pauperism would be nearly extinguished in England. We are convinced that if a statesman who heartily wished to do the utmost possible good to his country, were thoughtfully to inquire which of the topics of the day deserved the most intense force of his attention, the true reply —the reply which would be exacted by full deliberation— would be, that he should study the means by which the worst of plagues can be stayed.

The intellectual, the moral, the religious welfare of our people, their national comforts, their domestic happiness, are all involved. The question is whether millions of our countrymen shall be helped to become happier and wiser— whether pauperism, lunacy, disease and crime shall be diminished, whether multitudes of men, women and children shall be aided to escape from utter ruin of body and soul?

And yet the saloon is established by law, and licensed to wage war against the church and school, the library, and the home. More than thirty years have passed away since Buxton, viewing the traffic as an interested party, nevertheless could not forbear to proclaim it the highest duty of the Statesman who " *heartily wished to do the utmost possible good to his country,*" to direct his energies against the liquor traffic as " *the mightiest of all forces that clog the progress of human good.*"

Thirty-eight years ago John Dougall said before the Select Committee of the Legislative Assembly at Montreal:—

"The traffic should be regarded as a wild beast, which, if we cannot altogether destroy, should limit and hamper as much as possible, but in no case license. All history shews that the further legislation has been carried out against the baneful traffic, the better it has been for the people, and the more it has been relaxed, the worse.

It is the special licensing of what is evil that I decidedly deprecate; were the traffic unlicensed, it would doubtless soon be viewed as a kind of social piracy, and the person engaged in it would be looked upon as an Ishmael whose hand was against every other man. But the obloquy which would attach to it, if left to itself, to be judged by its fruits, is in a great measure taken away by the sanction and respectability thrown around it, by a legal license to carry it on."—*Report of Select Committee, 1849.*

Mr. Dougall struck at the root of the system when he declared against license. No greater error in public policy could be committed than to license an evil with a view to its suppression. Nothing is surer than that if an evil be endowed with the authority and sanction of law it will take a firmer grasp of the social habits of the people. No wrong can ever be regulated by sanction or permission. Any attempt to do so gives strength and vitality to the interests vested in it.

All history proves the truth of this, not only in connection with the liquor traffic, but with every other form of evil, which has ever been licensed by any country. We need only cite for illustration, the gambling system and prostitution. When vice is made the creature of law, and contributes to the State-purse it rears its head, with the assumption of right. Then indeed the law educates downward. The public conscience is lowered by the action of the State.

In every country where any form of vice is regulated by license this is abundantly apparent. See what sad results have followed the legalization of the social evil in certain countries under the license system. In Paris, Brussels, Rheims, Bordeaux, Marseilles, Berlin, Hamburg, Vienna, Italy, Hong Kong, and other places, the public mind has been so demoralized that the rising generation are brought into contact with, and readily acquiesce in the theory that evil is a necessity, and a right. An attempt to introduce the system secretly into England was so far successful that an Act* was passed in 1864, with operation over a very limited area, which however was enlarged in 1866, and again in 1869. By that Act a practical permission was given to the social evil, and it was raised to the dignity of a recognized trade in eighteen towns and districts in England and Ireland, where military camps were located.

The result was, as might be expected, a general lowering of the standard of morals among both men and women; public opinion was shocked and aroused, and after a long but vigorous struggle, headed by the Right Hon. James Stansfeld, M. P., and Mrs. Josephine Butler, wife of a distinguished Church of England

---

* "The Contagious Diseases Act."

clergyman, the Act was repealed by the late Gladstonian Parliament, that being one of the very first acts of the new Parliament elected under the enlarged franchise.

Similar attempts have been made in some of our neighboring States, and Bills have been introduced in St. Louis, New York, Cincinnati and Pennsylvania, but the active efforts of the moral guardians of society, warned by the stealthy actions of the advocates of license in England, have prevented them from becoming law.

Prof. Sheldon Amos, an able writer, and Professor of Jurisprudence in University College, London, England, has written an exhaustive treatise on this subject. In that work he says:—

"It needs all the persistent teaching of good early discipline, good examples, good resolutions, good laws, and good personal conduct, to drive home the lesson that 'man shall not live by bread alone.' A thousand influences are hourly teaching the opposite lesson, and it is not without a steady struggle both in individual men and women, and in society at large, that the everlasting truth is kept uppermost. Among the influences which give force to doctrines, either of the degradation or of the depravity of man, none are more potent than those due to public opinion. This subtle agency of public opinion does not owe its power to the width, the representative character, nor still less to the inherent worth of the opinion itself. It owes its power rather to the nearness of the public concerned, and to the concentration of its movements. * * * It need hardly be pointed out that, whether in the language of law or of literature, all formal recognition of social vice as anything but an evil, determinedly to be combated at every point as a gross, temporary and unnatural excrescence on civilization, buoys up the interested public opinion, already pledged to countenance it, and affords to vice itself the most direct and unremitting stimulus.—*Laws for the Regulation of Vice, pp. 12 and 13.*

Exactly so! When law sanctions an evil its interested advocates claim legal protection for capital invested, and at once assume the air and tone of legitimate traders, whose rights are infringed by any attempts to check them.

So also with the public generally. The patrons of a licensed evil are, sometimes unconsciously, but certainly, influenced by the sanction which law gives to it. It is difficult to convict the individual citizen of doing wrong in the performance of an act for which the State makes provision. There is inconsistency, in fact, in every law against drunkenness, so long as the law provides for its indulgence and participates in the profits of the liquor which causes it.

Moreover the very presence of a legalized traffic is a continuous, subtle, education in favor of vice. To quote from Sheldon Amos again;—after referring to the educating influence of religion, of traditional customs, social intercourse &c., he says:—

"But no one of these influences is so omnipresent, so enduring, so persuasive, so directly authoritative, as the voice of the State uttered either in its laws or in its administrative acts. These laws and acts speak with a deliberateness of purpose and a magniloquence of style which, while they compel the attention of all, powerfully impress the imagination in a way no other, private or public, utterances can. Of course most people do not read or study the law until it is brought into close contact with them; but on this account there is all the more need that the part of the law which they do chance to study should fairly represent the spirit of the whole; and therefore that the whole law, each part of which will be studied by some should be unimpeachable and harmonious. If then it be true that it is upon the sublimity, the simplicity and the tenacity, of the moral sentiments of the people that the fortunes of the State depend, and that these sentiments are sound and pure according as the law is clear and stainless, how can a body of Law which formerly and openly recognises, protects, licenses, regulates, and facilitates prostitution, be exempt from the grave charge of weakening and confounding the moral sentiment of the whole people and so conducing to the worst national misfortunes. A struggle will no doubt for a time ensue, between the lessons of the legislator and the lessons of every moral and religious teacher in the land. But * * the lessons of the legislator will be constant and uniform, only gaining force by time and custom and will finally dominate over every rival."

This passage in Prof. Amos' able work puts the case exactly and is quite as applicable to an evil so prevelent and so ruinous as drunkenness. Of course it will be said that the law does not call upon any man to get drunk. And precisely the same could be said of every other licensed vice. It may be further argued that drinking of alcoholic liquors is not in itself a vice. This also is true of every other habit out of which vices grow. If it happened that the vice of drunkenness was only a rare or occasional circumstance, it might be pleaded that the state need not interfere;—but the entire license system is based upon the fact that drunkenness is a gigantic evil and therefore proceeds to regulate it. This is the case indeed with all evils to which the quack legislation of license is applied. The evil is acknowledged, the grosser forms of it are deplored, and in the desire to lessen or to hide its worst phases, legislators, social reformers, vicious men, and interested parties have all joined in a comfortable compromise to regulate the wrong by license and restriction. Such a compromise works ruin, and has never failed to do so. The history of every licensed or permitted evil is a series of most conspicious failures.

From the first license law of England in 1552 down to the present, every attempt to regulate the liquor traffic has proved a disastrous failure, although over 400 acts have been passed in the British Parliament, some very stringent, others more lenient;—some to encourage the sale of beer and light wines, &c., not one but has proved to be a signal blunder. The same is true of the United States and Canada. High license, and low license, and every form of license adopted by the different States have all alike failed.

I have used the word "failed" but strictly speaking these laws have not failed. Whatever may have been the intention of their promoters it is clear that the only logical result of such laws would be to perpetuate the drinking system by educating the people into drinking habits and giving importance, respectibility, and permanency to the traffic. In all these respects the license system has been a success, and with that success there has grown a demand on the part of the priveleged traders that the business which receives the sanction of the State has also a right to the protection of the State against all attempts to abolish it. Happily for the nations there is an unanswerable answer to this, viz: that what the State permits the State can prohibit.

But in the meantime the license system remains an ever present factor of evil in the land, at war with every agency for the advancement of the people.

The Hon. Edward Blake appears to have overlooked the powerful influence of the law as an educator. In his recent address on the question of prohibition says:[*]

---

[*] Speech at Aylmer, Ont., Dec. 7, 1886.

"Suppose one of us is walking along the street behind a neighbor, a friend, or a stranger, and see his pocket being picked. He would make himself a special police constable at once, would try to prevent the crime, and, if he was big enough, would arrest the criminal. But supposing, in a Scott Act county, we pass an unlicensed house—for they are all unlicensed, no license being granted—and see some one going in and getting drink; we turn to the other side; we say nothing about that; we do not propose to enforce the law; we do not give the same support, the same sympathy, the same active investigation in the case of this law as is given in the other case. Now if that be the condition of the more advanced localities, what is the condition in the other parts of Canada?

Mr. Blake's contrasting picture is a little overdrawn. The general feeling of private citizens is that the thief had better be left to the policeman, and very few people are ready to make special constables of themselves, while most people will even avoid the unpleasantness and sacrifice involved in attending court as witnesses, if they can.

But, admitting the difference to be as great as portrayed in Mr. Blake's illustration, does not the relation of law to the evils respectively fully explain it. For ages the law has put its uncompromising veto upon stealing as a crime, and at no time has there ever been a law permitting, sanctioning, regulating, licensing theft. Thus the law has been a schoolmaster, educating all classes to respect the rights of private property. The present quality and quantity of public respect for the laws against theft has not always existed. Time was when organized theft had it pretty much its own way, and when private citizens did not dare to make themselves special constables to arrest crime.

On the other hand the liquor traffic has existed for hundreds of years with the sanction of law, and it has acquired an assumption of right, and of dignity, by the State having entered into partnership with it, not only by agreeing to the terms of sale, but by participating in its profits. Even in Scott Act counties Mr. Blake's comparison is not admissable. The Scott Act is at best only a partial prohibitory law. It does not declare liquor selling a crime. It simply narrows the circle and conditions of sale. It takes effect only in counties or cities by local option, so that the public see closed bars in one municipality, and open bars in the next. That is good as far as it goes. It is putting a broom into the hands of the people by which they may sweep their own sidewalks. It affords opportunity to test the question whether prohibition, as against license, is acceptable to the people or not. From this point of view the Scott Act is clearly a success, for no law has ever received such manifest approval from the electors.

As an educator of public opinion the Scott Act has had but little opportunity. If the educative power of a license law which has existed for ages, and still exists in the larger half of the Dominion, be contrasted with that of the Scott Act, it must be admitted that the principle of prohibition which is recognized in that Act has proved a wonderful success, comparatively. The Act is new, its machinery not yet adjusted to usages, and it is at present subject to numerous contentions and legal quibbles. Magistrates, officials, and citizens who have the courage of their convictions are constantly threatened with lawsuits on technical points, and judges have reversed decisions and declared unconstitutional some of its most important provisions and clauses. Magistrates and inspectors have been officially advised not to prosecute while these points were pending. Government itself has been worse than negligent as to its enforcement. Ruffianism, outrage, arson, and dynamite have been employed to terrorize citizens, and at least one judge has expressed sympathy with the accused outlaws, and severely lectured the detectives for inducing the criminal to testify against himself. Against the laws relating to theft all the police of the country are armed and marshalled. Against the Scott Act it has been difficult to get officers charged with unqualified instructions to bring offenders to justice. The law of the whole Dominion has long and uniformly said to the thief, " thou shalt not ;" to the liquor seller it has said, " under certain conditions thou mayest."

Thus the permission of the state has encouraged, if not created, the cry of vested interests. Archdeacon Farrar referring to this evil says:—

"In the days of the slave trade some one said to an abolitionist, "What! would you stand between a man and his vested interests !" " I started," he said, "as if one had trampled on my grave, and exclaimed, 'A vested interest in a human being !'" " Let it be understood, once for all, that there can be no vested interests in that which is the source of a nation's ruin, and a nation's wrong. Other selfishness may be as intense, but none is so unblushing, because none is so much tolerated as the selfishness of monopolists claiming a vested interest in public infamy."

Dr. Albert Barnes the great commentator in the course of an eloquent sermon on "The Throne of Iniquity," says :—

"A law which asserts that a thing is wrong and yet tolerate it, which attempts only to check and regulate it, without utterly prohibiting it which aims to derive a revenue from it for the purpose of government ; which make that which is morally wrong *legal*, is one of those things in human affairs with which the throne of God can have no fellowship. * * The true object of legislation is to *prevent* not to *protect* evil. God never instituted a government on earth with a view to its throwing a protecting shield over vice and immorality. He has never commissioned men to sit in high places to accomplish any such work. The end of government, so far as it bears on that point at all, is to suppress crime, to punish wrong-doers, to remove iniquity, to promote that which is just and true. And it matters not what the evil is, how lucrative it may be made, nor how much capital may be invested in it, nor how much revenue may be derived from it, nor how many persons may have an interest in its continuance—the business of the lawgiver is to suppress it—not to protect it; to bring it to as speedy an end as possible—not to become the panderer to it, or the patron of it. What would be thought of a government that should, under any pretext whatever, take under its protecting care, thieves, counterfeiters, and burglars."

Mr. Gladstone has said that it is the "duty of the Government so to legislate as to make easy to do right and difficult to do wrong."

But the licensing system is exactly the reverse. Under a prohibitory law it is easy to do right and comparatively difficult to do wrong. A licensed saloon is *drunkenness made easy*—a legalized invitation to drink. A secret unlicensed drink-shop is drunkenness made difficult—the law dodged in order to get drink. Licensed drinking produces legalized drunkenness. He who gets drink in a licensed saloon does so with the *consent of law*, but he who is drunken under prohibition is so *in spite of law*.

The duty of the state is to remove its sanction from all evil:—and the duty of the state is the duty of the statesmen—the politician and the individual citizen.

To this duty every man and woman is called. Already the brave and true are numbered by tens of thousands. The promise of coming victory is given in every assault made upon the enemy. It is reported in every Scott Act campaign ; it is proclaimed aloud from the ballot box and the City Hall of our Queen City Toronto. If there are those who say that we advance too rapidly we reply that he who has fashioned us for moral progress and intellectual growth, He who has given us a mission for home and country has fixed the bounds of our progress. If we are told that we are yet too soon with a reform against the mightiest forces of human corruption, of sorrow and of death, we answer that in a warfare against such a demon it is treason in us to delay.

John Bright, the eloquent tribune of the people, when declaring against the Crimean war closed his speech with the following words :—" The angel of death has been abroad throughout the land ; you may almost hear the beating of his wings. There is no one, as when the firstborn were slain of old, to sprinkle with blood the lintel and the two sideposts of our doors, that he may spare and pass on. He takes his victims from the castle of the noble, the mansion of the wealthy, and the cottage of the poor and lowly, and it is on behalf of all these classes that I make this solemn appeal."

The angel of death is still abroad throughout the land. From mansion and from lowly cottage he takes his victims. Happily there are men and women, by the thousand, to sprinkle with blood the lintel—to warn and counsel those who are in danger, but this angel of death passes not, nor spares, though the lintel and sideposts of our doors are sprinkled. The fairest and brightest, the first and last born sons of men, the hope and promise of our land are stricken down. Yet hope springs up in the hearts of the millions that this demon of death may ere long be shorn of his power, and the nations be freed from his mighty instrumentality of evil.

This is our hope, the hope of the mothers of our boys, the hope of the fathers and the citizens, the hope of every true and holy purpose.

That "the struggle of the school, the library and the church all united against the beer-house and gin palace" shall speedily end in the final overthrow of the former—that there shall be "*a school-house on every hill-top and no saloon in the valley*"; that the home shall cease to have a legalized rival in the saloon is the hope, the prayer, and the aim of every true citizen.

Appendix

A.

CONTAINING TABLES SHOWING AN APPROXIMATE ESTIMATE OF THE ACCUMULATED WEALTH OF CANADA.

LAND INTERESTS AND BUILDINGS.

Acres of Land	Owned		67,645,162
"	"	Occupied	45,358,141
"	"	Improved	21,899,181
"	"	Under Crops	15,112,284
"	"	In Pasture	6,385,562
"	"	Gardens & Orchards	401,335
Number of Occupiers			464,025

It is probably a low estimate to suppose that these 464,025 occupiers will have an average interest in the land amounting to a sum of not less than $500 each especially if their stocks of Agricultural Implements and working plant be allowed. This would give a total—

Value in the Land Interest amounting to upwards of $230,000,000

APPENDIX. 283

	NUMBER	ESTIMATED AT
Town and Village lots	419,116	$ 40,000,000
Houses	712,440	400,000,000
Warehouses, Factories, Stores	110,170	90,000,000
Barns, Stables, etc.	860,985	80,000,000
		$840,000,000

RAILWAYS.

" Whether it be regarded as industrial, financial, commercial or speculative, there is probably no material interest which, in Canada and in the world at large, has developed so rapidly and reached such immense proportions as the railway interest. There are thousands of people in Canada whose memories carry them back to the time when the only means of land transit at their disposal, whether for freight or passengers, were the stage coach, the express wagon, or the private conveyance. Men still in their prime have witnessed the growth of railways in Canada, from the first small and humbly equipped line to the vast system of to-day, with their mileage in operation of 9,575 miles, their solid road-beds and steel rails, and the costly and luxurious provision for the comfort of the travelling public."--*Government Report 1884*.

The following table is compiled from the Government report for the year ending June 1885.

[Note 1]—The Total amount of Insurance risks taken by the various Insurance Companies against fire, amounted in 1885 to the sum of $511,774,402.

[Note 2]—The above table is estimated, so far as the quantity of property interests is concerned, upon the census return of 1881. Of course the extent and value of property has greatly increased since then.

Rolling Stock and Traffic.

Miles of Railway completed	10,773
" " under construction	812
Number of Engines owned	1,490
" Passenger Cars	1,202
" Baggage, Mail and Freight Cars	37,200
" Passengers carried during the year	9,672,599
" Tons of Freight carried during the year	14,659,271

Cost and Earnings.

Total Capital paid up	$454,082,509
Gov't Bonuses and Municipal Grants Paid	171,672,194
Gross Earnings during year	32,227,469
Net Earnings	8,212,118
Total cost of Railways and Rolling Stock	594,723,219

Allowing for depreciations by wear and tear, it may be fairly estimated that the Value of our Canadian Railways at the present time is not less than $500,000,000

CANALS.

The Canals of the country are so constructed as to form one connecting chain with the great lake and river service of the country thus making a continuous navigable river line of 2,384 miles in length. The actual income or earnings of the Canals is at present very small, amounting in the year 1885 to only $344,135. But this forms only a very small part of the real value of the Canals to the manufacturing, industries and merchandise of the Dominion. The total cost of these canals as reported in the Government Returns of of 1885 is $46,263,130

SHIPPING INTERESTS.
Compiled from Census Report of 1881.

Steam vessels owned	721	Average tonage	277
Sailing " "	3,909	" "	220
Barges owned	1,792	" "	54
Total	6,422	Estimated value	$25,000,000

APPENDIX

In 1885 the total number of vessels had increased to 7,315 with a tonnage of 1,231,856. This is estimated at an average of $30 per ton, making the present estimated value of the vessels of the Dominion $36,955,680. *Official Abstract and Record 1886.*

INDUSTRIES.

The capital invested in various industries in 1881 amounted to a grand total of $165,302,623.

We thus see that the total value of the accumulated property of Canada will not be less than $1,500,000,000 or about $330 to every man, woman and child in the Dominion. This estimate does not take into account the amount of money in Banks and in the hands of private individuals, in excess of liabilities, or the private property of individuals such as house machines, tools in the hands of workmen, furniture, musical instruments, carriages, horses, cattle, &c., which will be worth fully as much more.

PRODUCTION OF THE FOREST.

The Census Report of 1881 gives no estimate of the value of timber produce but only the quantities for the year as follows:—

```
Pine..................................43,544,802
Oak...................................  5,670,894
Tamarac...............................  5,653,575
Birch and Maple.......................  4,414,795
Elm...................................  3,191,968
Walnut................................     13,224
Other timber..........................48,956,958
Pine and other logs...................48,349,991
Masts, Spars, &c......................    192,241
Thousands of staves...................     41,801
Cords of Lathwood.....................     98,311
    "    Tan Bark.....................    400,418
    "    Fire Wood....................10,993,234
```

APPENDIX.

Some estimate may be formed of the value of this timber produce on the following basis :—

The Export Returns for 1885 gives the value of our exports of timber at $22,373,305. In a valuable little work by H. B. Small there is a carefully prepared table compiled from the Census Returns of 1881 giving the details of 34 Industries which depend wholly or in part upon wood, or timber, for manufacture. The table shows that there were 17,557 factories employing 95,741 hands and producing a total value of $95,029,828.

The Trade and Navigation Returns show that less than two million dollars of our wood export is for manufactured articles, so that the amount of "wood manufactured" (less two million dollars) may be fairly credited to the value of our forest production. In addition to this the whole of the fire-wood is consumed at home, which if valued (first cost) at $2.00 per cord is worth about $22,000,000.

The total value of our lumber produce must therefore be at least $130,000,000.

ANIMALS AND ANNUAL PRODUCE.

The census returns of 1881 gives the number of animals and their produce for the year, but gives no statement of their value. The quantities were as follows :—

Horses, Colts and Fillies	1,059,358
Horned Cattle	3,514,989
Sheep	3,048,678
Swine	1,207,619
Cattle killed or sold	657,681
Sheep " " "	1,496,465
Swine " " "	1,302,503
Pounds of Honey	1,875,745
" " Wool	11,300,736

APPENDIX.

The following is a statement of our exports for the year ending 30th June 1885.

TABLE OF EXPORTS IN 1885.

Minerals	$3,836,470
Fisheries	7,976,313
Forests	22,373,305
Agriculture	19,120,366
Animals	26,503,994
Manufactures	3,794,224
Miscellaneous	658,487
Total	$84,263,164

Trade and Nav. Report 1885 p. 728.

VALUE OF INDUSTRIES 1881.

Wages paid during year	$59,429,002
Value produced	$309,676,068

VALUE OF FISHERIES.

"The Department of Fisheries" has issued a Report showing the value of the produce of the Fisheries of the Dominion in the year 1885.

Nova Scotia	$8,283,922
New Brunswick	4,005,431
Quebec	1,719,459
Prince Edward Island	1,293,429
British Columbia	1,078,038
Ontario	1,342,691
Total	$17,722,973

B

TESTIMONY OF EMINENT AUTHORITIES ON THE RELATION OF DRINK AND CRIME.

TESTIMONY OF BRITISH JUDGES.

Sir Matthew Hale, the venerated Chief Justice of England in 1670, said :—

"The places of judicature which I have long held in this Kingdom have given me an opportunity to observe *the original cause* of most of the enormities that have been committed for the space of twenty years; and by due observation, I have found that if the murders and manslaughters, the burglaries and robberies, the tumults, the adulteries, fornications, rapes, and other enormities that have happened in that time, were divided into *five* parts, *four of them* have been issues and product of excessive drinking, *of tavern and ale house drinking.*"

Judge Coleridge, at the Yorkshire Assizes in 1848, remarked :—

"Liquor has either been the temptation beforehand to robbery, to get something to purchase it, or it is the provocation under the influence of liquor that causes them to quarrel and perhaps commit murder; or it is the liquor upon which the fruits that have been obtained by robbery is generally spent; and it seems to me that but for the cases where offences have been brought on by the use intoxicating liquors *the courts of justice might be shut up.*"

Dr. Warren in his charge to the Grand Jury at Hull, Yorkshire, England, said :—

"To the best of my belief, no temperance man ever stood at that bar to receive judgment from this seat in my time at least, while seven out of every ten criminals who have done so, have been brought there by intoxicating liquor. I have talked with many of them afterwards in prison and they have owned it with tears of agony."

Judge Wightman at the Crown Court, Liverpool, in 1846, said:—

"Of ninety-two prisoners whose names were on the calendar, six were charged with wilful murder, twelve with manslaughter, thirteen with malicious injury to the person, sixteen with burglary, and eight with highway robbery, accompanied with violence to the person. He found from the perusal of the depositions one unfailing cause of four-fifths of these crimes was, as it was in every other calendar, the besetting sin of drunkenness. In almost all cases of personal violence and injury, the scene was a public house or a beer shop."

Baron Alderson at the York Assizes, 1844, made the following observations :—

"A great proportion of the crime to be brought forward, arose from the vice of drunkenness alone. If they took away from the calendar all those cases in which drunkenness had some connection either with the person accused or the accusing party it would leave that large calendar a very small one. If all the men could be persuaded from the use of intoxicating liquor, the office of judge would be a sinecure."

Mr. Justice Hayes at the Manchester Assizes, 1869, remarked :—

"When people come to inquire into the causes of crime, with a view to ascertain how crime might be diminished, the fact presented itself at these assizes, as he had remarked at the last winter assizes at Liverpool, when he had to dispose of five murders and eight manslaughters, it would be proved that they were chiefly attributable to drinking and drunkenness, and to nothing else. Crime was the immediate and direct effect of that besetting evil and bad habit."

On March 13th, 1854, Mr. Justice Talfourd while addressing the Grand Jury at Stafford Court House, suddenly expired. His last words were :—

No doubt the *exciting cause* in the far larger number of these cases, the exciting cause that every judge has to deplore in every county in the land—is that which was justly called in the admirable discourse to which I listened yesterday, from the Sherriff's chaplain. *The greatest English vice*, which makes us a by-word and a reproach among nations, who in other respects are inferior to us, and have not the same noble principles of Christianity to guide and direct them—I mean the vice of drunkenness. No doubt that this in most of these cases is the immediate cause, and it is a cause in two ways of the crimes which will come before you, and especially of the crime of highway robbery; for whereas, on the one-hand, *it stirs up evil, awakens malice, and kindles the slumbering passions of the human heart, and puts the reason into a state of twilight*, so, on the other hand, it points out the victim, as the person to be robbed by presenting temptations to those who see him exposing his money in public-house after public house, or in a state of drunkenness finds himself a sharer in a sin from which domestic ties should keep him, and is overtaken by his partner in that sin, who adds to it another crime, or he is marked out by some of his wicked associates. One great evil of this circumstance is, I think you will find, looking at the depositions one after the other, that is *a mere repitition of the same story over again—of some man who has gone from public-house to public-house spending his money*, and exhibiting his money, and is marked out by those who observe him as a fitting object for plunder, when his senses are obscured, and who is made the subject of an attack under those circumstances which enables the parties to escape from the consequences; because although the story may be perfectly true which the prosecuter in this case tells, although it may be vividly felt by him, yet he is obliged to confess."—

Here the learned judge suddenly ceased speaking, and in a few minutes the melancholy fact became painfully manifest that those who had heard him had been listening to HIS LAST WORDS.

Mr. Justice Deasy, at the Armagh assizes, 1871 observed:

"Drunkenness is the parent of all the crimes committed in Ireland."

The late Sir W. Bovill, at the Denbigh assizes, August 1872, made the following statement :—

"Drunkenness, according to my experience, is at the root of nine-tenths of the crime committed in this country."

Mr. Baron Martin, at the Liverpool assizes, 1886, remarked :—

"Drunkenness seems to be the cause of nine-tenths of the crime committed in this country."

Mr. Justice Hannen, in his charge to the jury at Liverpool, 1869, said :—

"I should suppose the testimony of every judge upon the bench would be the same as to the fact that a very large proportion of the crimes of violence brought before us are traceable either directly or indirectly to the intemperate use of intoxicating liquors."

Mr. Justice Keating, at the Norwich assizes, August 1874, bore the following testimony :—

"After a long experience, I can state that nineteen-twentieths of the acts of violence committed throughout England originated in the public-house."

"Drunkenness again! It's almost the case with every one that is brought before me."

APPENDIX.

AMERICAN TESTIMONY.

Chief Justice Noah Davis, of New York, writes: "Of all the causes of crime, intemperance stands out the unapproachable chief."

Dr. Elisha Harris, of New York, says:—

"After two years of careful inquiry into the history and condition of the criminal population of the State, I find that the conclusion is inevitable that, taken in all its relations, alcoholic drinks may be justly charged with far more than half the crimes that are brought to conviction in the State of New York, and that fully 85 per cent. of all convicts give evidence of having, in some larger degree, been prepared or enticed to the criminal acts, because of the physical and distracting effects produced upon the human organism by alcohol, and as they indulged in the use of alcoholic drinks."

The Board of Police Justices of the city of New York, in their report of 1874, says:—

"We are fully satisfied that intoxication is the one great leading cause which renders the existence of our police courts necessary."

Governor Dix, of New York, says:—

"Intemperance is the undoubted cause of four-fifths of all the crime, pauperism, and domestic misery of the State of New York."

Judge Allison, in a speech delivered in Philadelphia in 1872, says:—

"In our criminal courts we can trace four-fifths of the crimes that are committed to the influence of rum. There is not one case in twenty where a man is tried for his life in which rum is not the direct or indirect cause of the murder."

OPINIONS AND TESTIMONY OF EMINENT MEN.

Lord Shaftesbury :—

"Is there any one in the least degree conversant with the state of our alleys, dwellings, and various localities who will deny this great undeniable truth, which all experience confirms ; for if you go into these frightful places you will see there the causes of moral mischief, and I do verily believe that seven-tenths of it are attributable to that which is the greatest curse of the country—that which destroys their physical and moral existence, cut through their domestic ties, and reduces them to pauperism with all its various degradations—habits of drinking, and systems of intoxication."

Lord Brougham :—

"Of Intemperance, the baneful effects need not be dwelt upon in detail. It is the smallest part of the evil that at the very least ten times as much money is spent upon drink as upon publications of all kinds, newspapers included. The learned and enlightened Recorder of Birmingham makes this abundantly evident in his valuable charges to the Grand Jury. But the far worse effects of this propensity is producing disease, both of body and mind, and in filling our jails with criminals and our workhouses with paupers, are so dreadful as loudly to call for the application of repressive measures. The connection of intoxication and of drunken habits with crime is demonstrated in the the clearest manner. "Every one acquainted with criminal courts," says Mr. Hill, "must admit the truth of what our judges state day by day, and year after year, that by far the greater number of all offences have the origin in the love of drink." In the United States, we find a judge of Maine, the strenuous adversary of absolute prohibition, yet urging the necessity of restrictions upon the sale of liquors. He declares that nine-tenths of all crimes attended with violence arise from intoxication. In another State, Rhode Island, sixty per cent. of all offences appear to be caused by drunkenness, and 10 per cent. of insane persons is the proportion of those whose malady had this origin.

Cardinal McCabe, Dublin :—

" Intemperance is the source of nearly all our crimes and misfortunes. Thousands of permature graves tell of its ravages. Our work-houses are thronged with its victims. Its baleful tyranny is cramming our jails with criminals. The deep wail of woe, the moan of despair that burst continually from wretched homes tell of misery through the land, which God alone can measure."

Right Hon. John Bright :—

"If we could subtract from the ignorance, the poverty, the suffering, the sickness, and the crime which are now witnessed amongst us—the ignorance, the poverty, the suffering, the sickness, and the crime which are caused by one single but the most prevalent habit or vice of drinking needlessly, which destroys the body and mind and home and family—do we not all feel that this country would be so changed, and changed for the better, that it would be almost impossible for us to know it again?"

Bishop Ireland at the Catholic Church, St. Paul, Minnesota, on August 2nd, 1882, said :—

" Is the liquor traffic to be allowed to rule as sovereign over our fair country, and to deluge it with drunkenness and vice? This is the question upon which citizens of America ought seriously to ponder. I know well the value of moral suasion, of teaching by individual example and individual exhortation, in our battlings with intemperance. But it becomes plain that citizenship enjoins upon us other duties in the premises. The State must interpose its authority to arrest the evil. The State alone has power: the enemy is organized, determined: individual efforts are as pebbles thrown against a well-fortified citadel. The traffic conscious of the power of the State has striven to wrest it to its own ends, and the State must hurry to free itself from its evil-working captor. It is a matter bearing upon its own life: the liquor traffic threatens destruction to our republican institutions, and even now it has in many places made manhood suffrage a meaningless word. The State cannot be silent and passive while this traffic fills its jails and poorhouses, increases ten-fold its tax-list, robs its subjects of virtue, honor and life. THE SALOONS WILL RAISE THE CRY OF PERSONAL LIBERTY, OF PERSONAL RIGHTS; THE STATE MUST NOT BE FRIGHTENED BY VAIN WORDS FROM THE CLEAR, IMPERATIVE PATH OF DUTY. THERE IS NO RIGHT, NO LIBERTY FOR MEN TO PREY UPON THE BODIES AND SOULS OF THEIR FELLOW-MEN AND NOT TO LEVEL BLOWS AT THE VERY PILLARS OF SOCIETY. The claims of the traffic in the name of personal liberty, and of personal rights is the bitterest irony, a deadly insult to true liberty, and to the true rights of men. THE LIBERTY WHICH THE TRAFFIC DEMANDS IS THE LIBERTY TO ENSLAVE US, AND TO DIP OUT TO US ITS BEER AND WHISKEY IN EXCHANGE FOR OUR LIBERTY, OUR POSSESSIONS, OUR MANHOOD, OUR PURITY, OUR ETERNAL HOPES. AWAY FROM US THIS DEMON-LIKE LIBERTY!"

ARCHDEACON FARRAR in his sermon on the Nations Curse, which has been reprinted and published by the Citizen Publishing Company, Toronto, says:—

"Will anyone venture to say, for there is no end to the subterfuge of minds brazened by custom, that these are mere opinions? Well, if you want, not opinion, but hard, glaring, patent facts, untinged with any opinion whatever—facts black, rugged, comfortless, and horrible—facts in all their ghastly nakedness, denuded of all vesture of human thought and of human emotion in narrating them—it will be the most flagrant hypocrisy to say that such facts are not forthcoming for you, when every day and every newspaper teems with them. No one single day passes over one single town in England, without some wretchedness, crime, and horror, caused by drink. Week by week, in the *Alliance News*, is published a ghastly list, called "Fruits of the Traffic." It is not invented; it is not concocted; it is not garbled. It consists simply of cuttings from multitudes of perfectly neutral newspapers, the records of police courts and sessions. I cannot enter into these. The human hand can perpetrate, the human heart can conceive, the human frame can suffer, horrors of which the human lip refuses to speak. Take the evidence of two weeks alone; the blessed week in which we listen to the melody of angel songs, and the first week of the glad New year. For twopence you may purchase the record of events which drink caused for these two weeks in 1882, for England only. It fills a large double-columned pamphlet of thirty-six pages. Thirty-six pages of what—in this our Christian England, in Christmas week? Thirty-six pages of stabbing, cutting, wounding; of brutal assaults on men, on women, on children; of public peril and accident; of deaths, sudden, violent, preventible; of homicide; of parricide; of matricide; of infantcide; of suicide: of every form of murder. In four hours on one evening in one city 36,803 women were seen going into public-houses. The results formed a tragedy so squalid, and so deadly, as to sicken the heart like the impression of a nightmare, whose very memory we loathe. Read that hideous list and then prattle, and lisp, and sneer about exaggeration; read that list, and then, if any man can still quote Scripture for the purpose of checking temperance reformers, or of encouraging our immense capacities for delay and indifference, I can only say for such a man, that

> Though in the sacred place he stands
> Uplifting consecrated hands,
> Unworthy are his lips to tell
> Of Jesus martyr-miracle;
> The miracle of life and death,
> Thou holy one of Nazereth!"

LORD MORPETH, when Secretary for Ireland, gave the following statistics in a speech on the condition of Ireland, delivered after a public dinner in Dublin. Of cases of murder, assault with attempt to murder, outrageous offences against the person, aggravated assault, cutting and maiming there were in:—

1837............................12,096
1838......... 11,058
1839.............................1,097
1840............................. 173

It further appears that the number of persons charged with murder within the police boundaries of Dublin was in

1838................................14
1839................................ 4
1840................................ 2
1841................................ 1

The consumption of spirits for the year 1840 (ending 5th January, 1841) had fallen, in round numbers, to 7,000,000 gallons; whereas, in 1838, it was 12,000,000 gallons. Hence the falling of in the calendar.

C.

HOW DRINKS ARE DOCTORED.

The well known publishing house of David C. Cook, of Chicago, publishes a little book entitled "Drink from Drugs," by Eli Johnson. Mr. Johnson's character is guaranteed by the endorsement of such men as the Rev. Dr. Theodore Cuyler; Rev. P. Striker, Pastor of First Presbyterian Church, Saratoga; Dr. Hamilton, Principal Physician of Hamilton Medical Institute, N. Y.; Ex-President Hayes, Ex-Governor St. John. He gives particulars of a number of "trade circulars" and books together with the names of their publishers and price of the books designed for the use of spirit dealers and bar tenders. He says: "In London,

(England,)I went out shopping one day, and called upon seven druggists. In each place I inquired for the oil of cognac. Three of them said they had never heard of such a thing. Three others said, "You will find it with the wine and spirit merchants." The seventh one said he did not keep it, nor did he know anything about it. After conversing for some time, he turned to a drawer, and taking from it a small bottle, said to me, "That is port wine oil. I have been analyzing it; but there is one ingredient in it that I can't make out. If I could make out that one ingredient I could realize a fortune in a little while manufacturing that oil for the trade of London." After conversing quite freely upon the subject, and giving me all the information he was able to impart, he said to me, "Are you engaged in the liquor traffic?" "No," I replied; "I am engaged in the temperance cause." This closed our conversation, and I bade him good-day.

Following up my investigations, I next called upon a chemist in Finsbury Pavement, whom I knew. Having with me a bottle of the oil of cognac, I showed it to him and asked him if he could tell me where I could purchase that article. Taking the bottle in his hand, reading the label and holding it up between him and the light, he said, "I have heard of that thing many times; but this is the first time I have ever seen it. Yes, I think I can tell you. There is a namesake of mine over here in Norton Folgate, engaged in the same business that I am; some time ago, one of his letters fell into my hands, and I supposing that it was designed for me, opened it. It proved to be from a publican out in the country, who said : ' Please send me liquid enough to make thirty-six gallons of gin.' Now, sir, if you will call on Mr. Jones, I think you will find the article on sale."

Entering the store of Mr. Jones, in Norton Folgate, and inquiring if he kept oil of cognac, he replied in the affirmative. "What will you charge me for an ounce?" "Six shillings," was his reply. "O," I said, "I can buy it in America for four shillings. Do you keep gin oil?", "Yes, sir." "What will you charge me for an ounce of that?" "I would not sell you an ounce; but I would sell you a pint for eight shillings, and with the pint you could make one hundred gallons of gin." "Do you keep port wine oil?" "No sir; but I can tell you where you can purchase all you like." "Do you sell many of these materials for making liquors?" "O, yes," said he. "We sell great quantities of them." "How do you manage that? I thought your laws prohibited the use of all such things?" "O, no, sir. The law prohibits the use of anything that is injurious; but these are not injurious; they are entirely harmless." Then I said, "If that be the case, please let me have two bottles, and put them up good and strong, so that I can take them back to America."

For the oil of cognac I paid him six shillings; for the essence of rum, two shillings. With the former I can make twenty gallons of French brandy; with the latter I can make twenty gallons of Jamaica rum.

My next discovery was a firm which I was told dealt exclusively in materials for publicans. I called upon them and obtained their business card." Mr. Johnson gives a *fac-simile* of the card.

Mr. Johnson, among numerous other facts of a similar character discovered in London, says: "In the Licensed Victuallers year book for the year 1875 there appears an advertisement of the "Escortt Hop Essence Company," in which they say:—"Having secured the services of Mr. Escortt, who is the authorized city analyst for the city of Manchester, publicans using this Hop Essence may always be assured of having their liquors pronounced pure." This advertisement created so much furor in England that the books containing it soon disappeared; and it was said that they were bought up and destroyed. The copy that I saw was in the hands of a temperance man.

Purchasing a book of Mr. Loftus 146 Oxford Street London, entitled, *Loftus New mixing and Reducing book for the use of Publicans and Spirit Dealers.* Mr. Johnson says:—

When I had paid for the books, and had them in my hand, I said to Mr. Loftus: "Now please put up some of those essences of yours in small bottles. "Why," said he, "we never sell them, but I'll give you the address of the gentleman of whom I purchase them, and you can go there and obtain them just as cheaply as I do." He then wrote out the name on a piece of paper, "Bush & Co., 30 Bishopgate Street." Now I said, "please write your own name under that, and then I shall be sure of getting them." Picking up his business card, he said, "There, take that, and you will get all you want."

Going up to 30 Bishopgate Street, I found a building five stories in height; but when I entered it I found myself in a little room five by ten feet square, partitioned off from the remainder of the building, with a small hole in the partition, through which I could speak to the people on the other side. I presented the card with the address, and said, "I should like a few samples of your essences for flavoring liquors, put up in ounce bottles. "Well, what will you have?"—handing me their circular, with names and prices of a large number of essences, etc. I began calling off what I wanted, and he wrote it down. When I had finished, he said, "please take a seat, sir, and we shall have them ready for you in a few minutes." After sitting about fifteen minutes, he handed me out seven ounce bottles, each of which was sufficient to make six gallons of the liquor represented by the labels attached, and for each of which I paid him one shilling. So that for seven shillings—$1.75—I obtained the drugs for making forty-two gallons of assorted liquors.

If we are to believe the statements of several books published for the use of brewers, there are used in the manufacture of the different malt beverages, alum, copperas, tobacco, *cocculus Indicus*, capsicum, opium, henbane, salt of tartar, aloes, ginger, slacked lime, quassia, sweet-scented flag, wormwood, hoarhound, bitter oranges, salt, molasses, sulphate of iron, gentian, strychnine, alum, coriander, paradise seed, sulphuric acid, jalap, ammonia, maranta, etc.

In a book published in London, called "Brewing Malt Liquors," many of the articles already named are recommended for brewing malt liquors, and for improving them after they are brewed.

The liquors are not only drugged by the manufacturers, but they are in many instances again doctored by the retail dealers."

From a book entitled the "French Wine and Liquor manufacture" by John Rack, Practical Wine and Liquor manufacturer and for which Mr. Johnson paid Stone & Co. of Denver, Colerado the sum of $2.50, he gives the names of 40 articles of poison recommended in the 27 recipes which the book contains for making brandy. He says:—

"This book is a translation from the French, and reveals to us the deception practiced by the French in preparing liquors for foreign trade. In the introductory the author says:—"The manufacture of fictitious liquor is, and will continue to be, practised. Large quantities of corn whiskey are annually exported from this country to France, from whence it returns as French brandy, and so close is the imitation as to deceive the best judges."

Mr. Johnson's collection of facts on this subject are very extensive.

From a book called the "Bordeaux Wine and Liquor Dealers Guide" he quotes the remarks in the preface as follows:—

"It is well known to the trade, and generally supposed by those not engaged in the sale of liquors, that adulteration is carried on to a very great extent in the United States as well as in England. In France also—the source of more than three-fourths of the liquors imported to this country—it is conducted on a large scale.

"Were all liquors imported pure, and sold in the same state, the quantity sold would be a mere item compared with the amount now drank in this country. Indeed, France and the continental countries of Europe do not produce a sufficient quantity, if the entire products of their vineyards were exported, to supply the natural trade of New York City alone. So great is the demand for exportation beyond the supply, that the French are compelled to resort to imitations to supply the deficiency, and to such perfection has the system been brought, that by no test, chemical or otherwise, can these imitations be detected.

"The city of New York alone sells three times as many 'pure imported brandies,' and four times as many 'pure imported wines' annually as all the wine-producing countries export."

Upon these statements Mr. Johnson remarks:—

"NOW WILL MY READER PLEASE REMEMBER THAT THE FOREGOING STATEMENTS ARE PUBLISHED BY A LIQUOR DEALER, IN A LIQUOR DEALER'S BOOK, WRITTEN FOR THE LIQUOR DEALERS, AND THAT THEY ARE NOT THE STATEMENTS OF A TEMPERANCE FANATIC."

The following is taken from a letter published by the New York *Tribune*, and written by "An Occasional Correspondent":

"COGNAC, FRANCE, NOV. 27, 1879.

"This is Thanksgiving Day away off in the States, a festival of which these dwellers in the Charente probably never heard. If you were to ask them this year to assemble and thank God for the harvest and the fatness of the land, they would look incredulous, shake their heads and walk off whistling. For now that the vintage season of 1879 is over, there is no longer room for doubting what had before been almost a certainty—that their years brandy crop amounts to practically nothing; in short, that in Cognac annals the year 1879 may be regarded as a failure of the grape crop.

A severe frost came at the last moment and snapped up what few grapes had managed to survive the phylloxera and the rains.

"But strange to say, 'Old Cognac' is found to be just as plentiful as ever. That is, there is no end of casks and cases so labelled, and filled with a liquid which in taste and appearance so resembles the distilled juice of the grape as to defy all ordinary means of detection. Some months ago a French newspaper correspondent, writing from Bordeaux, to the *New Era*, of Cognac, made the startling assertion that enormous quantities of spurious brandy known as '*trois-six*'—a distillation from grain, beet-root, potatoes, or other substances—were arriving there from Germany, were put into brandy casks which had been sent back empty from London, and were then shipped to foreign countries, notably to England and Spain, as pure Cognac brandy·"

Numerous other books are quoted by Mr. Johnson such as "Hints to Liquor Merchants by Wm. Rudkins Sons' practical chemists" New York. "The Secret Process of manufacturing Whiskey, Brandy, Rum, Gin, Bitters, Wine, Champagne" etc., etc., published by John D. Hounihan, Buffalo N.Y., and others. He says: "In Canada I found the drugs on sale with the books and recipes for making the drink. I have one bottle that I purchased in Hamilton. * * "Mr. Griffin, of Canada, told me that at one time he purchased, of a druggist, a lot of wine for communion. A part of it was consumed, and the remainder set aside in the decanter for future use. On going to the cupboard to get the wine for the next communion service, he found what appeared to him to be an empty decanter; but, upon further examination, the liquid appeared clear as water, while the drugs had all settled to the bottom."

This testimony so amply given by Mr. Johnson could be strengthened by many others. Mr. Axel Gustafson in chapter 4 of "*The Foundation of Death*" gives some striking facts on this subject. He quotes from a leading article in the London *Times* Dec. 10th, 1873 as follows :—

"The correspondence which we have lately published on the manufacture of the liquid sold in this country under the name of "Sherry" seems calculated to shake even the robust faith of the British householder in the merits of his favorite beverage. The correspondence had its origin in the fate of a gentleman who was found by the verdict of a coroner's jury to have died from an overdose of alcohol taken in four gills of sherry: and as it proceeded it gradually unfolded some of the mysteries of the processes by which the product called sherry is obtained. In the first place, it seems that grapes before being trodden and pressed are dusted over with a large quantity of plaster of paris, (sulphate of lime), an addition which removes the tartaric and malic acids from the juice, and leaves sulphuric acid in their stead, so that 'must' contain none of the bitartrate of potash which is the natural salt of wine, but sulphate of potash instead usually in the proportion of two ounces to a gallon. Besides this the common varieties of 'must' receive an additional pound of sulphuric acid to each butt, by being impregnated with the fumes of five ounces of sulphur. When fermentation is complete the wine may contain from a minimum of about 14 to a maximum of 27.5 per cent of proof spirit * * and it receives an addition of sufficient brandy to raise the alcoholic strength of the mixture to 35 per cent as a minimum, or in some cases to as much as 59 per cent of proof spirit. When all this is done it is shipped in the wood for England where it is either bottled as 'pure' wine or is subjected to such further sophistications as the ingenuity of dealers may suggest."

Mr. Gustafson also cites the following advertisement from a prominent London journal Sept. 29th, 1886:

"*Partner Wanted.—A practical distiller having been experimenting for the last seventeen years, can now produce a fair port and sherry by fermentation without* a drop of grape juice, and wishes a party with from £2,000 to £3,000 capital to establish a house in Hambnrg for the manufacture of his wines. Has already a good connection in business."

Col. Dudley, of Boston, says in his work on "*Alcohol and its physical effect*":

"With few exceptions the entire liquor traffic is not only a fraud, but—perhaps without all dealers being aware of the fact—it amounts to a system of drugging and poisoning. The business of making adulterated liquors has been so simplified that any novice who knows how to make a punch or a cock-tail can learn in a short time to make any kind of liquor that will pass muster with nine-tenths of the community."

Mr. A. B. Richmond, a prominent member of the legal profession of Pennsylvania, in a little work entitled "Leaves From the Diary of an Old Lawyer," gives a number of recipes for making and mixing liquor with logwood, oil of cognac, turpentine, oil of juniper, cochineal, rosaline, red beet, poppy, etc., etc.

The *Scientific American*, vol. 39, page 344, says:

"There is perhaps no article of daily consumption that undergoes a greater variety of adulteration than wine. Indeed it is not only adulterated, but much of the liquid we know by that name is entirely innocent of any Grape Juice at all.

Mrs. Mary T. Lathrop is quoted by Eli Johnson as follows:—

"In place of passing resolutions *advising* the use of unfermented wine at the communion, the churches should pass a *law* that never again the cup of devils should be placed upon the Lord's table."

"Where I once lived, *pure* California wine was sold by a druggist (who was also a Sunday school superintendent) for sacramental and medical purposes. Some temperance men and women analyzed it; not a drop of grape juice did it contain, but that pious man made it in his cellar from whiskey and drugs."

Rev. Dr. James B. Dunn, of Boston, Mass., in his essay for which the prize of the Nationa Temperance Society was awarded, gives the following description of some of the ingredients used in the manufacture of intoxicating drinks :—

"COCCULUS INDICUS, or Indian berry. This article, which is rarely ever used in medicine, and of no importance in the arts, is extensively used for the purpose of adulterating malt liquors. To such an extent is this the case, that writers on brewing openly acknowledge the fact and give regular formulæ for its employment, and all recommend it on the ground that it increases *the apparent strength of the beer, and improves its intoxicating qualities.* It is a small, rough, and black-looking berry, of a very bitter taste and an intoxicating quality. In doses of two or three grains it will produce nausea, vomiting and alarming prostration. In ten or twelve grain doses it kills strong dogs by tetanic spasms and convulsions, and in still larger doses, death both in man and animals is speedily produced. In India it is employed by the Nagus and other Indian tribes to poison the water in wells and tanks, to impede the progress of an invading army, and also to poison 'the weapons used in warfare."

FOXGLOVE is a plant with large purple flowers, possessing an intensely bitter, nauseous taste. It is a violent purgative and vomit ; produces languor, giddiness, and even death. It is poison, and is used on account of the bitter and intoxicating qualities it imparts to the liquor with which it is mixed.

GREEN COPPERAS, a mineral substance obtained from iron, is much used to give the porter a frothy top. HARTSHORN SHAVINGS are the horns of the common male deer rasped or scraped down. They are then boiled in the worts of ale, and give out a substance of a thickish nature like jelly, which is said to prevent intoxicating liquor from becoming sour.

HENBANE, a plant of poisonous nature, bearing a close resemblance to the narcotic poison opium. It produces intoxication, delirium, nausea, vomiting feverishness and death, and appears chiefly to be used to increase the intoxicating effects of liquors. Grains of Paradise are also largely used. They are also narcotic, causing when taken in a state of effusion, sickness, general feeling of distress, and finally stupor, tremor, or general nervous prostration.

JALAP, the root of a sort of convolvus, brought from the neighborhood of Xalapa, Mexico. It is used as a powerful purgative in medicine. Its taste is extremely nauseous, and it is used to prevent intoxicating liquor from souring, and to counteract the binding tendency of some of the other ingredients employed by the brewer.

LIME, an earthy substance of a white color. It has a hot burning taste, and in some measure corrodes and destroys the texture of those animal substances with which it comes into contact.

MULTUM is a mixture of opium and other ingredients prepared by Chemists for the brewer, and used by him to create the intoxicating qualities of the liquor. It is of a highly poisonous nature, and doubtless contributes to the fatal effects of that liquor.

NUT GALLS are excrescences produced by the attacks of a small insect on the tender shoots of a tree which grow in Asia, Syria, and Persia. They have very little taste, and are used to color or fire the liquor.

NUX VOMICA is the powerful fruit of the strychnus nux vomica. Its name suffices to characterize it. It is a violent narcotic, acrid poison, and is extensively used in the manufacture of intoxicating liquors. It is such a dangerous poison that medical men rarely prescribe it.

OPIUM is the thickened juice of the white poppy, which grows most abundantly in India. It is the most destructive of narcotic poisons, and it is the most intoxicating. It is largely used in the manufacture of intoxicating liquors, because its very nature is to yield a larger quantity of intoxicating matter than any other beverage.

Oil of Vitriol, or sulphuric acid, is a mineral poison of an awfully burning nature. It destroys everything it comes in contact with. It is used by brewers to increase the heating qualities of their liquors.

Potash derives its name from ashes and the pots in which it is prepared. It is made from vegetables mixed with quick-lime boiled down in pots and burnt, the ashes remaining after the burning being potash.

Quassia is the name of a tree which grows in America and the West Indies. Both the wood and the fruit are of an intensely bitter taste. It is used by brewers instead of hops.

Tobacco is a narcotic poison of a bitter acrid taste; when it is distilled, it yields and essential oil of a most violently destructive nature.

Wormwood is a plant or flower with downy leaves and small, round headed flowers. The seed of this plant has bitter and stimulating properties."

D.

THE KNIGHTS OF LABOR.

PREAMBLE TO CONSTITUTION.

"The alarming development and aggressiveness of great capitalists and corporations, unless checked, will invarably lead to the pauperization and hopeless degradation of the toiling masses.

It is imperative, if we desire to enjoy the full blessings of life, that a check be placed upon unjust accumulation, and the power for evil of aggregated wealth.

This much desired object can be accomplished only by the united efforts of those who obey the divine injunction, " In the sweat of thy face thou shalt eat bread."

Therefore we have formed the Order of the Knights of Labor, for the purpose of organizing and directing the flower of the industrial masses, not as a political party, for it more : in it are crystalized sentiments and measures for the benefit of the whole people ; but it should be borne in mind, when exercising the right of suffrage, that most of the objects herein set forth can only be obtained through legislation, and that it is the duty of all to assist in nominating and supporting with their votes only such candidates as will pledge their support to these measures, regardless of party. But no one shall, however be compelled to vote with the majority, and calling upon all who believe in securing " the greatest good of the greatest number," to join and assist us, we declare to the world that our aims are :—

1. To make industrial and moral worth, not wealth, the true standard of individual and national greatness.

2. To secure for the workers the full enjoyment of the wealth they create ; sufficient leisure in which to develope their intellectual, moral, and social faculties ; all of the benefits, recreation, and pleasure of association ; in a word, to enable them to share in the gains and honors of advancing civilization.

In order to secure these results, we demand at the hands of the State :

3. The establishment of Bureaus of Labor statistics, that we may arrive at a correct knowledge of the educational, moral and financial condition of the laboring masses.

4. That the public lands, the heritage of the people, be reserved for actual settlers ; not another acre for railroads or speculators ; and that all lands now held for speculative purposes be taxed to their full value.

5. The abrogation of all laws which do not bear equally upon capital and labor, and the removal of unjust technicalities, delays and discriminations in the administration of justice.

6. The adoption of measures providing for the health and safety of those engaged in mining, manufacturing and building industries, and for indemnification to those engaged therein for injuries received through lack of necessary safeguards.

7. The recognition, by incorporation of Trade Unions, orders, and such other associations as may be organized, the working masses to improve their condition and protect their rights.

8. The enactment of laws to compel corporations to pay their employees weekly, in lawful money, for the labor of the preceding week, and giving mechanics and laborers a first lien upon the product of their labor to the extent of their full wages.

9. The abolition of the contract system on national, state and municipal works.

10. The enactment of laws providing for arbitration between employer and employee, and to enforce the decision of the arbitrator.

11. The prohibition by law of children under fifteen years of age in workshops, mines and factories.

12. To prohibit the hiring out of convict labor.

13. That a graduated income tax be levied, and we demand at the hands of CONGRESS.

14. The establishment of a national monetary system in which a circulating medium in necessary quantity shall issue direct to the people, without the intervention of banks: that all the national issue shall be a full legal tender in payment of all debts public and private; and that the Government shall not guarantee or recognize any private banks, or create any banking corporations.

15. That interest-bearing bonds, bills of credit, or notes, shall never be issued by the Government; but that, when need arises, the emergency shall be met by issue of legal tender, non-interest-bearing money.

APPENDIX.

16. That the importation of foreign labor under contract shall be prohibited.

17. That, in connection with the post office, the Government shall organize financial exchanges, safe deposits, and facilities for deposit of the savings of the people in small sums.

18. That the Government shall obtain possession by purchase under the right of eminent domain of all telegraphs, telephones and railroads ; and that hereafter no charter or license be issued to any corporation for construction or operation of any means of transporting intelligence, passengers, or freight. And while making the foregoing demands upon the State and National Government, we will endeavor to associate our own labors.

19. To establish co-operative institutions such as will tend to supercede the wage system, by the introduction of a co-operative industrial system.

20. To secure for both sexes equal pay for equal work.

21. To shorten the hours of labor by a general refusal to work for more than eight hours.

22. To persuade employers to arbitrate all differences which may arise between them and their employees, in order that the bonds of sympathy between them may be strengthened, and that strikes may be rendered unnecessary."

E.

FIRE INSURANCE AND DRINK.

Everyone knows that the life insurance companies discriminate sharply and unfailingly against drinkers. This fact is one of the strongest arguments for temperance. Almost equally strong is the fact (which, however, is not quite so generally known) that the fire insurance companies have strict rules bearing on the liquor question. Intemperance begets carelessness, obliviousness to danger, and, quite as frequently, destructiveness. Incendiarism is largely due to strong drink, and a very large proportion of accidental fires is to be attributed to the effects of drunkenness. Hence, the fire insurance companies invariably take into account the habits of men frequenting a place before they will insure it. Hotel-keepers and others, who harbor persons of whom a large proportion are, presumably, subject to intoxication, have to pay rates of insurance to cover this extra hazard.

F.

COMPENSATION.

For the full discussion of this question read the pamphlet by the author of this work entitled "Compensation and the Liquor Traffic," published by Hunter, Rose & Co. Copies may be had, price 10 cents, of the publishers of this volume, or of the author, Rev. W. Burgess, Listowel, Ontario, Canada.

www.ingramcontent.com/pod-product-compliance
Lightning Source LLC
Chambersburg PA
CBHW031906220426
43663CB00006B/784